Playable Hands by Position in Limit Hold'em

	Early-Position Hole Cards	Middle-Position Hole Cards	Late-Position Hole Cards
Pairs	Aces through 9s	Aces through 7s	Aces through 5s
Suited cards	Ace with King through Jack	Ace with King through 9	Any suited Ace
	King with Queen or Jack	King with Queen through 9	King with Queen through 7
		Queen with Jack through 9	Queen with Jack through 8
		Jack with 10 or 9	Jack with 10 through 7
			10 with 9
			9 with 8
			8 with 7
Unsuited cards	Ace with King through Jack	Ace with King through 10	Ace with King through 9
	King with Queen or Jack	King with Queen through 10	King with Queen through 9
		Queen with Jack	Queen with 10 or 9
			Jack with 10

Questions to Ask Yourself Before You Play

- **What is the purpose of my playing this session?** Whether it's to learn more, win money, or just hang with friends for a good time, make sure you know why you're there and that you're doing everything you can to accomplish that goal.

- **If I were to play an opponent who's exactly the same as a well-rested, un-stressed version of me, would that person have an advantage?** If the answer is "yes," hold off on playing until you're in a better psychological and physical state.

- **Can my bankroll handle this level of play?** If not, play a lower level.

- **Are there any distractions in my life that I need to get rid of before I play?** Pay your rent, walk your dog, call your significant other — whatever it is, get it out of your head so you can focus.

- **Do I know if the house I'm playing in has any bonuses for players such as bad-beat jackpots, high hands, free food and/or drinks for players, or freeroll tournaments?** If not, ask a floorperson before you start playing and find out about the details of how you can qualify.

- **Is there an aggressive person at the table I'll be playing at?** If so, try to get yourself seated to his left so you see the raises *before* your action and not after.

- **What do I know about the people sitting at the table?** Whatever it is, use it to your advantage.

Online Poker Abbreviations

- **86** To remove or ban
- **brb** Be right back
- **gc/nc** Slightly sarcastic phrase meaning good catch/nice catch
- **lol** Laughing out loud
- **nl** No-Limit
- **n1** Nice one
- **ne1** Anyone
- **nh** Nice hand
- **gg** Good game
- **gl** Good luck
- **ty** Thank you
- **:)** Smiley face (view sideways)

Texas Hold'em For Dummies® Cheat Sheet

Quick Bluffing Tips

- Only bluff where it makes a difference to your standing — either in a tournament or to your stack of chips.
- Be careful bluffing someone considerably worse than you are. He may call just to see what you have, or on some probabilistically low draw when he already has you beaten anyway.
- Bluff in situations where the board hints at the great hand you do not have: straights and flushes being hinted at by the board, the turn of an Ace, and so on.
- Don't try to bluff players who only play the most solid of hands if they're still in the pot.
- Don't bluff people who are extremely likely to call.
- Do bluff the timid or people who are likely to fold.
- Remember that it's easier to bluff in No-Limit than Limit because the bets (both implied and real) are bigger.

Poker Etiquette 101

- Always play in turn.
- Be aware of when it's your turn to post the blinds and do so promptly.
- Any time there is a discrepancy at the table, talk to the dealer — not the other players — about it. If you're not able to get satisfaction from the dealer, ask for a floorperson. Talking with other players about the problem you perceive may generate ill will among people who have no authority in the situation in the first place.
- Place your bets in front of you. Do not splash them into the pot.
- Do not show your hand to other players at the table while a hand is in progress.
- Tell the dealer when you intend to raise. In No-Limit, gather the amount that you're going to raise and either announce the total, or move it all forward with one motion. This prevents being called on a "string raise."
- Don't forget to tip your dealer. Dealers work for minimum wage and rely on tips for their livelihood.

Rough Odds at a Glance

- **1 percent (1-in-100):** Percentage of time that no player holds an Ace or a King at a table in a 10-handed game
- **1 percent (1-in-100):** Percentage of time that if you hold two suited cards, you'll flop a flush
- **6 percent (about 1-in-20):** Percentage of time that five community cards will give pocket suited cards a flush
- **6 percent (about 1-in-20):** Percentage of time that you'll be dealt a pocket pair
- **8 percent (about 1-in-12):** Percentage of time that you'll hit at least trips after having a pair on the flop
- **12 percent (about 1-in-8):** Percentage of time that you'll flop trips if holding a pocket pair
- **12 percent (about 1-in-8):** Percentage of time that two more cards will flop in the same suit as a suited pocket pair
- **19 percent (about 1-in-5):** Percentage of time that the five community cards will at least trip your pocket pair
- **32 percent (about 1-in-3):** Percentage of time that you'll pair one of your cards on the flop (with no pocket pair)
- **33 percent (about 1-in-3):** Percentage of time that you'll make a full house or better after having trips on the flop
- **35 percent (about 1-in-3):** Percentage of time that you'll make a flush on the turn or river if you have four cards to a flush after the flop

For Dummies: Bestselling Book Series for Beginners

Texas Hold'em
FOR
DUMMIES®

by Mark "The Red" Harlan

WILEY

Wiley Publishing, Inc.

Texas Hold'em For Dummies®

Published by
Wiley Publishing, Inc.
111 River St.
Hoboken, NJ 07030-5774
www.wiley.com

Copyright © 2006 by Wiley Publishing, Inc., Indianapolis, Indiana

Published simultaneously in Canada

For general information on our other products and services, please contact our Customer Care Department within the U.S. at 800-762-2974, outside the U.S. at 317-572-3993, or fax 317-572-4002.

For technical support, please visit www.wiley.com/techsupport.

Wiley also publishes its books in a variety of electronic formats. Some content that appears in print may not be available in electronic books.

Library of Congress Control Number: 2006927731

ISBN-13: 978-0-470-04604-3

ISBN-10: 0-470-04604-X

Manufactured in the United States of America

10 9 8 7 6 5 4 3 2 1

1B/RT/QZ/QW/IN

WILEY

About the Author

Mark "The Red" Harlan was born in Rawlins, Wyoming, and has lived exactly the life you'd expect as a result. Armed with a degree in Applied Mathematics (from a university he loathes so much that he refuses to even utter the name), he fell headlong into a 20-year stint in the Silicon Valley's computer industry.

Red's professional experience includes human-interface work at Apple Computer, development of the bidding schema used by eBay, overseeing application development at Danger (makers of the T-Mobile Sidekick), as well as co-founding CyberArts Licensing (suppliers of the poker software seen on the MANSION and GamesGrid sites).

At the tender age of 8, he won a pinewood derby competition in the Cub Scouts, giving him his first heavy swig of victory that would forever warp his oh-so-soft-and-pliable mind. Under the influence of this experience, he started playing poker that same year ("might as well win money if you're going to win") and became good enough by 2005 to be a net money winner in that year's World Series of Poker.

Red is a member of the American Society of Journalists and Authors and has an extensive writing background ranging from penning InfoWorld's *Notes from the Fringe* during the heyday of the Internet, to being lead author of the book he thinks everyone should own (his mom does): *Winning at Internet Poker For Dummies* (Wiley). Red maintains a Web site of poker articles at www.redsdeal.com and welcomes non-spam e-mail at RedsDeal+HEFD@gmail.com (be sure to include the +).

Dedication

This book is dedicated to my mom, Marijane, and my brother, J. Scott Harlan, mostly because you're two saintly islands in a world that could desperately use more of your type, and a little because you've put up with me all these years.

Author's Acknowledgments

Biggest thanks of this go 'round goes to Leslie "All Ska" Dill for providing the cheerleading, support, and total lack of advice that were all precisely what I needed during the most stressful time of my life. You know what you did. I'm glad you did it.

Super thanks to my agent Margot "The Sunny Negotiator" Hutchison, for suggesting that I write this text, as well as driving through all my crazy contract requirements.

Extra thanks to Elizabeth "Exclamation Points!" Kuball for acting as my project editor and not freaking out when I say crazy things in phone conversations.

A nod and a wink to Gridders: UCD Aces, ifoundnemo23, and yanksalex. You guys are the reason I worked on poker sites for a living, I just didn't know it at the time.

Lingering but totally necessary thanks to: Josh "Birdhead" Carter for continual computer expertise and extensive ideological support; Taqueria Eduardo (TE) for having the greatest carnitas on the planet; Max "You're Not 'Erik'" Francis for ongoing poker discussions, loans of his poker library, and companionship at TE; Dino for not selling Dino's after all; Konstantin Othmer for repeated favors and questions; Fishbone for not quitting; Chris Derossi for a zillionty and one things; Radiohead for being the only band that matters; and Clarus at the Bitmap Café.

Publisher's Acknowledgments

We're proud of this book; please send us your comments through our Dummies online registration form located at www.dummies.com/register/.

Some of the people who helped bring this book to market include the following:

Acquisitions, Editorial, and Media Development

Project Editor: Elizabeth Kuball

Acquisitions Editor: Tracy Boggier

Editorial Program Coordinator: Hanna K. Scott

Technical Editor: Jeremy P. Bagai

Editorial Manager: Michelle Hacker

Editorial Supervisor and Reprint Editor: Carmen Krikorian

Editorial Assistant: Erin Calligan, David Lutton

Cover Photos: © Cut and Deal Ltd/Alamy

Cartoons: Rich Tennant (www.the5thwave.com)

Composition

Project Coordinator: Kristie Rees

Layout and Graphics: Claudia Bell, Carl Byers, Denny Hager, Barry Offringa, Lynsey Osborn, Heather Ryan, Alicia South, Erin Zeltner

Proofreaders: John Greenough, Jessica Kramer, Joe Niesen, Brian H. Walls, Techbooks

Indexer: Techbbooks

Publishing and Editorial for Consumer Dummies

Diane Graves Steele, Vice President and Publisher, Consumer Dummies

Joyce Pepple, Acquisitions Director, Consumer Dummies

Kristin A. Cocks, Product Development Director, Consumer Dummies

Michael Spring, Vice President and Publisher, Travel

Kelly Regan, Editorial Director, Travel

Publishing for Technology Dummies

Andy Cummings, Vice President and Publisher, Dummies Technology/General User

Composition Services

Gerry Fahey, Vice President of Production Services

Debbie Stailey, Director of Composition Services

Contents at a Glance

Table of Contents

Introduction

*T*urn on the TV, drop by a news rack, spend ten minutes in any college watering hole, or for that matter walk into your local supermarket and you can see firsthand the stranglehold that Texas Hold'em has on the public. Twenty years ago, when I'd play Hold'em in a casino, it wasn't unusual for people to stop and ask me about the game. (I just have one of those ask-that-guy-he-looks-harmless kind of looks, I guess.) Now my *mom* tells me about it.

Hold'em is a game that is deceptively simple: There are four chances to bet (pre-flop, flop, turn, and river) and five ways you can act when you do (check, bet, call, raise, or fold). Yet within that simple mechanism, you'll find truth and trickery, boredom and fear, skill and misfortune — in other words, direct reflections of the things that make life worth living.

Hold'em is a game of both skill and chance — and infuriatingly, which of these things is the most important often changes without warning. Needless to say, this interaction is what makes the game gut wrenching at some times and great at others. If you want to find a sucker, don't hang out at a chess table. Then again, if you can't take being beaten by chance, it'll be better for your blood pressure if you spend your spare time knitting instead.

Amazingly, about 95 percent of the people who play Hold'em in a professional card room (be it online or at a casino), lose money — all because of the insidious nature of the *rake* (a small cut of every pot the house takes). Don't lose hope, though. Hold'em is a game that *can* be beaten, and by buying this book and referring to it often, you're absolutely taking the right first step.

About This Book

This book is a grand overview of Texas Hold'em.

All *Dummies* books are designed as references. You don't have to read it from beginning to end, cover to cover. My advice is to treat it like a salad bar: Load up on the things you're most interested in, and pass on the items that seem a bit too smelly.

In some of the later chapters, I make reference to concepts and ideas I cover earlier, but the cross-referencing here is heavy. I always point you back to the fundamental concepts for brush-ups.

Don't stress out as you read these pages. You're not expected to remember everything and, hey, you can always come back to anything you need to be recharged on.

Conventions Used in This Book

New terms are always written in italics, with a definition that follows close on its heels. If you're a text skimmer and find yourself running across a new word you don't know, back up until you find the italicized word (or just look in the glossary or index). You might also see italics used for emphasis — and I can definitely get emphatic from time to time.

`Monofont` is used for Web sites and e-mail addresses. There aren't a lot of site references in this book, and you certainly don't need to have access to a computer to learn or play poker, but there are some very valuable references out in cyberspace that you need to be aware of.

The sidebars you see in gray text are not required reading for the book, but will usually relate to the text being discussed to illustrate it more fully (or in some cases, it's just me trying to make you laugh). You'll find a sidebar at the end of this Introduction.

What You're Not to Read

Don't worry about any of the paragraphs labeled with a Technical Stuff icon. Those are present merely for completeness and to give more illumination to the terminally hard core.

There are two chapters you should bypass at the start. Get a little more general theory and practice under your belt before you tackle them:

- ✔ **Chapter 13:** This one is all about the concept of game theory and assumes you already understand the other poker concepts that are in this book.

- ✔ **Chapter 22:** Get solid in the other topics in this book before you go out and try to get even better. *Remember:* You need a good foundation before you can build a fancy house.

Foolish Assumptions

I've made several assumptions about you as a reader — might as well clear 'em up right here to avoid any future embarrassment. I assume that

- ✔ **You're familiar with playing cards.** You know that a deck has 52 cards, with 4 suits and 13 cards in each suit. You know what a Jack, Queen, King, and Ace are.

- ✔ **You would rather beat other people in poker than have them beat you.**

- ✔ **You have any range of poker experience going from none to a lot.**

- ✔ **You want to improve your game, no matter how good it is, right now.**

- ✔ **Trying in vain to get a cocktail waitress's attention is worse than having one stop by your table when you don't need her.**

How This Book Is Organized

I've organized this book in parts to make it more readily digestible. Yum.

Part 1: Everything's Bigger in Texas: Welcome to Texas Hold'em!

Chapter 1 gives a synopsis of larger concepts you'll run across in the book: how the game is played, how *to* play the game, and *where* the game is played.

The remainder of Part I talks about the hand rankings in poker, how to read a hand, betting, blinds, and etiquette. It's this section that also talks about one of *the* most important facets of the game: your bankroll.

Part 11: Texas Hold'em: Play by Play

This section covers, in detail, the betting and play surrounding your hole cards, the flop, the turn, and the river. It includes getting hints as to whether you're holding a winner or a loser and subtleties like check-raising.

Part III: Movin' On to Higher Stakes: Advanced Strategies of Hold'em

This is where things start getting really meaty. Knowing how to play other players at the table, bluffing, and trapping are all covered here. This part is also the one that deals with math (including pot odds) and game theory.

If there's one part you should really focus on in this book, it's this one.

Part IV: Casinos, Card Rooms, and the Internet: Places to Play Hold'em

If you can play poker someplace, I talk about it here. This is also the place where I fill you in on tournament play.

Part V: The Part of Tens

All great *For Dummies* books have a Part of Tens. In mine you find:

- ✔ A comparison between online and real-world play
- ✔ Common mistakes people make in Hold'em
- ✔ Great ways to make your home game better
- ✔ Bad beats (because everyone likes a good horror movie)
- ✔ Ways to get better

Glossary

Most *For Dummies* books don't have a glossary (and neither do lame poker books), but poker is *so* full of slang that I felt a glossary was almost mandatory. New expressions in the text will always be in *italics* followed by the definitions — the glossary wraps them all together in a nice, tidy package.

Icons Used in This Book

Icons are those little pictures in the margin that flag your attention for a particular reason:

When you see this icon, you'll find suggestions that save you time or money. When you see the Tip icon, think "clever."

Careful! These are things that if you ignore them could cost you time or money.

When you see this icon, you'll find information meant for the hard-core poker player. If you see something with a Technical Stuff icon that you don't understand, don't sweat it: You don't need to know it to improve your game.

Items flagged with this icon are things you'll need to know either at the poker table or later in the book.

While I highly advise against playing No-Limit ring games as a beginner, you could run across a No-Limit tournament situation when you're just starting off. I mark No-Limit special cases with this icon.

Where to Go from Here

Where you go is totally up to you. If you've never played Hold'em or poker before, just carry on into Chapter 1. If you have played, but you find yourself always losing, I suggest going to Chapter 8 and reading about the other players you're up against. If you've played a lot and just happened to pick up this book, either on a whim or at a friend's house, flip to Chapter 13.

And hey, if you ever want to check me out, go to www.redsdeal.com or send an e-mail to redsdeal+hefd@gmail.com. I'll respond to anything I get (as long as you aren't a spammer).

My bankroll, this book, and you

Before I started writing this book, the last time I played Hold'em was in the 2005 World Series of Poker (money winner, thank you very much). I figured I should be playing as I wrote, to keep the game more alive.

Playing only in tournaments, over the course of three months, and never playing in tournaments where my entry fee was more than $33 (although some of my wins were to satellites in bigger-entry-fee events), I have won:

✔ $3,596.85 in cash

✔ A $535 satellite seat for the World Series Main Event

✔ A $535 satellite seat for the World Series H.O.R.S.E. Event (Hold'em, Omaha, Razz [7-Card Stud Low], 7-Card Stud, 7-Card Stud Eight or Better [high hand splits with low hand])

I mention this not to brag (well, at least not too much), but to illustrate a point: Because you play Hold'em against *people,* the game is beatable. I won this using nothing more than years of practice combined with the exact concepts I put forward in this book.

If you practice and pay attention, you can — and will, over time — win.

Good luck to you.

Part I

Everything's Bigger in Texas: Welcome to Texas Hold'em!

The 5th Wave   By Rich Tennant

"We're studying arithmetic, Emily, not Texas Hold'em."

In this part . . .

Think of it as Texas Hold'em 101. I walk through the rankings of poker hands, the mechanics of Hold'em, proper poker manners, and bankroll basics. Your introductions to everything from flopping to dropping are all here.

Chapter 1

A Bird's-Eye View of Texas Hold'em

*T*wenty years ago, Texas Hold'em lived in relative poker obscurity. When I was playing in casinos, it was fairly common for people to come up and ask me about the game.

A few years ago, the perfect Hold'em storm was created: Chris Moneymaker won the $10,000 Main Event of the World Series (pocketing more than $2 million off of a $40 entry fee), the World Poker Tour became the most successful program in the history of the Travel Channel, and online play became prevalent.

The poker craze has gotten so out of hand that my *mom* is now telling me about watching poker on TV: "It's a lot like quilting. You really have to pay attention to catch the nuances." Not exactly the way *I* look at the game, but the fact that she's even watching says something.

In this chapter, I give you an overview of everything else you can expect from the book. Read on and then venture forth where you will.

Oh yes, and good luck to you! Let's shuffle up and deal.

Considering Why You Want to Play

Before you even cozy up to a card table, you should ask yourself a critical question: *Why am I here?*

There are several possible answers to this question:

- I want to make money.
- I'm just out to chill with my pals and have a good time.
- I want to sharpen my game.
- Hold'em has just crossed into my mental radar and I want to find out more about it.
- Baby needs a new pair of shoes.

Your reason may even be a combination of these things. Whatever your reason for being at the table, setting a main goal for your play and trying to reach it is critically important.

What I'm about to say will sound like I'm joking, but I assure you I'm not: You do *not* have to set a goal of making money at the table. The media pressure, and general public attention on Hold'em, has set up an expectation that you can, must, and should, win.

The sad fact is that roughly 95 percent of the people who play poker in professional establishments *lose* money. It's a devilishly hard game to beat because of the *rake* (a small percentage of the pot that the house takes to run the game — see Chapter 3 for more), and because the vagaries of chance even out over time, you have to truly maximize your wins and minimize your losses, or you'll watch your wallet slowly shrink.

It you decide from the outset that you have a goal other than winning, you won't beat yourself up when you don't. And believe me, *no one* at your table will argue with you if you don't mind losing.

Don't get me wrong, one of *my* requirements of sitting at a table is that I play to win — when I don't, it sets me in a foul mood for hours if not days. Because you're playing against other mortals — people full of pride and fallibility — you *can* beat the game. My friends and I have proven it over a mathematically significant period of time.

But winning takes perseverance, attention, and thought. Your reading this book is a great start. Keep going. Your will is already stronger than the average Friday-night player — now's the time to get your ability up there as well.

Working with Game Dynamics

In order to begin appreciating the complexities of Hold'em, you need to understand two basic elements of the game: your position at the table, and the particular way the game is dealt.

The importance of position

When Hold'em is played in a professional card room (be it online or in a brick-and-mortar casino), a dealer button acts as the theoretical point that the cards are being dealt from. This button moves one position clockwise around the table at the conclusion of every hand.

The player in the position immediately to the left of the dealer (that is to say, clockwise) *posts* an automatic bet called the *small blind,* and the player immediately to *his* left (or two places to the left of the dealer) posts an automatic bet known as the *big blind.* These are forced bets that players *must* make in order to get dealt into the game. All other players get to see their hands "for free." (To get a better understanding of the dealer button and blinds, flip to Chapter 3.)

Players decide whether to play or *fold* (quit) in a clockwise position, starting with the player immediately to the left (clockwise) of the big blind.

In Hold'em, your position relative to the other players is critical. When you're in the beginning of the betting order, your cards *have* to be of higher quality than the cards you would normally play in later position — especially if lots of players are left in the hand — because you have no idea what evil may lurk beyond. (For more detail on playing by position, see Chapter 4.)

Likewise, if you're riding at the back of the calling order, you can afford to play *looser* hands (those that aren't as high quality) and hope to catch cards to break people's dreams. In fact, *pot odds* (the amount you bet relative to the amount you would win) say that sometimes you *should* call, even when you have a lesser hand. (Chapter 12 gives you more detail on pot odds and all things mathematical.)

Playing move by move

Like all poker games, Hold'em has a very specific order in which the cards are dealt and played. (Chapter 2 has diagrams of Hold'em hands being dealt if you want to see what they look like in action on a table.)

Hole cards

At the start of a Hold'em hand, after the two blinds have been posted, all players are dealt two cards facedown. These are known as the *hole* or *pocket* cards. Players then make a decision to *call* the blinds (match the big blind), *raise* the blinds (increase the bet) or *fold* (quit playing and throw their cards away, facedown, to the middle of the table — known as *mucking*).

In the form of Hold'em known as *Limit,* the bets have to be of a certain specified amount. In *No-Limit,* players may bet any amount of their chips on the table. (You can find more on the different types of betting limits and how they work in Chapter 3. In Chapter 4 (and on the Cheat Sheet), you can find more on the types of hands you should play as hole cards, according to your position, as well as information on how to bet them.

If you've just been invited to a poker party and don't have the time to even read Chapter 4, here's a general rule I tell newbies that works remarkably well:

> If *both* of your hole cards are not 10s or greater (Jacks, Queens, Kings, or Aces), fold.

Yes, it sounds harsh, but it'll keep you pretty much only playing the cards that you should — and about the right frequency of hands.

Make sure not to show your hole cards to other players at the table (even if those other players are no longer in the hand). And after you've looked at your cards, you should protect them from being collected by the dealer by placing an extra poker chip (or some other small object) on top of them.

The flop

After the betting action is done on the round with the hole cards (also known as *pre-flop*), three cards are displayed by the dealer simultaneously to the center of the poker table — this is known as the *flop*. At this point, each player at the table has a unique five-card poker hand consisting of his two hole cards and the three community cards.

Because of the raw number of cards involved, the flop typically gives you the general tenor of the poker hand and definitely gives you a good idea of the kind of hand to look for as a winner. For example, an all-Spade flop (especially with a lot of players still in the hand) will be hinting at a flush as a strong possibility for a winner.

Betting begins with the first person still in the hand to the left (clockwise) of the dealer button. As a general rule, you want your hand to match the flop, and you should fold if it doesn't. (Chapter 5 is all about how to play the flop.)

In Limit play, the size of the bet you can make on the flop is identical to the amount you can make pre-flop.

The turn

After the flop betting round is completed, another community card is placed, known as the *turn* (or sometimes *fourth street*). Each of the remaining players now has a six-card poker hand made up of his two private hole cards and the four community cards. Hold'em is a game where only five cards count toward a poker hand, so everyone has a theoretical "extra" card at this point.

In Limit, the betting is now twice the amount that was bet pre- and post-flop.

Poker wags like to say, "The turn plays itself," meaning your hand gets better and you bet it, or it doesn't and you start giving strong thoughts to folding. This is more or less true. (You can find more details about playing the turn in Chapter 6.)

The river

After the betting round of the turn, a final community card is exposed, known as the *river* (sometimes called *fifth street*).

Each player left in the game has his final hand consisting of the best five cards of the seven available (two private hole cards and the five community cards). Players may use two hole cards along with three community cards, one hole card combined with four community cards, or just the five community cards (known as *playing the board*). Again, poker hands are made up of the best five cards — the other two available to any given player don't count. There is one final round of betting. (Chapter 7 washes you with the river details.)

The showdown

The *showdown* is what happens after the final river bets have been placed. Although it isn't formally required, typically the person who initiated the final round of betting is first to show her hand. The action then proceeds in a clockwise fashion with players either mucking their hands if they can't beat the hand exposed, or showing a better hand (at which point the dealer mucks the old, "worse" hand and continues around the table for any remaining hands).

Winners and losers are determined by the standard poker hand rankings. (Chapter 2 gives more details on those if you're not already familiar with them.)

If you're ever unclear about who is winning a hand, just turn your cards face up and let the dealer decide. *Never* take a player's word on what she has in hand until you've actually seen her cards with your own eyes — when you muck a hand, it's officially dead.

Moving Up a Notch

After you have the basics of how the game is played, it's time to move into the deeper levels of the game.

Gleaning your opponents

By *far,* the most important thing in a poker game is figuring out, and then playing specifically to, your opponents. When you've been bet into, what might be a raise against one player can be an easy and fast fold against another.

You need to factor in such questions as:

- ✔ How likely is your opponent to bluff?
- ✔ Does your opponent sense weakness in your betting action or in the way you're behaving at the table?
- ✔ Is your opponent's table position influencing the way he plays?
- ✔ Do the board cards hint at a good hand (or possibly a hand that has been "missed," and is your opponent now bluffing)?

If you read no other chapter of this book, look over Chapter 8 for *much* more detail on playing the players at the table.

Playing the roles

When it's your turn to bet, you really only have some subset of five choices:

- ✔ **Check:** If no one else has bet yet
- ✔ **Bet:** If no one else has bet
- ✔ **Call:** If a player in front of you has bet and you want to match the amount to stay in the game

✔ **Raise:** If a player in front of you has bet, but you want to increase the amount

✔ **Fold:** If you've decided you can't take it any more

With such limited choices, some people may think there isn't a whole lot to the game — but nothing could be farther from the truth.

Bluffing

One of the things poker is best known for is *bluffing* (acting as though you have a hand that you don't actually have, in an effort to get your opponent to fold). Bluffing is the point where your the psychological rubber hits the steely money road — and it's the glorious difference that separates poker from nearly any other game you can mention.

Bluffing works best when:

✔ You're playing against a weaker opponent (who is likely to fold).

✔ There is a large amount of money at stake, where winning the hand would make a difference to your stack.

✔ People have reason to believe you aren't bluffing.

✔ The community cards hint at a hand you could have (for example, a straight or a flush) but that you actually don't.

Bluffing is a bad idea when:

✔ You try to get a player to fold who is very prone to calling, "just to see what you have."

✔ There is no other obvious reason for you to bluff.

✔ You're playing with people who think, "Sure, I'll call — that guy always bluffs."

✔ You gain nothing (or nearly nothing) by doing so.

For more on bluffing, see Chapter 9.

Slow playing

Slow playing is the expression used to describe a player who has an extremely good hand, but doesn't bet it strong from the start, all in an effort to squeeze more money out of his opponent.

The good news is, if you slow-play it can help camouflage your hand, leaving the unsuspecting at your disposal. The bad news is it can backfire and give your opponent a chance to draw cards that can ultimately beat you.

Chapter 10 is your slow-playing headquarters. In the name of indirection, it's best to act like you're actually going somewhere else as you mosey on over to Chapter 10 and take a look.

Figuring in math

If playing your opponents is the most important thing to know at a poker table, the next most important is mathematics.

The math behind poker isn't complicated — much of it you can already do off the top of your head, assuming you know little things like the fact that a deck has 52 cards: 4 suits, each with 13 ranked cards (2, 3, 4, 5, 6, 7, 8, 9, 10, Jack, Queen, King, and Ace). What you can't (or don't want to) figure out you can memorize.

The two important things to pay attention to are the chances of making your hand on a draw (for example, you have four Clubs between your hand and the community cards through the turn — what're the chances of seeing one on the river?), and what are the pot odds if you do (that is, how much do you win relative to how much you bet?).

I cover mathematics in detail in Chapter 12 — and I promise it's not the yawner that it was in school.

Places You Can Play

Playing poker is easy, assuming you can find a game. Of course, thanks to the current poker craze, you can find a game nearly anywhere.

Home games

For poker, there's truly no place like home. For one thing, there's no rake. For another, you can slap on your Judas Priest album and bang your head — and your tablemates can just join in.

The upsides:

- ✔ You get to play with your pals. (This is an upside only if you actually *like* your pals.)
- ✔ You get to play as naked as you'd like.
- ✔ You call the shots on *everything*.

The downsides:

- ✔ Your dog might eat the food you spread out on the counter.
- ✔ The equipment isn't as nice as a professional card room.
- ✔ Your place tends to get a little bit trashed.

For more on home games, take a look at Chapter 14. Chapter 20 has some ideas on making your home games better.

Casinos and poker rooms

As far as a place to play goes, you can't beat the equipment, comfort, and cocktail waitresses of a professional card room. A professional dealer lets you focus all your attention on the game (and not having to fumble with the cards yourself), and gaming commission rules ensure that you're getting a fair deal.

When you go to a professional card room, you should check in with the *board person* (the person responsible for the waiting lists) to find out the limits and games that are being spread. The floor-person will seat you and help you get your chips.

Chapter 16 has the rundown on professional card rooms, and hey, don't forget to tip your dealer!

Online

The biggest poker room in the world is no farther away than your computer. All you need to do is transfer money from your bank account to a third-party transfer agent, and then from there to the poker site of your choice. (This is a process similar to using PayPal for buying stuff off of eBay.)

As soon as you have money in your account, you can be off and playing. The good news is, the rakes tend to be less and there are more bonuses than at brick-and-mortar card rooms. The bad news is, the physical absence of a player at your table makes reading tells *much* harder.

See Chapter 15 for more on the online world. Chapter 18 details some differences between the online and "real" worlds. And hey, if you *really* get into playing online, you can just pick up a copy of *Winning at Internet Poker For Dummies* (published by Wiley), which I wrote with Chris Derossi. It dovetails almost perfectly with this book.

Chapter 2

Ranking and Reading a Hand

In This Chapter

▶ Figuring out poker hands, from the lowly to the royal

▶ Delving into the hand that's been dealt

▶ Scoring a pot

*T*he main thing to remember about Hold'em is that it's still just poker. If you already know poker's hand rankings, you're already all over what beats what in Hold'em.

If you've played poker but not Hold'em, skip ahead to the "Reading a Hand" section of this chapter. There you get a feel for how to tell the value of a hand as well as the board.

Hand Rankings

When a Hold'em hand is fully dealt, you have ownership of seven cards — your two hole cards, along with the five community cards. Your poker hand is the best five cards of the seven. The other two cards don't count toward the hand in any way.

Figure 2-1 illustrates the way hands are ranked. Hold'em uses exactly the same hand rankings as all other standard poker games, and — assuming you're not playing at Crazy Larry's — there aren't any wild cards.

In the following sections, I walk through these hand rankings from lowest to highest. At a card table, whenever you get one of these hands for the very first time in your life, be sure to squeal with glee. It doesn't make your hand any better, but it's good entertainment for everyone else at an otherwise monotonous table.

Figure 2-1: Rankings of poker hands, best to worst.

High card only — no pairs

The technical name for this hand is "bad." It's any hand were you have, in a word, nothing. If the board shows 10♣ 5♥ 4♦ 3♦ K♣ and you hold A♥ Q♥, your hand is A-K-Q-10-5. Rank order of the unrelated cards determines the winner (Aces are high). So this hand beats A-K-Q-10-4 (all other cards tie, and 5 beats 4) but would lose to A-K-Q-J-4 (first three cards tie, but J beats 10).

One pair

This hand is two cards of the same rank with three unrelated cards. If two players hold the same pair, then the unrelated cards are compared to determine a winner.

Two pair

In this hand, you have two cards of the same rank along with two cards of another rank and an unrelated card. If multiple players have two pair, the high single pair of all the two-pair hands wins. If players have identical high pairs, the highest ranked second pair wins (K-K-Q-Q-4 beats K-K-7-7-A). If multiple players have identical two-pair hands, the person with the highest unrelated card (the *kicker*) wins (3-3-2-2-K beats 3-3-2-2-9).

Three-of-a-kind

This hand is three of one rank matched with two unrelated cards. Three-of-a-kind is also called a *set* or *trips*.

Straight

Five cards, not of the same suit, ranked in sequence are considered a straight. A-K-Q-J-10 (known in poker slang as *Broadway*) is the highest straight. A-2-3-4-5 is the lowest (called a *wheel*). Straights are always called by their high card, for example "7-high-straight." The highest ranked straight wins.

The wheel is the *only* case in Hold'em where the Ace is low. An A-2-3-4-5 straight is only 5-high, not Ace-high.

Straights are not allowed to *wrap around*. Q-K-A-2-3 is not a straight — it's a hand that is Ace-King-high.

How rare is a royal flush?

Assuming all seven cards get dealt out and you get to choose the five best (which is the way a full Hold'em hand is dealt), on average you'll see one royal flush every 30,940 hands. A royal flush on the board (meaning the five up cards in the middle of the table *only*) will happen only once every 649,740 hands. Better start playin'.

Flush

In this hand, you have five non-straight cards of the same suit. 2♥ 3♥ 5♥ 8♥ 10♥ is a "10-high flush." The highest ranked flush wins.

All suits have the same value. One suit is not worth more than any other (unlike a game like bridge where spades outrank hearts).

Full house

This is three-of-a-kind matched with a pair. A full house (also called a *full boat* or just simply *boat*) is always ranked and called by the three-of-a-kind rank first, so 5-5-5-Q-Q is called, "fives full of Queens."

Four-of-a-kind

As you can probably guess, this hand is four cards of one rank (also known as *quads*) with another loner. If two players have the same four-of-a-kind, the highest fifth card determines the hand.

Straight flush

This is five cards that are both straight and flush. Q♥ J♥ 10♥ 9♥ 8♥ is a "Queen-high straight flush." A straight flush wheel (a *steel wheel*) is the lowest straight flush.

Royal flush

A-K-Q-J-10 of the same suit is called a *royal flush,* but really, it's just a fancy name for the highest possible straight flush.

Reading a Hand

If you've never played Hold'em, you'll find that getting used to how to read a hand takes a while. Don't panic, just pick the best five cards of the seven.

Straightforward hands

Some hands are pretty obvious. For example in Figure 2-2, Dean has a pair of Aces, Jerry has a pair of Kings. The pair of Aces win.

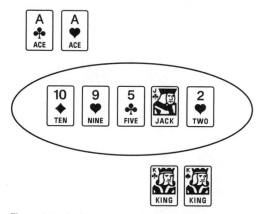

Figure 2-2: A pair of Aces beat a pair of Kings.

Figure 2-3 shows two players with a straight. David has the high end with 10-9, Tina has the bottom end with 5-4. David wins, Tina complains. A lot.

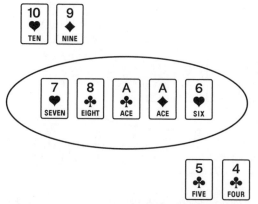

Figure 2-3: 10-high straight beats 8-high straight.

Figure 2-4 is an example of two people *playing the board*. Although Gilligan managed to get a pair of Jacks early on, and Ginger also ended up with an Ace-high straight, the highest hand, for both players, is the flush on the board.

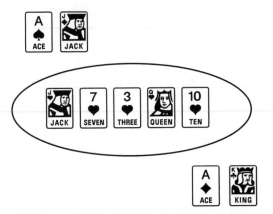

Figure 2-4: Both players have a Queen-high flush.

Subtle hands

These hands are the ones that have the ability to jump out and bite you if you're not careful.

Take a look at Figure 2-5. The river card is key here. It made Virginia's set of Queens, completed Robert's King-high straight, but made Scott's Queen-high flush.

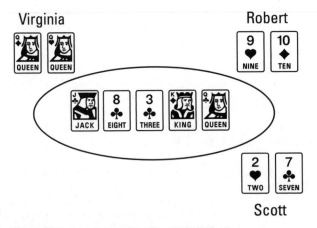

Figure 2-5: Scott wins with a Queen-high flush.

Consider Figure 2-6 carefully and see if you can figure out what each player has before reading ahead.

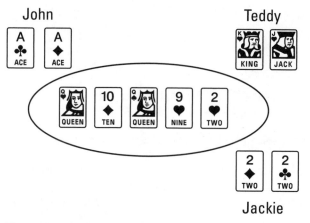

Figure 2-6: Which hand is best?

John had two pair — Aces and Queens — with a 10 kicker. This hand is the best starting hand of the three players, although it never improved. Teddy had a King-high straight on fourth street with the hand improving to flush in the river. Jackie, though, is the big winner with a full house, twos full of Queens.

Counterfeiting

I've played poker more than 30 years, and after all this time, counterfeiting is the _one_ thing about the game that has the ability to drive me insane. _Counterfeiting_ is what happens when a card, or series of cards, hits the board that somehow spoils your hand, or takes away from its inherent value.

For example if you were dealt pocket Aces, and the board eventually showed 2-3-4-5-6, your A-2-3-4-5 straight was counterfeited by a 6-high-straight on the board.

More diabolical versions of counterfeiting exist, though. Figure 2-7 shows an actual tournament hand I was in.

Figure 2-7 shows the final hand of a charity tournament, one card away from the finish. The winner would take home a money prize; the other two would get all-you-can-eat servings of crow in extra-large doggie bags. Because I knew both players were going to be involved in the hand, and we were right on the money cutoff, I was "forced" to play if I wanted a taste of the prizes (more on tournament dynamics in Chapter 17). All players had bet all their chips at this point, and the cards were exposed.

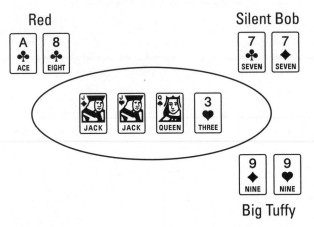

Figure 2-7: A board ready for Red's counterfeit river card.

The diagram is frozen in time at the turn. Silent Bob is holding two pair, Jacks and 7s and being *real* quiet about it (only because he's losing badly and only one of two 7s left in the deck will save him). Big Tuffy is going wild, thinking he's essentially locked the game as long as an Ace doesn't hit on the river.

Examine the hand and consider this: I win this hand (yay!), but I do *not* draw an Ace on the river. How do I win? How *can* I win?

The river card, Q♣, hits the board. Big Tuffy's friends went wild. They thought he had won the hand, and in fact the dealer began pushing the monster pot in his direction. I stopped her and explained the board. Forget what I said then — the short version is Big Tuffy had been counterfeited.

The river Queen gives Silent Bob two pair, and the lowest hand of the three players — Queens and Jacks with a 7 kicker. It gives Big Tuffy the same two pair, but a better hand with Queens and Jacks and a 9 kicker. Your hero (that would be me), however, was handed Queens and Jacks with an Ace kicker to win!

After some soul searching, and a deeper understanding of just *exactly* what the phrase "best hand wins" means, Big Tuffy and his pals turned a whiter shade of pale about the same time as my bank account turned a deeper shade of green. (For information on how to corral dealers as they start walking off into the weeds, as happened here, have a peek at Chapter 3.) Hey, I said that counterfeiting drives me insane; I didn't say that it stops me from playing.

Looking for Mr. Big

A very good trick to figure out early on is to take a deck of cards and practice reading boards. Deal a few sets of hole cards face up to imaginary players and deal five board cards face up in the middle. Take a long look at every hand to determine what the different players have relative to the board and figure out the winner.

Just as useful is to look at the board cards and get a feel for what the best *possible* hands are in order to get a better idea of what can happen on a board.

For example, let's take a board of A♠ A♦ K♠ 10♥ 9♣. The best possible hand (the *nuts*) here is four Aces (A-A along with the board).

The next best are the full houses. The best is A-K for Aces full of Kings. If you held this hand, you would have the best hand, because you know it's impossible for anyone to have quad Aces (you hold one), and you hold the nut full house.

From there, the full houses rate A-10, A-9. These are followed by pocket pairs K-K (gives Kings full of Aces), 10-10, and 9-9.

There are no flush possibilities (you have to have three board cards of the same suit), so that's out, but there is one straight, Broadway, if someone is holding a Q-J.

Below that are the trip Aces (A along with any card that does not match the board).

From there are the two pair. You don't really have to dig deeper than this, if for no other reason than it's not the low hands that beat you — it's the high hands.

Probably the biggest difference between a true novice (someone just learning how the game is played) and a beginner (someone who is actually playing) is having a feel for just how good your hand is relative to the board being displayed. Getting a feel for this is much easier if you have an idea of all the hands *possible* on any given board layout.

Paying a Hand

The only way to win is to get, as Beck says, "real paid." Paying a hand is fairly straightforward, although you need to be aware of some subtle nuances.

The winner

Best hand gets the spoils. If you're playing in a game with folks who are overly dramatic, awarding the loser(s) of any given hand a tissue is not a bad idea.

Normal situations

A "normal situation" (my term, not some crazy poker slang) is the case where all players in the pot have enough money to cover all the necessary bets being made. In this situation, which is by far the most typical, the best hand gets awarded the pot.

If you happen to win the pot (and honestly, after you read this book, how could you not?) and you're playing in a professional poker room, you should *not* reach out and scoop the pot toward yourself until the dealer has made the motion (for more on table etiquette, see Chapter 3). Doing so is considered bad form, and repeated abuse will get you thrown out of an establishment.

All-in

If a player wants to make a bet with all the money he has remaining on the table (be it an initial bet, call, or raise), he moves his money to the center and declares, "*All-in*." When a player has made this declaration, he is playing only for bets matching his original amount in the main pot — any remaining money goes into a *side pot.*

After the river card is dealt, and all final bets have been made, players playing for the side pot expose their hands first. Best hand is awarded the side pot.

This winning hand of the side pot is then compared to the all-in player for the main pot. The best hand of the two wins the main.

For example, say there's a game with Uncle Poison and Aunt Sally (both with $15), and Dorothy (with $1). Poison bets $5 and Sally calls. Dorothy wants to play in the hand and she calls all-in. The dealer will make two pots. The main pot has $3 ($1 from each of the players, including Dorothy's $1 all-in), and the side pot has $8 ($4 each from Poison and Sally — the amount left over after matching Dorothy's bet).

At the showdown at the end of the hand, the dealer first has Poison and Sally show their hands for the side pot. For illustration, I'll say Poison has two pair, beating Sally's pair. He wins the $8 side pot.

Sally's hand is then mucked and Poison's hand is left exposed on the table. The dealer then has Dorothy show her hand. Dorothy has a full house, beating Poison's two pair and she wins the $3 main pot. Toto does a flip to celebrate.

There can be as many side pots as necessary to cover all players, although you rarely see more than two on any single hand, even at a full table.

Tie hands

Tie hands are more common in Hold'em than most other forms of poker because all the players at the table are sharing five community cards. In the event of a tie, the pot is split evenly between all players still in the hand.

All players must have five identically ranked cards to tie, and the sixth and seventh card do not count. A♥ A♦ 2♦ 2♠ K♠ and A♣ A♠ 2♦ 2♠ K♠ are tie hands. A♥ K♥ 4♥ 3♥ 2♥ and A♠ Q♠ J♠ 10♠ 9♠ are not. (The Ace-King flush is better than the Ace-Queen flush.)

If the pot can't be perfectly split and there's a leftover chip (say $51 where the smallest chip is $1) the pot is split as evenly as possible ($25 to each player) and the extra chip ($1), goes to the player "closest to the dealer button," meaning the first person to act among the winners. Having to act first is a disadvantage (see Chapter 1 for why), so this person is given the reward.

Chapter 3

Just Tell Me How to Play: Texas Hold'em Basics

In This Chapter

▶ Playing in turn

▶ Determining the "dealer"

▶ Dealing the deck

▶ Becoming blind

▶ Betting, betting, betting

▶ Caring for your bankroll

▶ Playing properly

The first time you see Texas Hold'em played, it can feel a little bit like the inside joke that only *you* don't get. Don't sweat it, though. Hold'em is an easy game to understand.

What's not as obvious is how much money you should take to the table, as well as the social standards of playing. I cover it all in this chapter.

The Order of Play

As with all forms of poker, in Hold'em, cards are dealt clockwise from the dealer. All players are then subjected to a round of betting (see Chapter 1). Any players who fold are no longer eligible for the pot and are skipped over in subsequent betting rounds for that specific hand.

The Dealer Button

If you're used to playing poker at your kitchen table, you're probably familiar with rotating the deal from player to player at the end of every hand.

In a professional card room, the house employee that deals the cards isn't actually involved in the hand. That casino employee (also, a little confusingly, called the *dealer*) merely acts as a sometimes-wise-cracking card-distribution and pot-collection/distribution mechanism. The house doesn't have a vested interest in the hand; instead, it makes its money through the *rake* (a percentage of every pot — see the nearby sidebar, "The insidious rake").

When cards are dealt, the house acts as though there is a virtual dealer at the table, using a small round white marker with a *D* on it (for *dealer*) to signify the chosen dealer of the moment. Cards are dealt around the table in an order as though they're coming from the dealer marker, and all betting action starts immediately clockwise from that position.

The insidious rake

Professional card rooms don't have a vested interest in the game — they only provide the tables, cards, and dealers for play. But they do take what's known as the *rake,* a percentage of every pot that is won. The rake typically is 5 to 10 percent of the pot, with a maximum amount taken *capped* at $3.

On the surface, the rake seems like a pretty good deal. A loser is watching his money go away anyway, so it doesn't matter where it goes. And when a winner gets pushed a $97 pot rather than $100, it's not like she's going to complain.

The problem is that the rake eats at everyone over time. If ten people sit at a table for an hour with $100 each and 30 hands are dealt (not an unrealistic number) with a $3 rake each, at the end of an hour, $90 is gone. The equivalent of one player has been busted out just from the acidic corrosion of the rake.

Looking at it another way, imagine flipping a coin with someone where every time they won you paid them a dollar, but every time you won, they only paid you 95 cents. That's what's happening at a table with rake.

The only way to dodge the rake is to play in something like a home game that doesn't have it. Otherwise, you're under constant bankroll threat.

Moving the dealer button around the table ensures that all people get to play all positions throughout a long session of cards. (See Chapter 1 for more on why this is a big deal — pardon the pun.)

Dealing the Cards

The order in which Hold'em is dealt is very specific and, assuming you're playing with a table full of lucid, honest people, never changes.

The hole cards

Starting with the player clockwise from the dealer button, all players are dealt two *hole cards,* one at a time, in a clockwise fashion. You *are* allowed to look at your hole cards (in fact you should — unless your psychic powers are way, way up there, it would be hard to know exactly what kind of hand you had if you didn't). However, for the most part you should *not* show these cards to other players, even when folding — more on that in the "Poker Etiquette" section, later in this chapter.

Be very careful to not expose your hole cards to other players as you peek at them. You're allowed to use both of your hands to look at your cards (although you're not allowed to take your cards off the edge of the table) and should do so to help keep them shielded from prying eyes. Always memorize your cards when you look at them, including the suit — this will keep you from having to refer to them again when something like a flush or straight draw hits the board (if you do, it'll be obvious that you're looking to see if you hit your straight or flush draw).

When you're dealt your hole cards, it's not a bad idea to wait and not look at either of them until it's your turn to act. This way you can watch other players around the table as they glimpse at their cards for possible hints as to what they may have (see Chapter 8 for more on tells). This strategy also keeps you from being obvious about whether you're going to bet or fold well before it's your turn to act.

If you *do* decide to wait to look at your hole cards, nearly every player at the table will be looking at you as you glimpse your cards. Have your best poker face ready. (If you don't have the ability to generate a good poker face, sneak a peek at each of your cards, one at a time as they are dealt — or you could wear a Halloween mask, I guess.)

Protecting your hand

When playing in a casino environment, *protecting* your cards is essential. This means you should always have control of your hole cards either by keeping your hands on them (not a great choice, because forgetting and letting them go is too easy), or by placing something on top of your cards as they lie at rest on the table.

The protector you use can range from just an extra poker chip in your stack, to your car keys, or maybe even your niece whom you were supposed to baby-sit for the day (if you can get her to sit still). Greg Raymer, winner of the 2004 World Series main event, uses fossils. I use a Polish złoty (a coin) because it can never be mistaken for anything else.

If you don't protect your hand, and it's hit by cards being *mucked* (discarded) by other players, your hand is automatically folded. Another possibility is that the dealer assumes you have folded and just mucks the hand herself. (The underlying theory here is that you can prove what hand you had out of the mess of cards sitting in front of you.)

Get in the habit of dropping a chip on top of your facedown cards at the table. When you fold, pass your hole cards facedown to the dealer, and leave whatever you're using as a "protector" in front of you.

The flop

After a round of betting for the hole cards (see "Betting" later in this chapter), a card is *burned* off the top of the deck (meaning discarded without being looked at — this is done in case the top card had somehow been exposed or marked), and three cards are dealt faceup to the center of the table. This is known as the *flop* and is the start of the *community cards* on the table — those cards that everyone may incorporate in his hand.

Everyone who has not folded now has a five-card hand — two hole cards combined with the three community cards. A round of betting takes place.

The turn

After the flop betting round, another card is burned from the deck and a fourth community card is exposed. This card is known as the *turn* (sometimes *fourth street*).

All players still in the hand now have six cards to choose from to make their best five-card poker hands. There is another round of betting and one more card yet to be exposed.

The river

A card is burned and the most infamous of community cards, the *river* (sometimes called *fifth street*) is dealt. All remaining players have seven cards for selecting their best five-card poker hand (their two hole cards combined with the five community cards). A round of betting takes place, and the best five-card hand at the table is the winner.

To determine their five-card hand, players may use zero, one, or both of their hole cards in combination with five, four, or three community cards, respectively.

 Because a player is required to use at least three community cards to make a hand, there can be no flushes if there are not three cards of the same suit (multiple suits with no flush possibilities based on the current exposed community cards is known as a *rainbow*). Nor can there be a straight if there aren't three cards from a five-card sequence (for example, 5-8-9).

In Figure 3-1, George is playing the board and has a King-high heart flush. John is using one hole card for an Ace-high flush, but Ringo is the big winner using both hole cards for a straight flush.

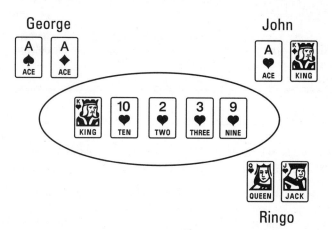

Figure 3-1: Each player using a different number of hole cards to determine a hand.

The showdown

If everyone in a hand has folded, leaving a single player, that person wins the pot by default and is not required to show his hand to any player at the table in any way.

Getting a peek at another person's cards

There is a little-known, but occasionally useful, tool at your disposal when playing in a Hold'em game. If a player has gone all the way to the river and then lost on the showdown, you can ask to see that player's hand, even if he's planning on mucking it.

To see it, make it clear to the dealer as early as you can that you want to see the hand (or all hands) in question. Even if the losing player mucks the hand, the dealer will isolate the two hole cards in question, tap them against the other cards in the muck (this demonstrates to security and floor personnel that the hand is dead) and expose the cards to the table.

The rules vary. At some houses, you have to have been in on the hand at the showdown to request a look. At others, you merely have to have been dealt into that hand (you're not allowed to ask to see a hand if you're merely observing).

There is a small catch to be aware of: If you've been declared the winner of a hand and you ask to see another player's hand, that hand is still live when it's exposed. In theory, if a player had mucked a hand that beat yours, and you asked to see it, you would lose the pot. Dealers tend to make a big deal about it, but in my years of play I have *never* seen this happen.

Don't be surprised to get standoffish reactions from people at the table if you ask to see the hand. For reasons that have never been clear to me, this request is a mildly unpopular one.

In online games, this request is much easier. At nearly all sites, when you request a hand history, you'll be shown the cards of all players from the showdown. (See Chapter 15 for more about online play.)

If more than one player at the table is still in a hand, and the final betting round has ended, the game has entered a phase known as the *showdown* (the part where people expose their cards to see who has won).

Anyone still in the hand may turn over his cards at this point, but people are usually reluctant to do so. If no one is making a motion to show his hand, the last person to raise (or the first person to bet if there were no raises on the river) in the final round of betting exposes his hand first — the theory being that this is the hand that everyone else called. (If no one bet on the river, the player closest to the dealer has to expose his hand first.)

Players are welcome, if not encouraged, to muck a losing hand without showing it. However, after a hand has been *mucked* (meaning turned facedown and pushed into the discards beyond the player's control), the hand is considered dead and no longer in competition for the pot.

After the first hand is exposed, remaining players expose their hands in a clockwise order. The dealer will muck losing hands one by one, leaving only the winning hand exposed for the awarding of the pot. When the dealer has determined a winner, she will push the pot in the direction of the player, and at that point, the winner is welcome to drag the pot in.

Don't *ever* trust another player when he announces a hand at the end of a showdown and muck your hand based on that information. After you've mucked your hand, it is truly dead and you can never bring it back. If there is an error on a player's call, other players *may* lie to you as a "joke." It's even more likely that they'll misread a hand. (I bet I've seen people read a combined hand of four spades and three clubs as a "flush" a hundred times in my life.) If you have *any* question as to who won a hand when you're involved in a showdown, merely turn your hand over and let the dealer make the decision.

Posting Blinds

In order to start betting in Hold'em, forced bets (known as *blinds*) are made by the two players immediately clockwise from the dealer button. The person immediately clockwise from the dealer has the *small blind,* and the next player clockwise has the *big blind.* Making blind bets is known as *posting* and this is done before any cards are dealt.

The size of the bets are determined by the *limits* of the game that you're playing and the small blind is nearly always half of the big blind (for more, see "Betting," later in this chapter). So a $2/$4 Limit Hold'em game has a small blind of $1 and a big blind of $2.

Blinds are forced bets. The players in these positions *must* make these bets or they aren't dealt cards in the hand. These blinds, in turn, force betting action on the table after everyone has been dealt their hole cards.

Figure 3-2 shows a $2/$4 Limit Hold'em game. The hole cards have just been dealt, with Groucho as the dealer, Zeppo the small blind, and Chico the big blind. Harpo is the first to act and must now either call the $2 big blind bet, raise to $4, or fold (turn to "Limit

Hold'em," later in this chapter, for a description on Limit betting). Checking is not an option for Harpo, because the big blind counts as a bet. Harpo's position of being first to act is known as being *under the gun.* Honk-honk.

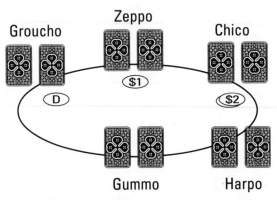

Figure 3-2: Blinds are in place, and Harpo is the first to act.

Fine points of posting first blinds

When you first sit down at a Hold'em table, the rules vary as to whether you have to post blinds (even if you're out of the normal blind positions for that hand) in order to be dealt a hand.

In Las Vegas, you're dealt a hand as soon as you sit down and have shown that you meet the table's minimum buy-in. You're not required to post a blind in order to get hole cards.

Conversely, in most California card rooms, you're required to post a big blind in order to get your starting hand.

In cases where you're required to post a big blind before you're dealt cards, you're mildly better off just waiting until it would normally be your turn to get the big blind anyway, rather than jumping straight into the hand. Waiting like this keeps you from making an extra forced bet and gives an added bonus of being able to case the players at the table while you aren't actually playing. Dealers are used to this behavior and will probably ask you if you want to *sit out* (that is, wait until it's your turn to post the big blind).

How soon you post is a fine point, though, that doesn't really make *that* much difference. If you're itchin' to play, or if you've got a very limited amount of time to play, go ahead and jump in. The dealer will tell you whether you're required to post a big blind.

Betting

A *bet* is when a player makes a wager on a poker hand. In Hold'em, there are four betting *rounds* (times when players make betting action around the table). These rounds always come after players seeing cards: after the hole cards are dealt, after the flop, after the turn, and after the river.

When it's a player's turn to *act* (meaning it's his turn to bet), the player has a few choices. If no bets have previously been made in the round, he may:

- ✔ **Check:** That is, choose not to bet at the moment but still be in the hand.
- ✔ **Bet:** Make a bet on the hand.

If someone has already made a bet when it's a player's turn to act in a round, the player may:

- ✔ **Fold:** Muck his hand and lose any chance at winning the pot.
- ✔ **Call:** Match the bet that has been made previously. He still has full rights to winning the pot.
- ✔ **Raise:** Match the bet that was made previously and then add more (being careful not to *string raise* — see the "Poker Etiquette" section of this chapter for more). Everyone left at the table must call the size of this raise or fold.

A betting round ends when all players have put the same amount of money into the pot (with the exception of all-in, described in Chapter 2) and all players have had an opportunity to act.

The amount and the style in which you can bet in Hold'em are determined before the game has started. The betting types are known as Spread-Limit, Limit, Pot-Limit, and No-Limit.

Spread-Limit Hold'em

In *Spread-Limit* games, you're allowed to bet any amount, within a given range, during a betting round. So in a $1 to $5 game you're allowed to bet $1, $2, $3, $4, or $5.

About the only place you find Spread-Limit Hold'em is playing at other people's kitchen-table home games. Professional card houses dealing a Spread-Limit game are very rare, indeed, tending to happen only in places sitting in poker backwaters (Blackhawk, Colorado, for example).

Typically in Spread-Limit, your raise must be at least equal in size to the bet in front of you. If someone bets $3 in a $1 to $5 game, and you want to raise, you can raise by $3, $4, or $5 *only*. Don't be afraid to ask a dealer what the betting rules are if you come across a Spread-Limit game.

Usually, the minimum *buy-in* (the amount you need to start playing the game) in a Spread-Limit game is ten times the lowest betting amount — so $10 in a $1 to $5 game. There is no maximum.

Limit Hold'em

When you run into a Hold'em *ring game* (that is, a game where people are playing for money on the table, as opposed to a tournament with a prize structure) in a professional card room, the most common game you'll find (especially in the lower betting ranges) is the form known as *Limit*. In Limit, assuming you don't check, you must bet *exactly* the amounts prescribed by the game in each round — no more and no less.

Limit is always described by two numbers: The biggest is twice the size of the smallest — for example, $10/$20 (said, "ten-twenty" with the $ ignored). The smaller of the two numbers is the exact amount players must bet (or raise) after seeing their hole cards and the flop. This means the smaller number is also the size of the big blind (because that is the forced first bet in Hold'em) and the small blind is half that amount ($5 in a $10/$20 Limit game). The larger number is what must be bet (or raised) on the turn and the river.

In casinos and card rooms, Limit games typically start at $2/$4 and run up into the hundreds of dollars (see Chapter 16 for more on professional card rooms). Online games can get extreme in the other direction and be as small as $0.05/$0.10 (Chapter 15 talks about online games).

Limit typically has a minimum buy-in of ten times the smaller bet size. So a $2/$4 game requires a buy-in of at least $20. There is no maximum.

Limit tends to be the hardest variation of poker to *bluff* (bet as though you have a good hand when you actually do not in an effort to get others to fold) because the bet sizes are regulated. (See Chapter 9 for more on bluffing.)

Pot-Limit Hold'em

Pot-Limit is the rarest form of Hold'em played today. I'm listing it just to be complete-ist, but don't sweat the details — you'll probably play a lot of Hold'em before you run across a Pot-Limit game.

Like Limit, Pot-Limit is always listed as two dollar figures, say $1/$2. You're typically allowed to buy in for a minimum of ten times the smaller dollar figure with no maximum.

In Pot-Limit, the amount you're allowed to bet is the same as it would be in Limit, but the amount you're allowed to raise is equal to the size of the pot. For example, say you're playing in a $1/$2 Pot-Limit game and you're under the gun. The blinds in front of you are $1 and $2. If you want to play in the hand, your minimum call is $2, just as if it had been a Limit game.

If you want to raise, the pot is calculated as though you already had called. You're allowed to raise anywhere between the amount of the bet to call and the size of the pot. In the $1/$2 game I've been talking about here, if you're under the gun, you could raise anything from $2 up to $5 (the pot being the two blinds [$1 + $2], plus the theoretical "call" you would have made of the big blind [$2]: $2 + $2 + $1 = $5). Additional raises are handled similarly

As you can see, it gets pricey fast (and man, with all this calculation, it's no wonder people never play it).

No-Limit Hold'em

It the olden days, say 20 years ago, *No-Limit* was a rarely played version of Hold'em — mostly, if not exclusively, attended by the extremely well heeled and the terminally vicious. Learning was an exercise in how far you were willing to drain your checking account.

Today, thanks to televised poker broadcasting, running the gamut from the *World Poker Tour* to *Stars You Never Really Liked Play Poker!*, No-Limit is probably the best-known version of the game.

No-Limit Hold'em is a vicious and diabolical game, where the rules are only slightly more complicated than "you can bet any amount at any time."

The most common way to see a ring game No-Limit table described is something like "$1/$2." When you do, these are the amounts of the blinds and the lower limits of the betting. The upper limit that can be bet on any given hand is however much any player has sitting on a table.

Buy-in is typically limited to a minimum of ten times the lower dollar figure and 100 times the upper dollar figure, so for a $1/$2 No-Limit game, your buy-in could be anything between $10 and $200. (The other way you'll sometimes see No-Limit described is by the maximum buy-in, say "$200." If you see a single number describing a No-Limit game, this is the maximum buy-in for that game — ask the dealer what the blinds are.)

As a general rule, you want to have something very close to the upper limit of the buy-in when you sit down at a table so you're not immediately intimidated (or just flat cleaned out) in a hand by someone with a considerably larger stack.

When you sit at a No-Limit table, you're not allowed to remove chips from the table (that is to, say, pocket some of your winnings) until you leave the game altogether. When you *do* leave a game, you're typically not allowed to reenter for a specified time limit (usually 30 minutes or more).

In case you haven't figured it out by now, No-Limit is an extremely dangerous form of the game. Just like doing trapeze without a net, the lack of limits on the betting doesn't make the tricks any more difficult — it just makes the penalties more severe. Starting out your Hold'em career with something like a No-Limit ring game is a very good way to watch your wallet walk south.

If you're interested in learning No-Limit, you should play Limit first until you're comfortable, and then either move along to micro No-Limit buy-ins online (see Chapter 15) or small buy-in tournaments (Chapter 17).

The Importance of Your Bankroll

You have to pay to play, but all that play isn't going to last very long if you don't have enough supporting cash behind your game to survive the bad times.

You don't *have* to play poker to win. It's perfectly fine to just have your time at the table as a form of entertainment, but if you're playing to win, the total cash available to you (your *bankroll*) will make the difference between ongoing enjoyment of the game and sitting on the rail wondering what's on TV.

If you've never been exposed to the basic concept of necessary bankroll before, you're probably going to be shocked about the amount of money I'm talking about here. So I need you to take a deep breath. Meditate. Go to your happy place. That's right, play with the cute puppy. Okay, now, read on. . . .

Recommended bankroll sizes

A bankroll is what will help you prosper when you're winning and stave off the poor times when you're losing. Because of the vagaries of luck, you need to have a thick cushion under you if you take a big fall.

Bankroll for Limit

If you begin as a Limit player, you should have a bankroll that is *at least* 300 times the maximum bet size. So for a $2/$4 game, you should have $1,200 earmarked for your poker play.

That's not to say you should walk up to a $2/$4 table with $1,200 in your pocket (in fact, you definitely should *not* do that), but that amount should be the amount of cash that you think of being at your disposal against your poker quests as a whole.

The nasty truth of poker

There is a truth about poker that you'll never see on the glamorous TV shows, nor hear from the seasoned professionals waxing poetic about the old days: The *vast majority* of poker players are losers. When I say "losers," I don't mean in the slacker sense of the word, I mean in the bottom-line, ask-your-accountant sense of the word.

How many? The commonly accepted figure is 95 percent. That's right, 19-out-of-20 poker players lose money in the long run. Kinda gives you a whole new perspective of the number of people you see playing on a crowded poker site online or what you're watching on TV, doesn't it?

Much of the loss is due to the rake (see the sidebar "The insidious rake," earlier in this chapter), but a nearly equal portion is due to bad bankroll management. If you're playing to win, even if you're an extremely good and talented player, you're asking for trouble if you're not fully prepared for the vagaries of fate with a nice, cushiony bankroll.

It's not unusual for a beginning player to lose as many as 50 big bets over the first several hours of poker play. A bigger bankroll will let you ride over the top of this initial loss to watch things grow later on.

Bankroll for No-Limit

As you would guess, No-Limit, due to the brutal nature of the game, requires even more cushion. You should have an absolute minimum bankroll of ten maximum buy-ins for the game you're interested in playing. A $1/$2 No-Limit ring game will probably have a maximum buy-in of $200, so a minimum bankroll for this game would be $2,000 (and double that would actually be safer).

Bankroll for tournament play

Tournaments tend to have wilder swings — especially multi-table tournaments where you might have a dry streak that runs for weeks, only to hit a big one to win it all back. (Chapter 17 has more on tournament play.)

For single-table tournaments (like those online, or satellites for bigger tourneys), you should have 100 times the buy-in. If you play in $10 tournaments, that means $1,000.

For multiple tables, you need even more. A bare minimum of 300 times the buy-in is more appropriate (and don't forget to count rebuys as part of the tournament fee). So if you're playing in $10 tournaments where you're rebuying twice, from your bankroll's point of view that's actually a $30 tournament. This means you need — yes, that's right — $9,000 to weather the storm. Told ya this would get your blood pressure up.

Moving up and moving down in limits

When you've got a nice cushy bankroll under you, you still have to be able to adjust to your wins and losses as you play merrily along.

Keeping records

Assuming you want to be a winning player, in order to keep tabs on how you're doing overall, you *must* keep records of your play. You can be as sophisticated as you'd like (who was playing, time of day, what you ate), but really the most important thing is to track your wins and losses across each poker session.

A simple spreadsheet or even just a small hard-bound notebook (spirals lose pages too easily) that you take with you will do the trick. Write down *every* session, no matter how big or how small the losses. And don't make an excuse to not record something, "I was really drunk at the time" doesn't matter to a diminishing stack of George Washingtons in your bank account.

How important is keeping records? If two players have exactly the same level of skill — one keeps records, and the other doesn't — the record keeper will win more money over time because he's more aware of how his game is affecting his bottom line and can adjust accordingly. Funny isn't it, how one player can beat another over the long run, using a technique that doesn't involve a deck of cards?

Going down

You need to be more leery of losing than winning, so it's the red ink in your ledger that you should be keeping an eye on. If you find that you've lost half your bankroll for the limit you assigned yourself, you need to move down one level in the limits that you play. So if your $2/$4 bankroll was $1,200 and you've seen it whittle down to $600, you need to move over to the $1/$2 table.

You also should examine your play in general for any *leaks* in your play — that is, mistakes that are costing you money.

Max: A record keeper becomes a winner

My pal Max is a big-time computer geek, and over the last few years he's developed a deeper interest in Hold'em. He started playing regularly online, keeping meticulous records rivaling those of even the most obsessed serial killers.

One day he came to me pretty dejected. "I'm losing. It's not a lot, but it's steady."

We both frowned at his gradual sloping downward line. There was no way to argue — he *was* losing. But the line was so slight, that it piqued my curiosity. "Hey, Max, run those numbers with the rake taken out."

He did, and sure enough, the line was now showing a winner. Max's problem was that he *was* beating the other players but he was *not* beating the rake.

I said, "If you move up one limit, the rake will become a smaller percentage of the total take of any one pot. I bet if you move up one level in limits, you start winning."

That's exactly what he did. Without meticulous records, we never would've figured it out.

Max bought me lunch at my favorite taqueria to celebrate. Now *that's* what I call winning.

Movin' on up

If you're in the envious position of having doubled your bankroll, you're now able to move up one limit at will. Yes, doubling your bankroll is a lot to win before moving, but it will prove, without a doubt, that you're not on a lucky streak and give you both the experience and confidence you need for the next level.

Moving up one limit in poker is *always* harder. If you assume that after you move up you'll automatically be as successful as you just were, you're opening yourself up for a (small) world of heartache.

Poker Etiquette

Poker etiquette goes beyond just being nice, being pleasant, saying "excuse me," and not chucking your chair at the dealer when he turns an unfriendly card. It's mostly rituals and customs for what happens around a card table. Repeatedly ignoring any of the rules listed in this section may get you removed from a professional poker room.

Handling your cards

To play cards, you first have to know how to physically handle them.

- ✔ **When you get your hole cards, don't take them beyond the edge of the table.** Look at them quickly, memorize them, and then protect them.

- ✔ **If the cards you're playing with are cardboard-based (like the kind you messed around with when you were a kid), be careful not to bend or warp them.** If you notice a deck is being warped, notify your dealer. (All-plastic playing cards, such as Kem brand, can be bent considerably more without warping effects.)

- ✔ **Keep your cards visible at all times.** This lets the other players and the dealer know that you still have a vested interest in the game.

- ✔ **Don't rip your cards in half when you take the most unbelievable beat of your life from the guy who started dating your ex-girlfriend and who is now mocking you.** Well, maybe.

- ✔ **Don't fold out of turn.** When you do fold, push them face-down to the dealer across the felt. After you've pushed your hand and let go of it, it's officially mucked and dead.

When should you show your hand?

In Hold'em, you only *have* to show your hand when you have a showdown winner. The rest of the time your exposure is at your option.

You *may* want to show a hand if you had a very strong hand or you were beaten by a lucky draw.

You *may* also want to show a hand if you pulled off a successful bluff to make your opponents slightly more incendiary.

Remember: When you show a hand, you're showing the tiniest bit of philosophy about you and your play — you're literally saying, "Yes, I play this kind of hand in this type of situation."

If you're comfortable with that, and *especially* if it's helping create a table image you want to convey (for example, "I only play the best hands — I *never* bluff"), then go for it.

My advice, and certainly the way I play, is to *never* show a hand I don't have to. I just prefer to keep my opponents guessing.

Don't ever show a hand to anyone at the table when the hand is still in play. Yes, this includes the girl with the low-cut blouse or the George Clooney look-alike who's sitting to your right and who isn't currently in the hand.

Handling your chips

You should know poker chip basics as well.

✔ **Keep in mind that only the chips on the table are eligible for that given hand.** You are not allowed to pull chips out of your pocket to play in a hand after cards have been dealt.

✔ **In No-Limit, you're not allowed to take chips off the table until you've decided that you're going to leave the game.**

✔ **In tournament play, you must keep your keeps stacked and readily visible/countable to all players and tournament officials.** You also have to carry them in full sight of everyone when you move from table to table.

✔ **When you want to raise a player, say "raise" to the dealer and then place the bet on the table.** If you're playing No-Limit, you must move the total amount of the raise in one motion *or* you should call the exact amount you want to bet. (Putting money on the table as though it were a call and then saying "raise" to put more money out is strictly prohibited. Doing so is known as a *string raise*.)

✔ **Place your bets out in front of you on the table, not mixed in with the rest of the pot (mixing with the rest of the pot is known as *splashing*).** Placing your bets in front of you lets the dealer make sure the pot has the correct bets and amounts from all the players in it.

✔ **Do not touch another player's chips.** Even if your halo is glowing that day.

✔ **Do not start moving a pot toward you until the dealer has declared your hand a winner and is moving the pot toward you.**

✔ **Do not bet out of turn.**

Playing in turn

Poker is played clockwise, with the first person to act being to the left of the dealer button (or to the left of the big blind pre-flop). The closest player to your right must act before you do, so you should be cuing off of her play. If you're sitting next to a player who tends to act out of turn, base your movement on the player to her right.

Playing in turn is especially important on the river. Be certain that all betting action has ceased and no one is still waiting to make a betting decision before you turn over your cards.

Tipping the dealer

In ring game play, tipping the dealer a buck when you win a hand is customary. Most dealers only make minimum wage and depend on your tips to make a living. Not to play the guilt card or anything. . . .

Keeping an eye on the game

When you play poker, especially if you're in an unfamiliar environment, keep an eye on what's going on around you. You have two people you can turn to, your dealer and the floorperson.

Talking to your dealer

If you run across any problem at a table — be it the way a hand was declared or an incorrect deal — talk to the dealer immediately. The dealer is the boss of the table. You'll be amazed at how many know-it-alls on a table will try to straighten out problems or solve big messes. They don't have any authority in a poker room, but the dealer does. Again, talk to the dealer.

Glimpsing someone else's cards

You'll be surprised how often you'll see someone else's cards when you're sitting at a table. It seems like nine times out of ten it's either someone who is drunk or some-one who's otherwise out of it.

I always approach this "problem" the same way. At the conclusion of the hand where it happens, I say, "Excuse me, you need to protect your hand — I could see your cards there," and I say it loud enough that most people at the table can hear it.

This strategy nearly always gets a "thanks" from the player you tell it to and for me at least, clears the conscience. If the player exposes his hand again, I figure I've warned him and just use this as another piece of information in my game.

Asking for a floorperson

In my experience, dealers are most likely to make mistakes in one of two ways:

- ✔ By incorrectly paying a board that has been counterfeited (see Chapter 2)

- ✔ By getting too deeply involved in a conversation with some-one else around the table

If the dealer has made a mistake — for example, paid a hand off incorrectly, called a winning hand incorrectly, or allowed some type of action at the table that you think is clearly egregious — ask for the *floorperson*. The floorperson handles any problems at the table and is essentially the dealer's supervisor.

If you *do* need a floorperson, the demeanor of the table is likely going to be fairly aggravated and hot. Explain the situation with the floorperson and only speak when spoken to. Don't argue with other players, even if those players are talking directly to you.

Watching your manners

If you play poker long enough, you *will* be beaten by the turn of an unlucky card. It's not a question of "if," it's a question of "when." If you can't deal with the pure concept of chance, you should seri-ously consider taking up an all-skill game like chess. (You think you got it bad? Take a look at what happened to the people in Chapter 21.)

Nobody wants to hear someone whine about a beat he just took, and if you're new to the game, you can be certain someone else sitting at the table has just had exactly the same kind of horror unleashed upon her. Just suck it up and live with it.

It's never okay to insult another player, throw cards at a dealer, or hurl your beer bottle through the mirror behind the bar. If the game is getting too tough or too intense, take a walk or call it a night. There's *always* another game somewhere.

It's just a game, unless you're a professional. And if you're a professional, you should behave like one.

Part II
Texas Hold'em:
Play by Play

"Sorry, counselor. You can 'check', 'fold', 'call', 'bet', or 'raise'. You can't 'sue'."

In this part . . .

Here you'll find several pages devoted to each card in a Texas Hold'em hand. I cover hole cards, flop, turn, and river in detail. I talk about the best hands to play, as well as the hands that should make you walk away.

Chapter 4

Beginning with Two

● ●

● ●

*B*oth the tease and the terror of Hold'em is the fact that you start with two hole cards. It's a lot like looking at the brochure for the house you'll ultimately own. Maybe the place that looks so great in the picture actually turns out to be on top of a toxic-waste dump. Or maybe that ratty little trap actually sits atop a gold mine.

Regardless of how you feel about the concept of judging a book by its cover, with starter cards in Hold'em, that's essentially what you have to do.

The start of a hand also determines your *position,* that is, your place on the table relative to the deal.

In this chapter, I take you on a stroll around the different positions at a table and talk about the relative strength of a hand according to where it sits.

The Importance of Position

Before I dive into talking about the hands you *should* be playing, it's worth just understanding the general concept of position. Position will help decide if you should raise, call, or fold. Your position can leave you stumbling blindly through a hand, or make you surprisingly educated about what's happening around the table.

The easiest way to think of a poker table is by position relative to the dealer button and then group those seats into sets (see Figure 4-1). I use these groups throughout the book.

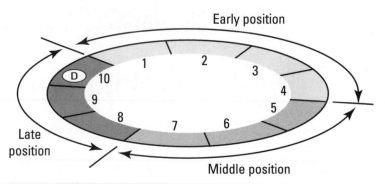

Figure 4-1: Relative position of early-, middle-, and late-position seats.

Early position

Seats in the *early position* are the ones that are first, second, third, and fourth from the dealer button. The problem with these seats is that you have no idea what cards the people behind you have, and worse, there are a lot of people behind you. When you're forced to act in early position, you'll continually be acting early for every betting round. For this reason alone, you should act *only* when you have premium cards (and fold everything else). Jack-Queen might look like a sweetheart here, but over the long run, it'll rip you to pieces when you play it from early position.

You may have noticed that early position has an interesting anomaly, and that is seats 1 and 2 from the dealer button are already covered by blinds. So in Seat 1 with the small blind, you may get a chance to see a hand for what is essentially half a bet (another small blind to see the big blind). In Seat 2 you might get to see the hand for "free," because if no one raised you're already in.

When you're in the big blind, watch the betting round as it comes to you. If you try to fold when it's your turn, the dealer may push your cards back at you and say, "You can check for free," but all the people at the table will know that you're now holding a hand that you have no interest in. Players can, and will, try to force you to fold based on this information.

In the blinds, you may be interested in playing hands because you already have a portion of a bet on the felt — and in some cases, that intuition is right (see Chapter 12 for more about mathematics and pot odds). Never forget, however, that after the pre-flop betting round, the blinds are the first hands that will see action — and for this reason they're continually at more risk of being attacked than other hands at the table.

Unless you're playing No-Limit, where you have the ability of putting down a mercilessly large raise, raising from the blinds will almost never get other players in the game to fold. So although you'll essentially gain a round of betting by raising, you've also switched on a bright neon sign that blinks "Hey look! I've got a hand!" Although that may gain you one bet in the short run, it will lose you more in the long run. (Only the masochistic and the terminally dull will repeatedly call a player they *know* has a great hand throughout all the betting rounds.) With a big hand, you're better off not raising and slow-playing instead (see Chapter 10 for more).

Middle position

The fifth, sixth, and seventh seats are known as *middle position,* and here things start to get interesting. You've already had a chance to see about half the table act (you can't be sure what the blinds are going to do unless you see a tell — see Chapter 8) and in some cases if you place a bet, you'll be the first person to do so because everyone else has folded.

Because you're sitting farther back in the order, you can run a little wilder. Play cards that are a bit worse — then when you actually do manage to hit a hand, the people in front of you may try to bet and you can return with some neighborly favor like a raise.

"Take Seat 4 on Table 33"

If you're waiting for a seat in a professional card room (or if you've drawn a seat to play in a tournament) you'll be given a seat and table number.

Most tables are identified by number, either right next to the chip tray on the felt, or from signs hanging above them on the ceiling.

The seats are numbered clockwise from the dealer starting with 1 and going up to however many, and the seats hold that number irrespective of the position of the dealer marker. If you ever have a question about the table you should be going to, ask your floorperson; if you ever have a question about sitting in the right seat, ask your dealer.

This isn't like being in Candyland, though. You still have about half the table to act behind you, as well as those pesky blinds.

As you play from the middle, be sure to keep an eye on the actions of the people behind you, especially the people who are raising. Those people are indicating hands of strength and you don't want to go out blindly betting in following rounds only to get raised, yet again, by the guy who has already nailed you once pre-flop.

Late position

The eighth, ninth, and (if there is one) tenth seats (lots of online tables have only nine seats) are *late position*. These are the rumble seats on the poker jalopy and are *way* fun. Because you've already seen all the action in front of you, you can make decisions like making calls purely on pot odds (see Chapter 12), raising with not-so-great hands when no one else has played, or folding marginal hands when it's clear there's going to be bloodshed in front of you.

Even if those bratty little people sitting in the blinds decide to raise you pre-flop (because they act after you), you'll be all over them like ugly on an ape after the flop because you get to act last *repeatedly*.

In a poker game, money tends to flow around the table in a clockwise fashion. The reason for this is due almost exclusively to the concept of position, and especially late position. The last people to act bring in the most because people either fold to the late-position bets or call the late-position raises and lose.

The only real difficulty of playing in late position is that everyone *knows* that it rocks. Just like Lovers' Lane, it has a reputation for being the spot where somewhat seedy things, such as *stealing the blinds* (raising from late position with garbage merely to try to gobble up blinds when no one else has bet) happens.

The Hands You Should Play, by Relative Position at a Table

Table 4-1 shows the starting hands you should play relative to your position around the table in Limit Hold'em.

Table 4-1 Hands You Should Play by Relative Position

	Early-Position Hole Cards	Middle-Position Hole Cards	Late-Position Hole Cards
Pairs	Aces through 9s	Aces through 7s	Aces through 5s
Suited cards	Ace with King through Jack	Ace with King through 9	Any suited Ace
	King with Queen or Jack	King with Queen through 9	King with Queen through 7
		Queen with Jack through 9	Queen with Jack through 8
		Jack with 10 or 9	Jack with 10 through 7
			10 with 9
			9 with 8
			8 with 7
Unsuited cards	Ace with King through Jack	Ace with King through 10	Ace with King through 9
	King with Queen or Jack	King with Queen through 10	King with Queen through 9
		Queen with Jack	Queen with 10 or 9
			Jack with 10

Although they're in early position, the small and large blinds do have a bit of play in them, exclusively because you were forced to play a bet when you were dealt the hand.

From the small blind, if you have *not* been raised, you can play:

- ✔ Any set of suited connectors, even if they're gapped (for example, 7♥ 10♥)
- ✔ Any set of connecting cards greater than 6 (for example, 6-7)
- ✔ Any two cards if more than half the table is playing (good pot odds for you)

From the big blind you can call any single raise with anything in the preceding list.

No-Limit modifications

The guidelines in the section "The Hands You Should Play, by Relative Position at a Table" are for Limit, as opposed to No-Limit. I *strongly* recommend you cut your Hold'em teeth on Limit (instead of getting them busted out in No-Limit), until you get a feel of the game. Then move ahead to No-Limit.

For No-Limit tournaments, consider moving the bottom rank of every category *up* at least one (for example, only play a suited Ace through Jack in early position rather than Ace through 10). This helps protect your bankroll (because after you lose all your chips, you're out). (See Chapter 17 for more on tournaments.)

For No-Limit ring games, consider moving the bottom rank of every category *down* one (for example, play a suited Ace through 9 in early position rather than Ace through 10). This gives you more of an ability to play spoiler hands after the flop, but requires considerable skill to do well. No-Limit ring game play goes well beyond "beginning" poker, so I don't cover it much in this book.

If either blind is raised multiple times, call with any of the cards listed in the early position (refer to Table 4-1).

When playing either the small or large blinds, particularly if there are a lot of players in the hand, be ready to fold post-flop if your hand doesn't improve significantly.

Be aware of a few things relative to the table I've supplied:

✔ **If you figured out your original Hold'em hands from *Poker For Dummies* by Richard Harroch and Lou Krieger (Wiley), you'll notice that I advocate playing a tighter subset than they have in that book.** (They list hands that I don't recommend playing.) I've done this because it's easier to start with a tight game and then loosen a bit than it is to start loose and tighten it up. Those authors themselves admit their recommendations are loose in that book — and I agree. Early in your poker career, your big goal will be to cut your losses to a minimum — and my recommendations will help.

✔ **Many people recommend playing an Ace with a weak kicker out of a later position (known as a *dangling Ace*), but in my experience, especially with players just learning the game, these hands will lose you more over time than they win (usually from someone in the blinds having an Ace with a**

bigger kicker). *Remember:* The more people who fold in front of you, the more implication there is that good cards are still left in the deck (or in the players' hands waiting to play).

✔ **Call any bet if there is a raise behind you, but be ready to let that hand go if you don't improve post-flop.** Your decision to play forward will be based partially on how you classify that player. (See Chapter 8 for more on those tricks.)

✔ **If there is a raise in front of you, you should only call if you have hands that are the equivalent of sitting one positional group in front of where you are.** For example, from a late position, you should no longer call with a J-10, but can call a bet and a raise with Q-J. Again, be ready to let the hand go if it doesn't improve post-flop.

✔ **Be certain to vary your starting cards relative to the other players at the table if that makes sense.** (See Chapter 8 for more on this.)

Considering the Players in a Hand

After you've figured out what hand to play and where, you're only beginning to get a true, deeper feel of the game. You have to keep track of a whole bunch of other things, too. I cover some of them in the following sections.

Keeping track of the number of players

The number of players in a hand is critical for your chances of success. Keeping track of the people in front of you is pretty easy, because you're always hearing them yap it up about checking, betting, or raising.

The danger is it's sometimes easy to lose track of the players playing *behind* you because the pressure and excitement of your declaring your action has passed and you can easily drop into a low form of stupor waiting for your next turn to act.

You don't have to be a math wizard to know that the more people you see staying in a hand, the more likely you are to lose. Also, if people are staying in against multiple raises, either they're suicidal or, more likely, they have great hands.

Watching the types of players

The players in a hand make a huge difference as to whether you should be raising, checking, or folding. The madman who will play any two cards under the gun is to be treated in a very different way from the woman who will only play A-A in the same position.

If you have a choice at a poker table, you always want the most aggressive player sitting to your right. Although it's true that if this person is a bit of a monster you'll see a whole lot of raising (much of it probably causing you to fold), it's *much* better to know that action is coming along than to have it happen behind you. Because when the Hell Raiser is behind you, you bet, and he raises, and then you may have to fold and just give a bet away.

Also, it's pointless to raise another player if he's continually going to call you when you don't think you have a better hand (or at least, are trying to convince him that you do). True, it sweetens the pot, but if it's not clear in your mind that you have a good shot at winning said pot, that extra money you're betting could just as easily walk away from you.

How good *is* that guy's starting hand?

Imagine you're playing at a table and everyone has folded to a person just in front of you in middle position and that person raises. You look at your hand and you're holding an off-suit A-Q. A good hand and you can definitely call, but you may be able to get a better feel for what the other guy has by raising. If he's playing something close to the hands that I outline in this chapter, that hand could be anything rang- ing from A-A to J-Q off-suit (or even worse depending on his current mindset and how much he values a hand like 4-4).

Now, it's true that your reraise helps indicate to the table that you have a very high-quality hand, but that's kind of the point. A lot of people behind you (maybe even all of them at a tight table) will fold. When the action comes back down on the original raising player, his action will tell you something.

If he does *not* reraise, that indicates he has a very good, but not great hand. If he comes right back at you with a raise, it may mean he has something very hot, or just doesn't want to be pushed around.

It's certainly not a foolproof method, but you'll be surprised how well it works — especially over time and at lower-limit tables.

The harder a person is to bluff, the less you should try to bluff him. Keep an eye on those players and, when they are in, their position relative to you.

In general you want to get a good classification of the players sitting around a table. Just be careful that you don't become prejudicial about it.

For example, if you're playing and you notice that a person raises with pocket threes under-the-gun, that's a good indication that either she overvalues pocket pairs, or she doesn't fully understand the importance of position. As long as there aren't extenuating circumstances (like being a significant chip leader in a short-handed tournament), keep track of that in your mind — and your position of that person relative to your play. *Remember:* As the dealer button orbits the table, sometimes that person will be behind you in turn, and other times in front of you.

In Chapter 8, I go into more detail on playing and classifying players, but here are some general things to watch for when it comes to the starting hole cards:

- **Loose players:** These are players who either play too many hands or bet too much on the hands they do play.

- **Tight players:** These players play only the very best starting hands — very possibly a smaller subset of the list I've described by position in Table 4-1.

- **Aggressive players:** These are people who raise, raise, raise.

- **Bluffers:** You should try to establish, very roughly, every player's likelihood to bluff at a table.

- **Timid players:** These players are the ones who are likely to fold.

Hands You Should and Should Not Play

I've already shown the hands you should play earlier in the chapter, and everything outside that list shouldn't be played. It's time to look at some more-specific examples.

Probable winners

There are a few big hands that when you have them, you have a very good chance to walk all the way through the hand with a winner. A-A, K-K, and Q-Q all fall in this category. But always be aware that the fewer players at the table, the more likely you are to win.

Big Slick (Ace-King) is a great starting hand, more so if it's suited, but it is purely a drawing hand. As I cover in Chapter 5, the flop determines the quality of that hand.

Quite possible losers

Small pairs are very dangerous. Especially on lower-limit tables, it's common to see people over-bet hands such as 5-5 and 6-6.

Riding the pocket rockets

On average, once every 220 hands you'll be dealt American Airlines — it is special enough of a hand to merit its own discussion.

If you're dealt A-A at a table and *everyone* calls all the way through — the odds are less than 50 percent that you'll win the hand. This is part of the reason it's important that you not only raise with this hand early to drop a few competitors out but also be aware that it's vulnerable. Yes, it's true that your raise will let people know you have a hot hand, but it may prevent a few less suckouts.

Pocket Aces get beaten (*cracked*) all the time and are particularly vulnerable to people with smaller pairs catching trips as well as flushes in unmatching suits and lower straights.

The beauty of the hand is that it's the best possible starter. The bad thing is that it's not a very good drawing hand. There are only two more Aces in the deck and for straights or flushes you have to have four community cards of that type.

Be happy when you have pocket rockets and don't be afraid to bet them. Just be aware that they're vulnerable and sometimes they *will* be beaten.

If you get in a hand that's starting to look bad, you can help dampen your losses by checking and calling. Or wet them down even more by getting out altogether.

Interesting side note: If you know, for certain, that your opponent has A-A, the best possible hand you can have in defense is a 6-7 in the suit that is *not* the same as either Ace. Such a combination has flush possibilities, lots of straights, and caps any 2-3-4-5 community cards for the wheel play.

There also seems to be an infatuation with pocket Jacks and the *only* reason I can think of (I know it sounds like I'm joking, but I'm serious) is that it has a lot of paint on it so it looks better than it is. In fact, if you're playing J-J against two other players with one having a King-X, the other having a Queen-X (*X*s being any card less than Jack), and the players play to the end, the pocket Jacks have about a 50 percent chance of winning. And you're going to be running into hands that are *much* better than that.

Gapped connectors can also cause you problems, especially ones with triple gaps such as 6-10. The problem with this hand is the only way you're going to make it straighten out with both cards is to end up with a community play of 7-8-9. If someone is playing 10-Jack here, you're dead meat.

Small suited connectors have similar problems. A little diamond mine like 2♦ 3♦ can be beaten by any two higher diamonds. Worse, you want to see the community cards come out with *exactly* three diamonds — because if there are four, anyone with another diamond beats you automatically. Gross.

Again, keep an eye on players at the table. If someone is playing extremely limited hands under the gun and you see him raise, you should be folding *any* hand that is not A-A, K-K, or A-K; because that's the only hand he would be playing out of that position.

Borderline hands

If you're playing any of the hands toward the bottom of Table 4-1, you're definitely down into borderline territory.

There's an interesting irony here because those hands are all much stronger against a fewer number of players, simply because they don't have to beat more people. But they pay better if you're up against multiple players.

The answer to this is conundrum is to go ahead and play them in both situations, but the flop is where the truth will start to be told. If you're up against multiple players, you must flop extremely well. If you're up against only one opponent, you may be able to bet in such a way that your opponent *thinks* you flopped well. (Read Chapter 5 to find out about flop play and what it means.)

Using "Fold or Raise" to Make a Call

Before ending this chapter it's worth mentioning a general rule of poker that you should incorporate deeply into your mind: It takes a better hand to call than it does to place an initial bet.

The easiest way to understand this rule is to look at an extreme example: Imagine playing at a table with ten players. Everyone is still in the hand, and with all five community cards faceup, nine players in front of you have called. You have the third highest pair with the board. What should you do?

Fold (of course). Someone has a better hand. In this situation there are just too many cards and too many players. The farther back you are in that ring, the better your hand needs to be because you're playing against *so many* players.

There's a good trick you can use with deciding to call — ask yourself if it's better to fold or raise in that position. If you don't feel good about raising ("There's no way this is a raise"), then it may well not even be a call. This isn't to say that you *have* to raise with your hand — you certainly can go ahead and call — but it sets a very good litmus test for you.

This theory applies across all forms of Hold'em, but it's a particularly good guideline in No-Limit. There, I take this theory one brutal step farther and instead of simply calling, I raise.

Chapter 5

Flopping 'Til You're Dropping

*O*n the whole, the flop is the most critical part of a Hold'em hand. You go from having two hole cards to — *boom!* — having a full poker hand. Love it or hate it, at least one of the cards you're staring at on the table will now be a part of your poker hand.

The flop is also the place where you make your last "cheap" bet, because betting rounds on the turn and river will cost you double what they do here.

Fitting or Folding

When the flop hits the table, you have definition of your hand. Five-sevenths (or about 70 percent) of all the cards possible for the hand are now known.

A flop relative to your hand is a lot like the weather. When you wake up and look out the window, you don't have a guarantee of what the rest of the day is going to be like (or that you won't be hit by lightning), but the general patterns give you a pretty good idea of what's up for the day.

The thing you need to be most concerned about is whether the flop (to borrow from *Poker For Dummies*) *fits* your hand. In other words, does your hand improve with the flop you see? Likewise, you want to think about how that very same flop may or may not improve the other people's hands around the table.

Great flops

The flop fits your hand very well if any of the following are true (in descending order of greatness):

- ✔ **You've flopped a straight flush.** It's always thrilling when it happens — and, if you're overtly emotional, it may give you a chance to see what your skeleton looks like when it jumps out of your body.

- ✔ **You've flopped a full house.** Fun. Especially when it's something bizarre, like you hold 3-8 on the big blind (no one has raised, so you're playing for free) and the flop is 3-8-3.

- ✔ **You've flopped the nut flush.**

- ✔ **You've flopped the nut straight.**

- ✔ **You've flopped quads.**

- ✔ **You've flopped trips.**

- ✔ **You've flopped two pair, with one of the pair being top of the board.** For example, you're holding A-3 and the board is A-10-3.

Good flops

The flop is definitely good for you in any of the following situations:

- ✔ **You've flopped a flush or straight that is not the best possible for a given board.** You probably have a winner here, but you have to be just a tad leery of people holding cards over yours — this is particularly true for those players who are now holding a four-flush with a singleton that is above your best hole card.

- ✔ **You've flopped two pair that do not include the bottom pair.**

- ✔ **You've flopped top pair with the best kicker.** For example, you're holding A-K and the flop is A-8-4, or you're holding A-9 and the flop is 9-2-7.

- ✔ **You hold a pocket pair that's higher than the board.** Say, you're holding 10-10 with a low-ball flop of 2-3-7. You still have a mild vulnerability here to trips and two pair (particularly from the blinds).

Very borderline flops

Then there are flops that do make your hand better but leave you possibly exposed:

- ✔ **You flop a pair that isn't the best possible.** Say you hold Q-J and the flop is K-Q-9, or you hold J-10 and the flop is A-Q-10.

- ✔ **You flop a four-flush or a four-straight.** Odds are you won't make this hand on the next two cards, but you may be forced to play it for pot odds reasons (see Chapter 12 for more info).

- ✔ **You flop top pair but have kicker trouble.** This situation is particularly a problem with Aces, because the whole table likes to hold onto them. If you're playing a suited A-2 from late position with five people still in the hand and the flop is A-7-5 rainbow, I guarantee you that you have a loser. (Right this second, all it takes is an opponent who has an Ace and any card bigger than a 5.)

From a bankroll perspective, you should think of the hands listed here as being some of the most dangerous hands at a poker table. The problem is that they tease you along to play more (sometimes even jacking with your mind in such a way that you become more convinced that your opponents are bluffing), but they're rife with holes.

Downright dangerous flops

Then there are those little places in Horrorville that occasionally crop up:

- ✔ **You've hit the bottom end of a straight, but the flop is also flushing.** For example, you have 8♦ 9♦ and the flop is 10♠ J♠ Q♠.

- ✔ **You hold a great pocket pair and bigger cards hit the board (especially when they're in quantity).** For example, you have Q-Q and the flop is A-A-K. If there is more than just a player or two in the pot, guess what? That's right, your great starter of pocket Queens is now a loser.

- ✔ **You have a flop that misses your hand, but still gives you over cards.** For example, you hold A-K in middle position and you see a Q-5-4 flop, with immediate action from the small or large blinds.

Just plain bad flops

Any flop that doesn't fit your hand at all (and you don't have a pocket pair) is bad — more so if you don't even hold an Ace. The answer in this situation is almost always exactly what you'd guess: Fold.

In Hold'em, especially until you get a better feel for the game and your opponents, you want to start off with the fundamental concept that if the flop doesn't fit your hand, you should fold. Yes, you will occasionally be bluffed out, but caution and folding will save you money as you learn. Watching *other* people see if that guy who's betting is bluffing is less costly for you and will give you more objective feel for the other players at the table (because your money isn't at stake).

The best of both worlds

You may get flops that play into your hand in multiple ways. For example, if you have A♣ 5♣ with a flop of J♣ 5♦ 3♣, you're now holding second pair (with best kicker) and the nut flush draw.

There are three obvious ways this hand can improve on the turn or river:

- ✔ If you draw a club, you have the nut flush.

- ✔ If you draw another 5, you have trips.

- ✔ If you draw an Ace, you have a strong two pair.

(There's also the freak runner-runner of drawing a 4 and a 2 on the turn and river for making the wheel. But this possibility shouldn't be part of your decision making — it's not likely enough to happen, but it *is* part of the hand.)

Any time your hand works in multiple directions, it's far better than having only one path to victory, and you should be more eager to play it. This rule is especially true in No-Limit. You may have an instance where you know you have an identical hand with an opponent. Say you're holding A♦ K♦ and the board has Q♦ J♦ 10♠. From the play at the table, you're certain your opponent also has A-K. You should move as much money on the table as possible — not because you're trying to make your royal flush — but because any diamond turned will give you a flush and beat your opponent's Broadway straight.

In poker slang, this situation, where you can draw cards at the mercy of your opponent with a currently identical hand, is called a *freeroll*. (Yes, it's the same term used to describe a tournament with no entry fee.)

Betting the Flop

Now that you have an idea of what category your flop falls into, we come down to the little details of betting. Unlike with your hole cards, where blinds force action at the table, checking all the way around the table after a flop *is* possible.

The way that players bet on the flop, and *especially* your position at the table, will come into play here.

When you're playing Hold'em, on the hole card and flop rounds, you bet one set amount. The amount you bet doubles on the turn and the river.

Because of this, you may want to make some bets now, in an effort to not make more costly bets later. You may also want to wait and not represent a good hand just yet — this strategy may give you a chance to make more money later.

Sizing up the table for a bet

The prime rule of anything economic — but *especially* poker — is to maximize your wins and minimize your losses. With *all* betting actions at a poker table, this concept should ride paramount in your mind (*well* above the fact that the cocktail waitress has really nice hair).

I think asking yourself a few questions helps. And don't sweat it: At first these questions may seem like a lot to consider, but after you've played some, they'll all become second nature.

How many players do you want?

If you have a very good hand, you may well want as many players in the hand as you can keep. The amount you're betting will double next round, so anyone who is still in the hand at the end of this round will be forced to decide to play for double in the next. This is great if you're on top and sucks rocks if you're not.

If you make any fence sitters fold now, you definitely won't get their bets next round.

However, if you have a hand that can be beaten with a draw (or a wide number of draws), you may want to bet to get people out of the hand now — or at the very least make them pay to see cards.

Who is still left to act in the hand and how do they behave?

If you have some monster opponent at your table who *always* raises and *always* plays to the end, don't go out firing a bet if you lack confidence in your hand. You *know* that guy is going to raise and there's no need to squander an extra bet.

Likewise, if you know that a player at the table only plays post-flop when she has a nut hand, go ahead and set a bet out right now. If she folds, you're done. If she calls, you know your hand has to get significantly better on the turn or she has you beat. It's still been a good bet on your part, though, because you found out the strength of her hand *now,* while the betting is half-priced.

Make sure to see Chapter 8 for more information about getting an understanding of the players at a table.

Making the bet

If there has been heavy raising and reraising pre-flop, especially if any of it has come from behind you, you're better off checking around the table than letting that player bet again — regardless of what happened with your hand on the flop. Nine times out of ten the raiser will be on some kind of adrenaline rush anyway from looking at a nice pair of hole cards, and he'll go ahead and fire a bet right on out when given a chance.

By checking to him, you save yourself a raise, and even if you *want* to raise, the check-raise will almost certainly work here.

Assuming you don't have any maniacal super-aggressive beasts prowling at your table, if the flop has fit your hand, you should bet it. If you're playing the cards I recommend in this book (and you should be, at least until you get supremely comfortable with the game), you're going to be folding the vast majority of hands. You'll be folding so much that when you *do* play a hand, you need a return on your betting investment.

In general, it takes a better hand to call than it does to bet, so by betting you're gleaning (somewhat imperfect) information about the hands around the table. You're also taking control of the game, which has some value.

If you get raised when you make a bet, consider both your opponent (for example, is she the kind of person who typically does this) and *especially* reexamine the flop (is there something in the flop you're missing?).

Straight draws and flush draws are the obvious threats, and they can easily sneak up on you. The other thing that will nail you is hidden trips. Someone (usually in late position) holds a smaller pair and may have managed to match the board.

If you have four cards to a straight or flush, from a purely mathematical point of view the best thing to do is to check because the odds are that you will *not* be making your straight or flush (see Chapter 12 for more on the math here). However, if you think that you have a pretty good chance of getting people to fold by betting, you should go ahead and bet the hand here.

If you're the last person to act and everyone has checked to you, you should bet if the flop fits your hand in any way. This bet implies to the table that you do, in fact, have a hand — and on extremely tight tables, it may win the pot for you outright.

From later position, check only if you have a true monster hand (which will guarantee a win on the next card at double the betting value) or the flop missed you entirely.

Calling a Bet

This is the edge of a more complicated territory.

If someone else has bet, you know a couple of things about his hand: He thought that his starting hole cards were good enough to play in the first place (or he was forced to play by being on the blinds), and now he's implying that the flop has somehow fit his hand.

The most important thing to consider on a call is the character of the person who has placed the original bet. Is he aggressive? Timid? Hotheaded? Mad about losing the last hand? Drunk? Get a good feeling about this before you make a decision to call. (See Chapter 8 for more about understanding your opponents.)

Hands that *somewhat* fit the flop can call. After all, this is still a cheap betting round and the turn may produce a card that fits your hand even better. Plus, your betting opponent *may* become less aggressive on the turn because he may not have that strong of a hand either and may have been just testing your mettle.

On the other hand, the turn card may come up anemic, making your not-so-great-fitting flop seem even worse — and making it easier to fold.

Hands that fit the flop well can call and can even consider raising, which I discuss in the following section.

"I *know* that guy is bluffing"

Several times in my poker career I've run across people who either, by their tells or their pattern of play, I *knew* were bluffing. I only had one problem: I didn't have a hand either.

Consider this scenario: You're on the button with a 5♥ 6♥, the small blind raises and the big blind folds. You've played at this table for six hours with the same guy on the small blind and the only time he has raised from that spot was when he was trying to get the large blind to fold and bluff down another lone player.

The flop is A♠ A♥ 9♦, and he bets.

Now you know for sure he doesn't have a 9 or an Ace. He shakes like a leaf when he has a good hand and he's sitting there solid as a rock. In fact, he's talking to you, and he only talks when he's bluffing. You know that if you raise, he'll call and check-call you all the way through the hand. He's done it eight times at this table, and he'll do it again. He wants to see what you have.

He doesn't believe you have an Ace, because you always raise from late-position pre-flop when you do (oops — that's a tell) and you didn't this hand.

The real problem here is that your hand isn't good enough to call him on his bluff. If he has a card bigger than a 6 (and he almost certainly does), you're beat. Which means the bitter truth is that you're right, he's bluffing — and even so, you have to fold. Just accept the fact that the flop missed this hand and go on to the next one.

You do not have to have the winning hand of the moment to be correct in calling. In fact, you can *know* that you're an underdog — but as long as you have pot odds in your favor (see Chapter 12 for more on those), you're still right in making a call.

If calling seems to be too hard of a decision, I always fall back on my old standby question: *With a bet in front of me, would I rather fold or raise with the hand I'm currently holding?* If you ask yourself this question and the answer is "raise," then you at least have a call. If the answer is "fold," then just give up the hand right now. The hand will only get more expensive and complicated from here, not cheaper.

It is a supremely bad idea, especially in Limit, to decide on the flop that someone is bluffing and start calling them from now until the last bet on the river. If you think someone is bluffing it's possible that:

✓ **You're wrong.** She actually *does* have a hand and you're watching your money walk away.

✔ **She doesn't have a hand yet, but she'll end up making one.** This scenario is possible with a semi-bluff (see Chapter 9) or if the player just gets lucky.

✔ **She may have a hand that's better than yours — even if she *is* bluffing.**

Raising the Dough

The rough guidelines of raising are to (a) consider how you want the person you'll be raising to react to your bet, and (b) make the action that will most help you with these interests.

Ask yourself how likely a person is to fold to a raise, and then:

✔ **If you want that person to fold and you don't believe she will, don't bother raising and just call.** You're not helping your situation.

✔ **If you don't want the person to fold, but you believe she will, wait and just call the hand for now.** The river round will cost twice as much money and you'll make more that way.

✔ **If you believe she may raise you back, and you don't want to call that raise, don't raise her right now.** The best way to stop a raising war is to not do it yourself.

✔ **If you believe she may raise you back, and that's what you want, what are you waiting for?** Go go go. (Hey, are you *sure* you know what you're doing?)

✔ **If you don't care whether the person raises or folds, you should raise.** You must have a pretty good hand, and if she folds, you know you win right now. If she doesn't fold, you'll probably just win even more money later.

✔ **If you're not sure how she'll react, raise.** Then you'll find out — and you'll almost certainly control the hand on the turn.

Bluffing is much more difficult in Limit than it is in No-Limit, because the penalty for calling — at least in the short term — just isn't that severe. For now, you should hold back on your aspirations of getting people to back away from the pot with your 2-7 off-suit.

Check-Raising

If you check during your turn, then raise when someone behind you has bet, this is known as a *check-raise*. It is, very rightly, considered to be one of the most aggressive things you can do on a card table (but not as bad as, say, throwing your drink in someone's face).

You should check-raise on the flop in just a few, very specific circumstances:

- ✔ **You have a very good hand, but the number of players currently playing is too big and needs to be reduced.**

- ✔ **You're playing against someone whom you know you're beating and you're certain he'll call *and* be the first person to bet next round.** If he will *not* be the first to bet next round, you should simply call and raise on the turn — you get an extra bet out of him that way.

- ✔ **You have the best hand, it's most likely going to remain the best, and you're playing at a table full of maniacs who will most likely cap all betting rounds, until . . . you pull down the largest pot of your life!** This is a level of thrill that is virtually unmatched in poker.

- ✔ **You think a check-raise will very likely work as a bluff now and get your timid competitor to fold before this same little stunt doubles in price next round.**

- ✔ **You think you can get a "free card" by check-raising.** (See the "Getting a Free Card" section of this chapter for more.)

- ✔ **You know that someone is playing for a draw, and you're beating him right this second, but you'll lose the hand if he's successful in getting the card he needs.** The reason to raise after checking is because you may be able to get him to fold right now — and even if you don't, you want to make him pay as dearly as possible to see each following card.

In any other situation, you're better off just calling and waiting for the next round. Check-raising always draws attention from even the sleepiest of players at the table, and it may well not be attention that you want.

The best hand *does* win a pot, you don't have to bet it repeatedly to make it better, and on the flop round (which is only half-price), you very likely are losing extra money.

If you think of a bet-raise-and-call being worth 4 units from a total of two people after the final call (bet 1 + call 1 + raise 1 + call 1), that same play is worth 8 on the turn (bet 2 + call 2 + raise 2 + call 2). Even if your opponent folds on a check-raise on the turn, you've still made an extra 2 units from what you would have on a folded check-raise on the flop. (You would have called your opponent's single bet on the flop and then raised his 2-unit bet on the river — he put in 3, rather than 1.)

The impropriety of check-raising

In the early days of poker, check-raising was considered to be ungentlemanly and unsportsmanlike conduct — so much so that the act was considered to be a brusque form of general unfairness and not allowed in many professional card rooms.

Over time, check-raising was allowed, in an effort not only to up the house take but also to make more customers happy.

Even today, you can see the vestigial remnants of this rule. Many of the older professional card rooms around the United States have "Check and raise is allowed" written into their card-room rules. Next time you wander into a brick-and-mortar place, have a look and see if that rule is still there if you're in need of a chuckle.

And if you want to see a *really* interesting reaction, call a floorperson over and ask if his card room allows check and raise.

Check-raising definitely does have its place, but usually you'll find it later in the game.

 No-Limit is a bit different. You want to *consider* using a very heavy check-raise on any opponent who's on a draw. The problem here, of course, is that you have to be dead certain that he *is* drawing (instead of just having you flat-out beaten), and there are many players who will semi-bluff back at you with an all-in.

Getting a Free Card

There is one big exception to the check-raising rule: If you think you can get a *free card* by doing it, it's worth trying. This exception is easiest to describe by example.

The free card setup

Typically, you want to try for a free card if you're trying to make a straight or flush draw.

Say you're playing J♦ 10♦ out of a late position and there was one flat-caller pre-flop from a middle position — meaning, three people are still in: you, the flat-caller, and the big blind.

The flop is Q♦ 5♣ 2♦ .

The big blind checked, the middle position bet, and the action is on you. You have a flush draw here, but most likely you don't have the best current hand (all it takes is one player with a card bigger than a Jack). A call might barely give you pot odds (see Chapter 12).

But if you *raise* here, what's likely to happen?

- ✔ Both players could fold and you win. That's pretty great.

- ✔ One player could reraise you, in which case you know she has some form of a smokin'-good hand (either trips or an A-J in this situation). Assuming you don't have pot odds for drawing your flush, you could fold.

- ✔ *Most likely,* one or both players will call. They perceive you as having a good hand (or maybe just trying to bluff), but the flop has slightly fit their hands as well. They call you, waiting to see the turn.

And here is where the beautiful part happens. On the turn, anyone still in the hand checks to you. If that player has made a hand, he's going to wait for you to bet so he can check-raise you. If he missed, or if he's still just in a so-so position, he's waiting for you to bet and then he'll make a decision on what to do. But because you're last to act, you don't *have* to bet. If you miss your card on the draw, you simply check and the dealer will summarily bang out the river card. If you made your hand, you just go ahead and bet.

What this effectively means is that you get a free river card. *And* you saw the turn for half-price, because your raise was less than a call on the turn would have been.

Defending against a free card

Now that you know the trick to get a free card, you can also defend against it. Any time on the flop that you see a raise behind you, with what appears to be a board draw — again, flushes and straights — you can either reraise before the turn if you have a very good hand, or simply call and then bet (instead of checking) when it's your action on the turn.

Notice that I'm talking about *draws* here, not made hands. Raising into a person with an all-club board showing is foolish at best, and suicidal at worst.

Chapter 6

Taking Your Turn

* *

In This Chapter

▶ Filling out your hand on fourth street

▶ Chronicling the action

* *

*A*ll in all, the turn isn't as pivotal a card as its name makes it seem. The flop holds the major moment of the hand, the river sets the stage for a victor, but the turn lies in the nether world. It's a nasty place of bad economics where the prices double and the number of cards is reduced.

Poker wags like to say that the "turn plays itself." That's a statement that's more true than it is false, but it doesn't mean it's not worth talking about.

Watching a Hand Fill Out

Of all the cards you receive in Hold'em, the turn is the least momentous. Only the clinically insane would have stayed through the flop for a double draw — meaning, drawing two cards to a straight or a flush — so it's unlikely that this is the point that your hand will suddenly be broken in *that* fashion.

However, bets double here and on the river, so if you make a mistake or a loose call here — as opposed to on the flop — it will cost you twice as much. And in the long run, the incorrect call on the turn is what will endanger your bankroll.

In broad terms, on the turn your hand will either be improving or getting worse. This isn't *quite* as stupid as it sounds, because when you stop and think about it, if your hand is staying the same, it's potentially degrading relative to the field (if there are a lot of players in the hand, it *definitely* is degrading).

Odds are that your hand won't be improving on the turn because you have to either pair a card or improve a straight or flush. And in Hold'em, for any given hand, the odds are always against that improvement happening. Therefore, when you *do* improve, you're very likely gaining with respect to the rest of the table, and (assuming that card isn't helping your opponent even more) you may well be passing them.

That's great because these are exactly the kinds of problems you want to have in poker. This particular one being the what-do-I-do-when-I'm-winning problem. Your big decision is whether you should check-raise or bet.

To check-raise or bet: That is the question

Here's a very good rule of thumb for check-raising (see Chapter 10) on the turn: If you think your opponent behind you will initially bet *and* call your check-raise, you should check. If not, you should bet — and do it right now!

Looking at a hand that's good enough to check-raise, say Q-Q on a rainbow 2-4-9-Q board (the best possible current hand), if you check and your opponent checks, you've lost a bet.

If you check, your opponent bets, and you raise, your opponent may well pass — check-raises tend to do that to people. And it's true that you gained two units (remembering that the bet on the turn and the river is double what it is pre-flop and on the flop), but you've also given your opponent a chance to simply check. Your Q-Q may well have come with a pre-flop raise and a post-flop bet. For sure, people want to see another free card — and if you check, that's exactly what they'll get.

If you bet, people *could* call — in fact there is a whole classification of people who will call — but won't make a bet if you check to them (for example, someone holding a tail-wagging K-9).

Made flushes: The notable exception

A flush is a big powerful hand that, if you're lucky, has been made by the turn. (Dang. You are *so* lucky. It seems like you *always* do that.)

Treat these hands as described in the "To check-raise or bet: That is the question" section, but with one *big* exception: If you have a tiny flush that is potentially threatened by a larger four-flush held by someone to act behind you, you need to bet it *now*. Think of it just like doing business at your local newsstand: absolutely no checks, cash only.

Consider, for example, that you're holding J♣ 10♣ in eighth position, but the other two people still in the game are behind you in the ninth and tenth seats. You're the first to act and the board shows 4♣ 7♣ Q♦ 2♣.

This is a great setup because you hold a club flush right now and it's possible that either person behind you (one of whom opened the betting on the flop) hit a pair of Queens. Unless the player drawing with a pair of Queens has another pair to go with it (or holds the Queen of clubs), he'll be drawing dead here. And even if he *does* have two pair, he still has to pair one of the board cards to make a full house on the river.

The lurking danger is a person holding something higher than your Jack still being in the hand. The Queen, King, and Ace, to the best of your knowledge, are all still in play — and those are *precisely* the kinds of cards people hold and play (especially if someone paired a Q♣ in his hand with the one on the flop).

Betting your hand right now will force anyone on the draw to decide if the pot odds (see Chapter 12) are such that a call is feasible. Your betting leaves lots of room for other players to make mistakes:

✔ They may make a mistake calculating pot odds and fold when they should call (or do the equivalent of making a mistake by not knowing what pot odds are and simply making the wrong choice to begin with).

✔ They may make a mistake calculating pot odds and call when they should fold. (Again, they may not know and may just make the wrong choice.)

✔ They may try to bluff you by reraising right now with a hand that's drawing dead.

If you do get raised when you bet a made flush, you should call and check-call on the river. It's possible someone is trying to bluff you; if so, you'll beat that person on the river. It's also possible someone is holding a larger flush than yours (for example, K♣ Q♣), in which case you're just unlucky — but you need to minimize your losses by not firing the first bullet on the river.

And, of course, the smaller your flush is (like holding a suited 2-3 — shame on you!), the more dangerous the four-flush on the river is.

In No-Limit, because so much more of your stack is at risk, you need to be more careful and really consider the types of hands your opponents have been playing behind you, as well as their pre-flop action:

- ✔ Suited Aces will probably have raises associated with them, as will a suited King-Queen. Back off and check-call any bet made on the turn and river.

- ✔ Other suited Kings and Queens are less clear and may well not have pre-flop raises. Your best action here is to bet enough so that a person on the draw doesn't get pot odds and stick it out for the river draw, but you need to be ready for beats.

- ✔ If you have a notorious slow-player (Chapter 10) behind you, you should check through and call any bet that is made on both the turn and the river.

- ✔ If you have a big-time bluffer playing behind you, check. If they bet on the turn, push all-in (don't call and then push on the river — this gives them a chance to see the river card before they decide). If they don't bet, wait for fifth street:

  - If it's a club, check and call any bet made.

  - If it's not a club, place a minimum bet to induce a bluff there. Reraise heftily, all the way up to all-in, if he acts behind you.

Watching for "hidden" improvements

On the turn, you need to keep your eyes open for opportunities that are making your hand better in ways that you didn't expect.

For example, if you were dealt 10♠ 10♣, a Q♣ 8♣ 3♥, flop isn't very exciting. As long as no one seems overly perky to see that Queen hit, and there seem to be a lot of stragglers, you've got good reason to be here for the turn card.

But when the J♣ turn hits, things are both better and worse. You now have a fairly good flush draw. Because the Jack and the Queen are both exposed, the only clubs over your 10 are the King and the Ace. You also have a gut shot straight draw of any 9 (with the 9♣ being your beyond-magical straight-flush draw — worth mentioning for novelty only, but not likely enough to change your mind in the overall scheme of things).

This means there are

- ✔ Nine clubs left in the deck that will make your flush. This wins as long as there isn't one of the three bigger clubs sitting at the table.

- ✔ Three more 9s left (we already counted the 9♣ above). This will be good enough to win as long as you're not fighting a flush already on the table, or a stray K-9 that is barking up a straight (except for the super-great 9♣ that's an automatic winner).

- ✔ Two 10s left in the deck. This is probably good enough as long as someone isn't playing a 9-10 for a straight (fairly unlikely because that means all 10s from the deck would have to be in play, *and* that last 10 would have to be paired with a 9, *and* someone would have had to play it). Not impossible, just very unlikely.

Assuming your pair of 10s isn't any good right now (and it almost certainly is *not* if there are a lot of players — there's both a Queen and a Jack on the board), that means you have 14 outs in the 46 remaining cards (not all guaranteed winners — depending on the composition of other players' hands; see Chapter 12 for more) on the draw.

This hand isn't good enough to bet straight-out, especially against a bunch of players — but if you're getting better than 3¼-to-1 pot odds (see Chapter 12) on your call, you can stay in to see the river. Keep in mind that the odds are against you in this situation — this means you probably *will* lose the hand, but mathematically you'll win money in the long run if you call here.

If you see betting *and* raising in this situation before the action even gets to you, you should fold. It almost certainly means you're either drawing dead or you're under-drawing (meaning that the same card that helps you also helps someone else who will end up better — say someone holding a higher club).

Keeping Track of the Action

The most important job you have on the turn is to remember the betting action you see on this round and try the best you can to equate it with the actions you saw on the hole cards and the flop. You also need to etch all the betting plays you see here into your mind. The number-one most common place for players to set a trap is on the turn — because they just miss a hand on the flop and then make it on fourth street.

If you saw someone attacking a pot earlier, and then backing off on the turn, it's likely one of two things has happened: They've either hit a hand, or they've missed and they're trying to save some cash.

Determining a hit

Many people will anticipate a straight or a flush draw by betting — beginning players will oftentimes raise. When they hit a hand, they'll often back off, hoping to check-raise you.

Trapping opponents who flush

Consider a flop of 2♠ 5♠ 10♦ with a turn of Q♠. Big hands in early positions, like A♠ K♠, will have raised pre-flop and may have come out initiating betting on the flop (or maybe check-raising). These players are sitting on a spade four-flush, with two dominant over-cards. That is enough to make the eyes of many players spin back in their heads and bet bet bet. When the other spade hits on the turn, they suddenly see the riches of the world on their doorstep and back off with the idea of check-raising you.

People in later positions like to play suited connectors, say 9♠ 10♠, and they too might get excited. Especially if they're catching top pair *and* a flush draw (also an example of a hidden improvement).

From a betting perspective, the event you're looking for is a ton of action, and then suddenly none. Again, it depends a *lot* on the players involved (see Chapter 8 for more on reading other players), but all other things being equal, I'd say this person is setting a trap by checking in front of you.

To test the theory, your best bet is to check through on the turn and see what happens on the river. If your opponent comes out betting on the river first again, she probably has a hand and was trying to trap you. If she checks again, it means that she had something good (trip 5s, trip 10s, two pair?), but backed off when the spades hit the board because she thought she was bested.

Of course, if *you* have the best hand (like the nut flush on the turn), then absolutely you should fire a bet off — especially if you're in the end of the betting order.

Putting you in a straightjacket

The other hand that gets made in the same fashion is a straight. Again, consider your opponents and their position around the table.

If someone very commonly plays connectors, or suited connectors, watch out for the player who limps in pre-flop, then gets excited by a set of cards like 5♥ 6♣ 10♠, but suddenly backs off on a 9♥ turn.

If you think about it, that kind of behavior doesn't make sense, because a 9 isn't a threatening card here. If someone had a hand they liked with a 4-5-10 board, how is a 9 going to make it any worse?

Easy. Either that person was bluffing, and has now backed off because he's afraid you're going to call again or, more likely with many opponents, because his 7-8 just went straight. Now, instead of bullying you with raises and hoping you might fold on semi-bluffs, he can back off because he has a made hand.

Comprehending the miss

Don't get so wrapped up in your inner psychic powers of analysis that the turban falls over your eyes and blinds you to the obvious signs that someone is afraid he's just been bested, or he's missing on a draw he was hoping for before.

Smelling someone's fear

For example, consider a flop of Q♠ 2♥ 4♥, and someone's betting strong. The A♠ hits on the turn and your adversary seems to back off. It's not because she just made a wheel, it's probably because she had paired the Queens and is now afraid that the Ace has counterfeited her in someone else's hand.

Although it's a fairly rare occurrence, another place you'll see people back off is when their trips have just been bested by a better set.

Here's an example that's easy to see: Nearly everyone who holds a suited K-Q pre-flop (some will bet it heavily). If a raising battle ensues, it's nearly always someone who is holding an Ace with a big kicker (say a suited A-Q). Lesser pairs on the table will eventually back off — they just assume that there is a bigger pair over them.

A flop of A-K-K will bring heavy action from the player holding three Kings, and the player with the Aces will back off a tad (but almost certainly still stay in the hand) assuming that the other player is *maybe* holding a King, and only vaguely considering that his opponent really *does* hold the nightmarish trip Kings.

A turn of an Ace will bring the player with the K-Q to a screeching stop. It's true, he now holds Kings full of Aces; but any opponent holding even a singelton Ace now has Aces full of Kings. So when the man with the cowboys quits betting, he isn't trapping, he's trying to figure out how he got so unlucky.

Gazing at the unfortunate

Big bets pre-flop and on the flop but then backed off on the turn could also mean your opponent has been anticipating a straight or flush and has missed — or he was trying to bluff that he had hit early, and he's afraid that the bluff isn't working because it was *you* who had actually hit the hand when you called.

These types of boards will have slightly different looks. What you're looking for are single-suited flops, say 2♥ 4♥ J♥ followed by an 8♣.

The siblings to the flush-not-making-it board are the ones where the flops that had hinted and teased at a straight are now walking away from making those wanting hands successful. Q♥ J♦ 3♣ followed by a lame 4♣, would be one example.

In the cases of straights and flushes that are not coming to fruition, if you have a hand (even a medium-strength one) you need to fire bullets. When someone folds, you automatically win — everyone else should *always* pay to see cards they're drawing for.

Chapter 7

Dipping in the River

*T*he river is where your poker hand, both literally, and figuratively, all goes down. Good luck! I hope you win — unless you're playing against me, in which case I hope you *barely* lose. And you better believe I'll be sincere in my sympathy. Really, I will.

Final Betting

From a pure theory point of view, the river card is very different from all the others in that your hand is determined. The card distribution is over and now it's just a matter of figuring out who has the best hand.

Well, almost. There is this little final betting detail left.

Fifth street is probably most akin to pre-flop action, in that it's the place where occasionally you'll see the bets really stack up. The variations mean that the river can take on a few different betting personalities, ranging from a nice quiet beer float trip, to a life threatening white-knuckle shoot through Class IV rapids.

All-checking, no dancing

Usually rivers are checked all the way around for one of three reasons:

✔ The board is threatening (for example, five hearts or a full house is showing).

✔ Extreme betting early on has caused people to back off (especially if the draws people were shooting for didn't come through).

✔ Players' hole cards just missed the community cards entirely. (This is especially common when it's only the blinds that were left in the hand.)

If you're in a later betting position and everyone is checking, this can be a very good time to pick up a pot. In fact, your ability to pick up the stray pot in these situations may very well make the difference between being a winning and losing player. If you consider the action you've seen in the hand up until now and take into account the types of opponents that are still in the hand (as you've decided, using the super-clever Chapter 8), you can then decide whether to check or bet in the following circumstances:

✔ If there was heavy action and raising surrounding a flop with two of the same suit (say, J♣ 8♣ 3♥), but things have since cooled off, you may well be looking at a broken flush. Fire a bet out if you have a pair that matches the middle rank of the community cards or higher.

✔ If the only people in the hand are the blinds, make a bet if you have any pair.

✔ If someone has been betting heavily up to this point but suddenly backs away from betting on the river, they probably will *not* check-raise you (this is much more of an expert play), and instead have been bluffing by over-betting. Make a bet if you have middle pair or better; or you believe there is a better than 50/50 chance your opponent will fold.

✔ If all else fails, or if you get flustered, or if you're just filled with doubt, check. It doesn't cost you anything.

Walking through the firestorm

Sometimes the river is the place where people sort of go insane and just start hurling bets at each other. You only want to get mixed up in this madness if you either have the nut (*maybe* second nut) hand, or the player you're up against is known to be looser than a broken jar of pennies in the bed of a pickup truck on a gravel road.

The most important thing you can do in this situation is make sure you're reading the board correctly (see Chapter 2). Make sure you're not getting caught up in a situation where your good hand is blinding you to bigger possibilities. Because pots can grind up so high over the course of a hand, one mistake here can wipe out an entire week's (or more) worth of poker winnings. Here are but a few examples that I've seen people self-destruct on:

- **You've hit the nut flush on a board of 10♠ 10♣ 9♦ 6♠ 2♠ with A♠ 9♠.** Started off pretty good with two pair, and then you runner-runnered into the nut flush. Don't get so wrapped up with your flush that you ignore the full house possibilities here. A common starting hand, especially from late position, is 9-10. Likewise, anyone tripping his pocket 2s, 6s, or 9s is sitting full. For sure you should call any bets, but don't raise and reraise. If people seem really eager to move any money into the pot, just call.

- **You trip on the board, holding a singleton.** For example, the board is Q♦ K♦ K♥ 7♠ 6♥ and you're holding K♣ J♣. Yes, you've got trip kings, but anyone who's tripped up with a pair (Q-Q, 7-7, 6-6), now has a full house. A good friend of mine had this exact hand happen to him the other day, when to his all-in dismay, his opponent was holding Q-Q. My pal even went so far as to call it a "bad beat" — it's not because his hand was *never* ahead at any point; *that* is hand myopia.

- **You play into a gapped straight like so: You hold Q-9 and the board shows K-J-10-2-4.** The good news is you're holding a King-high straight. The bad news is A-Q is a bigger straight than yours. Good slow-players love these kinds of set-ups. For some reason, the gapped straights are easier to be fooled by than holding 6-7 with a board of 10-9-8, I guess because it's so obvious there's another possibility (J-Q) on top.

Yes, you might look at these hands right now and say, "Yeah, yeah, whatever," quickly blowing off the advice I'm giving. Unfortunately in the passion of betting — especially big betting — when you have a hand that's made, it becomes remarkably easy to overlook another (better) hand. And if you *do* overlook another hand, you will not only pay, but pay *dearly*.

The telltale sign on No-Limit games on the river is if someone raises you the minimal amount, instead of pushing all-in, and (especially) if she does it *again* when reraised. What's happening here is the other player *knows* she has the nut hand and she's trying to maximize her return on the hand — she's afraid that if she pushes all-in, she'll lose equity in the hand by your folding.

Betting in moderation

The most common thing to see on the river is a bet, maybe two, with people deciding if they're going to call. If a bet has been made in front of a player deciding to act, unless he's one of the world's great actors, what he's always doing is looking at the board and answering the following questions, probably in order:

- ✔ What was the betting pattern of the person who placed the initial bet throughout the hand?

- ✔ How does the pattern apply to the position of that player relative to the dealer (the cards the bettor would have started with) and the cards I see on the board?

- ✔ What kind of player am I up against? Loose, tight, aggressive?

- ✔ Can the hand I'm holding right now beat the hand I *think* this person has?

These are the steps you should be going through as well, but the reason I talk about watching someone *else* do them is it can give you a very good feel for the strength of *her* hand as she makes the decision. For some reason, even very top players will drop their emotionless facade on fifth street, sometimes even if there are players still to act behind them. And if you're acting even later than the person considering, you have the ability to make an even better read on the overall power of your hand.

As a general rule, it takes a better hand to call than it does to make a bet. The more people calling, the better your hand has to be to win.

Deciding if you're being bluffed

A savvy player, especially if he's aggressive, or if he senses weakness in an opponent, will do exactly one thing when the river has determined he has a crappy hand: Bet. That is the *only* possible way to save the money that he's already put in the pot.

You now know this. The catch, of course, is that the person betting will *also* bet when he has a hand. So how do you know which is which? Again, the most important thing is to consider the player and ask yourself the following questions:

- ✔ Is this person prone to bluffing?

- ✔ How long has it been since this guy bluffed and does it seem like it's time again?

✔ Is there something very clearly wrong on the board or the cards that would hint at a bluff (like two cards to a flush or a straight that never materialized, or possibly a low-ball board such that someone holding two large pocket cards would never have paired)?

Even if you've determined that you believe your opponent *is* bluffing, you still have to be able to beat his "non"-hand. Any reasonable pair should be plenty.

The generally accepted rule is that you should look at the pot odds of your call. If there's $36 in the pot, and it costs you $6 to call, you can ask yourself if you think there's better than a one-in-six chance that you're being bluffed, and if so, call. And whatever you do, make sure to keep track whether you were right or wrong against that player. Because even when you guess wrong, there may well be something in what happened that will keep you from making that mistake again.

Showing a Hand . . . or Not?

After the betting round of the river — even if there's no betting and all everyone has done is the boring action of "check" — there's still the *showdown.* It's that heart dropping moment when people expose their cards.

It's not unusual, especially in games where tensions are running high, for players to be overly reticent to show a hand — even when it's nothing more than a showdown. People are *so* protective of their hands that they don't even show them when they're supposed to. It's also not usual when this happens for dealers to say something smarmy like, "First hand over wins."

There is, however, a progression that is followed if the whole table suddenly gets deadlocked with the heavy task of just turning their friggin' cards over.

1. **Technically, the person who made the last raise (or initial bet, if there were no raises) is the person being called, so he exposes his hand first.**

2. **The dealer displays this hand to the center of the table and calls out what it is — for example, "Two-pair, 3s and 2s."**

   At least the dealer is *supposed* to do this — he doesn't always.

3. **In a clockwise fashion, every player either shows or mucks his hand.**

   Any hand that is mucked, without being shown, is officially dead and no longer eligible to win the pot.

   - If the newly exposed hand is beaten, the dealer turns it face down and mucks it, moving to the next hand.

   - If the hand exposed beats the first hand shown, the newly exposed hand is moved to the center of the table and declared — for example, "Three 3s." The original hand that was shown is then turned face down and mucked.

4. **The process continues until one hand is left face up on the table (or multiples if there is a tie), the dealer pushes the pot to the winning player, and the hand is mucked.**

If there are any side pots (see Chapter 2), a winner is determined for those first, working all the way back to the winner of the main pot.

During the showdown, you'll want to keep in mind the following:

- ✔ **Unlike the rest of a poker game, you do *not* have to expose your cards in order (unless no one else is showing, in which case you *must* when it's your turn).** If you think you have a winner, you can turn it over immediately.

- ✔ **Be sure to keep your cards in front of you.** Don't send them sailing out into the middle of the table (it's also bad form to chuck them in your opponent's face). You need to be able to easily prove the hand is yours.

- ✔ **You must expose *both* of your cards.**

- ✔ **Even if you're heads-up and the other player immediately mucks her hand but has gone all the way to the showdown on the river, you still *must* expose your hand.**

- ✔ **You *might* have the rights to see another player's hand if he's made it all the way to the showdown.** At some card houses, you must have a hand all the way to the showdown yourself to be able to ask and see it; at others, you merely have to have been dealt a hand. Ask your dealer what the house policy is. Strangely, asking to see the other player's hand is always considered to be a mildly socially unacceptable thing to do in a professional card room. (I have no idea why and it most certainly has never stopped me.)

- ✔ **The most important rule: Never believe a player has the hand he orally declares until you see it with your own eyes.** Every day someone, somewhere, misreads his hand. And this is cutting your opponent slack, assuming you're not dealing with someone who has sinister intent.

✔ **After you muck your hand, the hand is dead.** Be *certain* you have a loser before you throw it away, or just let the dealer handle it for you.

✔ **Do not begin to scoop the pot toward yourself.** Let the dealer make the first motion.

In general, I don't like to expose any hand that I'm not forced to show, but I also like my poker games to move right along. Here's my quick list of how I behave at showdown:

✔ If I think I have a winner, or if I was the person who started the last betting round, I turn my cards over immediately.

✔ If someone else shows a hand that beats mine, typically I just muck.

✔ I only show a hand if there was a hideous beat involved and even then I do it *only* if I think it will give another player an impression that I play extremely tight.

✔ If players are being slow to show hands, I just go ahead and show mine to move things along.

If you have a hand that has been declared a winner and you ask to see an opponent's hand that is headed for the muck, you're techni-cally at a minor amount of risk. Because you've requested to see it, and you have a hand that has been declared a "winner," the hand you're asking to see is still considered to be live. If the hand that was going to be mucked beats yours, you lose the pot. Dealers will yap on and on about how dangerous and foolhardy this move is, and I'm sure it *can* happen, but in two decades of professional card room play, I've never seen a winner come back out of the muck — not on my table, not on any table around me.

People don't throw away winning hands — just be aware that it *could* happen. Oh yeah, and I highly recommend *not* asking to see hands of really drunk people.

If you make it to the river and no one calls your final bet, don't show your hand unless:

✔ You're convinced it will change (or enforce) an impression that you want to give other players about yourself, whatever that may be (you play tight, you play loose, you were bluffing, you weren't bluffing, and so on).

✔ There is a potential prize associated with it, such as a high hand. (See Chapter 16 for more on these.)

All mucked up online

In the online world (see Chapter 15), the showing of cards is a wholly automated process, including "auto-muck" check boxes that throw your cards in if they aren't winners. Just like everything else about the online world, it just speeds things right on along.

If you *want* to show a hand, make sure to turn the auto-muck check box off. At the end of the hand you'll be offered a chance to show.

Also if anyone has gone all the way to a showdown and then mucked a hand, you can see what those player's cards were through the "hand history" function of your poker site. Use your site's "help" function to find out more about how to do that.

Watching for Mistakes

 Because the river is the place where the payouts happen, and it's the final stop of the (potentially crazy) train ride that this hand has represented, you need to really keep your eyes peeled for any last-minute weirdness that can happen. Although it's true that professional card rooms are required by their gaming laws to keep things on the up-and-up, mistakes can (and surprisingly often do) happen. Of all the people in a card room, *you* are the only person who has your best interests at heart.

In all the cases mentioned in this section, if you see something amiss, call the dealer's attention to it. If the dealer is of no help, ask for the floorperson. You don't need to be an ass about it — be friendly, but firm, and point out the discrepancy you see.

Things to watch for include

- ✔ **Dealers who are raking too much:** Rakes in most establishments are posted on the tables themselves and capped at some amount. If you see a dealer taking more than the permissible rake, call him on it.

- ✔ **Not being paid for your winning hand:** If you have the winning hand, be sure you're being paid for it. The most common thing dealers overlook is a counterfeit of this type: You hold A-Q, your opponent holds 8-8, and the board is K-K-9-9-3. You win with two pair, Kings, and 9s with an Ace kicker; your opponent has Kings and 9s with an 8 kicker. (Another is when you hit a straight flush and your opponent holds the Ace-high flush. Something like 4♠ 4♦ versus A♦ K♦ with a board of J♦ 8♦ 6♦ 5♦ 7♦.)

✓ **Other players stacking your chips:** In a professional card room, don't let other players help you stack your chips. You'd be surprised how dexterous some people can be with their palming of a chip. (In home games, it's no big deal.)

✓ **Exposing your hand before betting action is done:** Be sure that all betting action is completed before you expose your hand. If you're uncertain of the state of the action, ask your dealer.

✓ **Other players trying to get cards back from the muck:** Make sure players aren't trying to retrieve cards from the muck. I've seen this happen about two dozen times at tables I've been at — once, unbelievably, a dealer was actually allowing it.

✓ **Errors in huge tournaments:** Extremely large tournaments, such as the main event of the WSOP, tend to be more error prone. This is partially because everyone — all the participants, including the dealers at the table — is nervous. It is also due to the fact that, because large tourneys have to bring in an unusual force of dealers from elsewhere, large tourneys commonly use dealers who are off their normal work schedule (or from a different card rooms entirely). Communications with the dealers who are there tend to be "less than ideal."

✓ **When you win an all-in, you in fact win it all:** In No-Limit, be certain you have *all* chips of another player when you bust them out (including any house chip they were using to protect their cards). Ensure too that you have any paper currency that was part of the betting.

✓ **When you lose an all-in, you pay the proper amount:** Also in No-Limit, if you lose an all-in and you have more than your opponent, be sure that you're paying an amount equal to his stack (and not just pushing all of yours over with no leftovers for you).

✓ **Flaws on the cards:** If you see flaws on the cards — nicks, folds, bends, or creases that make them stand out — point them out to the dealer. It's not very likely that people at your table are intentionally marring the cards, but Aces do get an unusual amount of wear and warp because of their importance relative to hole cards.

Part III

Movin' On to Higher Stakes: Advanced Strategies of Hold'em

The 5th Wave   By Rich Tennant

Having never learned the difference between a black bear and a brown bear, Stuart couldn't be sure whether his opponent's bet was aggressive, or false-aggressive.

In this part . . .

*T*he most important aspects of Texas Hold'em are in this section. If you're serious about playing cards, you need to study this section carefully. If you think of poker as a low form of war (and you probably should), this would be the armory where you gather your weapons.

You'll find a chapter dedicated to reading your opponents, as well as one dedicated to keeping your opponents from reading you. You'll also find a primer on bluffing, as well as the mathematical know-how you need to be a statistically successful player. The final chapter of the section is the most theoretically complex of the book and digs even deeper into the game to consider "larger" strategies of Texas Hold'em.

Chapter 8

Playing the Players

*I*f you ask me to give you the single most important factor in learning and playing poker, it has to be gaining the best possible understanding of the people you're playing against.

If there's one chapter in this book you absolutely need to read and fully digest, it's this one. Think of this entire chapter as being covered with a huge Remember icon.

A common assumption made by people who are just learning Hold'em is that it requires some high degree of mathematical skill. The implication is that if you're not a math genius, you don't really stand a chance at the tables. This misconception is further reinforced by TV shows giving you running percentages on hands as they're dealt and played (which also ignore little details like the fact that the players have no idea what their opponents are holding, but you do — making the numbers nonsensical in a way).

Although the math part does have a bearing on your play (see Chapter 12 for more on math), it is *heavily* overshadowed by just knowing the traits of people you're playing against.

If you can identify the traits of your opponents, and interpret the way those traits are presented to you at the table, you've found the master key to the game. Make no mistake about it, understanding your opponents at the table is *the* most important aspect of poker.

Classifying Players

When you play against people on a poker table, to the best of your ability you want to try to classify their play. Beginning and intermediate players tend to think of players by general categories of classification, I talk about those in this section here and that's certainly a great place to start. Eventually, though, you'll want to get to a point where you classify each and every player individually. The more you can say about an individual player whom you're competing against, the more likely you are to beat her in the long run.

Aggressive versus passive players

In broad terms, many players tend to be either aggressive or passive in their play. Figuring out where your opponents are in the passive-aggressive spectrum can help you not only win more when *you* have a good hand, but also lose less when *he* does.

All aggression, all the time

Aggressive players are the easiest to pick out at a table. And by this, I don't necessarily mean they're the ones who are most likely to throw an empty beer bottle across the room when bad beat. Aggression can certainly be well defined but you'll *feel* aggression as much as you actually see it, and the symptoms are fairly blatant.

Aggressive players tend to:

- ✓ **Raise and reraise fairly often when they're involved in the betting action.** Raising is what makes the aggressive players easily identifiable because dealers will *always* announce "raise," and all eyes on the table immediately turn there.

- ✓ **Play from their position more heavily.** An aggressive player in late position will raise even more often than her usual trigger-happy self, based solely on her position (see Chapter 4 for more on the importance of position).

- ✓ **Start the betting rounds.** When given a choice between check and bet, an aggressive player usually bets.

- ✓ **Check-raise.** Check-raising is the second most aggressive act you can do on a poker table (the most aggressive act is reraising). And check-raising is sneakier, because the original check implied that the player didn't have a poker hand — the raise indicates very clearly that the person does.

- ✓ **Be not at all intimidated by anyone at the table.** Aggressive players by their very nature are also more self-assured.

- ✓ **Be less likely to fold a hand after they're playing.**

✔ **Be more experienced poker players.** As a rough rule, people become more aggressive the more comfortable they get with the game. This is especially true of people who have read a lot of poker theory books (they repeatedly hammer home the importance of aggression at a table).

Those wimpy passive players

Passive players are a bit harder to spot at a table, mostly because their lack of aggression makes them easy to overlook. These are the players who:

✔ **Call rather than raise.** The passive player believes she has a hand — she just isn't interested in pushing it forward.

✔ **Check instead of starting the betting.**

✔ **Have a greater tendency to fold the hands they're playing.**

✔ **May seem intimidated by one or more players at the table — or maybe even playing the game itself.**

✔ **Typically have less poker experience.** For a passive player, just the act of sitting at a table and betting is scary enough. He doesn't want the added tension of raising. His inexperience also means that he hasn't had any exposure to advanced poker texts that recommend raising.

Deciding tight versus loose

In addition to aggressiveness, you should try to be making some sort of determination of how loose your opponent's play is.

Hearing the tight squeak

A player is considered to be *tight* if he plays an extremely limited set of starting hands. The starting set of hands I outline in Chapter 4 would be just a tad on the tight side. And although you can't see a player's starting hand very often, you do see how often he decides to play a hand — and this in itself is a clue.

The starting set of hands I describe in Chapter 4 will have you playing somewhere between 15 and 20 percent of all hands (including when you have the blinds and get to play for free or at a greatly reduced rate). If you see a player playing 1-in-5 hands or less (especially over a long period of time, or several sessions), you're looking at a tight player.

Watching the loose rattle

Conversely, *loose* players will play a wide variety of starting hands, and as result, you'll see them in the pot more often. Any player playing something like a third of her hands, or more, over a long session would definitely be considered a loose player.

Combining your evaluations

The implication is that there are four different types of players, but that's true only from the very widest of standpoints. Again, as you gain your poker experience, you'll probably find yourself fine-tuning your evaluations to each individual, but the following are a good set of evaluations to begin with — along with some advice on how to combat them effectively.

Battling aggressive/tight players

Playing against an aggressive/tight player is fairly simple. Because he's tight, he'll play only the highest quality hands. When he does, your response is fairly straightforward: Fold unless you have a hand that is extremely good.

Tight players tend not to bluff much, so don't be afraid to throw away the occasional hand that's only okay by your estimation. And if you're going to start aiming your hold cards at the trash can, the earlier you can throw it away, the better — their raising and reraising will gnaw on your stack in a big way.

Playing a bit looser against a tight player will get you more small pots (especially if you're raising, where he tends to fold quickly early on). But when you do play loosely against him you need to be very quick to drop a hand when you see aggression coming back at you.

Keep in mind that if a player *thinks* you're bullying him on the table, he *will* change his style of play — probably by loosening up a little and getting even more aggressive.

Playing against aggressive/loose players

Aggressive/loose players may seem a bit scary when you first come across them, but you'll quickly learn to think of them as one of the biggest assets to you on a poker table. The aggressive play will bring money out on the table; the loose play will mean that it just keeps on coming.

An aggressive loose player will have an interesting side-effect of making the other players on the table loose and aggressive as well.

And although you may be tempted to jump on the bandwagon yourself, your wallet will like it better if you instead opt for tighter and more passive play. Because your opponent is loose, if you play tight, you're more likely to win on any given hand (because you have a better set of starting cards). Over time, you'll take down more pots and find your stack ratcheting right on up.

Don't complain on the odd times you get a bad beat. Just think of it as the tax of doing business with one of your best customers.

Skewering passive/loose players

On the surface you may think that a passive/loose player is a rarity, but actually it's probably the most common category that beginning poker players fall into. These people are the ones who play too many hands and then have no idea how to bet as the hand progresses.

If the player seems passive enough to fold merely by someone else being aggressive, that's what you should do every time you enter a pot. Her continual folding will float your bankroll pretty quickly.

Be careful, though, some beginning players *never* fold, which means bluffing against them serves no purpose. Against these players you should instead tighten your play (so you're only playing higher-quality hands) and fire away unmercifully when you're holding the good stuff.

Dealing with passive/tight players

Passive/tight players are an interesting anomaly because what they will tend to do is stay in the hand when they have a winner, but not bet it. These types of players won't pad your bank account very much, but they're also easy to play against — just check through whenever they're in a hand.

Because he's playing tight, he may well have a winner over your hand, making betting mildly suicidal. However, you *should* bet if he's the passive kind of player who tends to fold.

Watching for the "unusual" play

There is one thing you need to watch for: any unusual play from a player you believe you have classified correctly. Here are some examples:

> ✔ **If you see a raise from a normally passive player who *never* raises, that means she has a hand.** Unless you have something *really* good relative to the board you're seeing, you should fold.

✔ **If a typically aggressive player who is normally Mr. Bet-Bet-Bet suddenly checks, he's either playing for a draw or (probably more likely) trying to trap you.** Only bet against a player like this if you're willing to call a reraise.

✔ **If an extremely aggressive player ever check-calls you, it almost certainly means she has a trapping hand.** If it happens to you, you definitely should *not* bet the next time you see action.

In No-Limit be especially careful of a player who flat-call the blinds from early position, when the typical action you've been seeing from her is raising pre-flop. This is a classic trick of someone holding a very large pocket pair (A-A or K-K). Don't fall for it.

As you're classifying players, try as best you can to get a read on how their play changes according to position as well. As you can see from the list of starting cards in Chapter 4, even a basic poker strategy encourages you to play tighter in early position and looser in the back. Keep your eyes out for people who violate this guideline in either way — either looser in front (especially those who play Aces with no kickers from early positions) or tighter in the back.

Looking for Tells

A *tell* is a hint that a player gives you as to what the strength of his hand may be — either through the way he bets, or the way he physically behaves around the table. Successfully interpreting the tells of your opponents will make a huge difference in any given session you have at a poker table.

Watching the right place at the right time

It *almost* goes without saying that in order to watch for tells in the first place, you need to be watching people. This tends to be easiest to do when you're not playing in a hand, but rather just sitting back and taking it all in. Although the other players not in the hand are watching television or reading the sports pages, you should be keeping an eye on your opponents. See how they face each other and how they react as they win or lose, bet or fold.

I find that I pick up more watching the table when I'm not involved in the hand because I don't have that evil mix of paranoia combined with my undeserved poker-playing superiority that's present when it's *my* money on the line.

Also, you need to get out of the habit of immediately looking at your cards as soon as they're dealt, as well as the community cards as they're exposed. Instead you should watch the players around the table and see how *they* react as they see the cards for the first time. (By waiting until it's your turn to look at your hole cards, you also avoid creating a tell on yourself — see Chapter 9 for more.)

Who's acting and who isn't?

Of course people *know* you're looking for a tell and will intentionally try to throw you off. What you need to figure out, then, is who is actually inadvertently showing a tell and who is merely trying to make your poker experience even more confusing. (As you read through this section, remember that all these things apply to you as well — read Chapter 9 for more on not exposing your own tells.)

The number-one rule of tells

Because people associate bluffing with lying, they tend to interpret that as meaning you should act in the *opposite* manner to what people would expect. And this is the biggest tell of all, especially in beginning-to-intermediate play: *Players will most often intentionally act as though their hands are the opposite of what they are.*

A player who is bluffing will bet in a very aggressive fashion and stare you right in the eyes. A player with a strong hand will casually lay a bet and look away. This tends to be especially true of players who have cut their Hold'em teeth on the Internet — they may have thousands of hours of play, but they've never sat in front of another human being to do it. They have no idea how to act.

A whole lotta shakin' goin' on

Another thing to keep a close eye out for is someone who is physically shaking as she goes to place a bet. I've seen many beginning players assume that this means a player is bluffing, and nothing could be farther from the truth. A shaking player *always* is holding a good starting hand or has made a big hand on the board — it's nearly impossible to fake the nervous rattle of someone with a great hand. When you see it, it's the real thing, and you're in trouble. Fold and ask questions later.

Watching other people's hands

There is so much surveillance and counter-surveillance in the world of tells — especially if you're playing against more experienced players — that I find it difficult to get a truly accurate read on the players involved. Did I really just catch something, or are they faking it? Hmm.

There does, however, seem to be one fairly reliable version of a tell and that is how people use their hands at the table. I don't mean *hand* as in the two cards they're holding, but rather *hands* as in that part of the human body that is attached to a wrist — those funny looking things that have five fingers on them.

Shaking hands typically indicate a crushing hand, but you can pick up a surprisingly larger amount of information from watching people's hands:

- ✔ **Many people will hold their cards in a certain way (for them) if they're planning on folding a hand.** This gives you a chance to look behind you on any given betting action to see how many callers you might get.

- ✔ **People thinking of betting will often fondle their chips before it is their turn to bet.** Many intermediate players do this to make you think they're either going to bet or call, in an effort to get you to *not* bet because they would actually fold otherwise — yet another version of acting in a way that's opposite of how they're actually thinking).

- ✔ **People who suddenly hit big hands, especially on the flop, will often flinch with their hands.**

- ✔ **People who recheck their hole cards after an all-suited flop (for example, all spades) were not holding two spades to begin with or they wouldn't be rechecking.**

- ✔ **People who check their hole cards twice pre-flop (or give their hole cards an exceedingly long stare) often have a very big pair.** For some reason, people with large pocket pairs need to look at them again — I guess they just want to make sure they aren't running away somewhere.

- ✔ **One signal for checking is to tap the table when it's your turn to bet; some people, as hard as this is to believe, will tap it one way for a true check (say with just an index finger), but do another (say, rap the table with a fist) if they intend on check-raising.**

- ✔ **In No-Limit, players who are becoming short stacked will often count out their stack relative to the size of the blinds.** What they're doing is figuring out how many big blinds their stack represents, and on a surprising number of occasions you'll find these people pushing all-in soon afterward. Anytime you see someone counting out a stack in such a fashion, you should be leery of the all-in play behind you when you're first to act. Be sure to play tighter in these situations so you won't be afraid to call the raise.

Listening to what people say

You can find out quite a bit just by listening to people talking at the table.

When people say the obvious

A couple years ago I was playing in Las Vegas, completely card dead, and as I folded hand after hand I spent my time watching the players for tells to keep myself from going even more insane. I found a few here and there, like the guy up the table who would always put his thumb on the lower-left corner of his cards before he folded.

But it took me a surprisingly long time to find the most obvious of all: There was one guy who would, literally, announce his hand every time the cards were exposed. He'd say things like, "Now I've got two pair," "I'm sittin' on a big flush draw," and so on. The most amazing thing, though, was that everyone at the table was either ignoring him or not believing him. Hand after hand he would announce his way through and then take his opponents down on the river.

I thought it was nothing more than a funny freak occurrence, but about a month later, I ran across yet another player who did the same thing.

When you run across a player who's decided to become the MC of the poker table, your task becomes pretty easy: Hand him the microphone and listen to what he says. On those rare times when you *do* see his cards, see how they line up with what the player is saying. It's very possible that you're hearing nothing more than some player spewing static that he somehow finds "funny," but you'll find a surprising number of times when it's actually a tell (whether it's lying [which you then mentally reverse] or telling the truth).

Also when players show a big hand at a table to prove they weren't bluffing, it's fairly common for others to chime in about what they were playing. And while this isn't 100 percent foolproof, the things the other players say tend to be more accurate than not (because those people don't really gain anything by lying about the hands that they folded). Keep track of what those players said they had, what their relative position around the table was, and try to remember the way they acted as they went through the betting phases.

Listening to those who already know

Also keep an eye on how players who are very well acquainted with each other, react *to* each other. For example, if you visit Las Vegas in the off-season, it's common to sit at a table with four or five retirees who know each other. These people play often enough, and know each other well enough, that it's not unusual for them to know (and often openly announce) the tells of all their pals.

In these cases, if you see one player always backing away from another in a given set of circumstances, you should start doing it too. There's no need to play against Lonnie for 20 years just to find out that he always snorts when he has Big Slick — especially when Big Sal has already done the investigation (and reporting) for you.

Keeping track of the mundane

Keeping track of mundane conversations that have nothing to do with the card game you're playing is a good idea. The way people behave when they're responding and reacting to the world around them can be revealing.

For example, someone takes a sip of coffee and says, "This is the best cup of coffee I've ever tasted!" If it is a great cup of coffee, then you know what the person sounds like when she's telling the truth. You can watch her body posture and any other little detail that seems relevant. Likewise, if the coffee is actually closer to sludge, you've just seen how she reacts when she's lying.

Don't just take my word for it, Amarillo Slim Preston claims to have won a world title by using exactly this kind of investigation.

Involuntary reactions

Many people have involuntary reactions to their play. I mention hand shaking earlier in this chapter, but there are also things such as sweating (people with big hands pre-flop tend to sweat) and racing heart rates. Phil "The Unabomber" Laak plays with a hooded sweatshirt, sometimes drawing it all the way up like Kenny from South Park. Phil Hellmuth plays in a track suit with the collar turned up. Both of them do this expressly so you can't see their veins pounding in their necks. (**Note:** I *am* assuming this isn't just something peculiar about people named Phil.)

When you watch for involuntary reactions from your opponents, don't forget to factor in the raw importance of the event you're seeing. Anyone making the final table of a major tournament will, by default, be wound up tighter than usual.

In general, though, the more keyed up a person is, the more likely he is to have a big hand.

Failing all else . . .

You can sit and analyze and analyze your opponents and the situations you're in, and if you're not careful, you will *over*analyze them. If you find that you're driving yourself bonkers and you're not able to get a proper read, you do have a couple more options.

Look at the hand positionally

If you find yourself getting overly confused with the situation, forget trying to read your opponent for a tell. Instead consider her betting pattern on this particular hand and how it could relate to starting hands of different types. Consider nuances such as trips, flushes, and straight draws. Don't forget to factor in her actions on the hand pre-flop and be certain to consider the player's position at the table.

Trust your gut

The reason you're able to live, breathe, eat, drink, and play poker is because your ancestors made it through some pretty dark times. They did this by fleeing from the big scary things that could eat them and pounding on the little annoying things that were threatening but beatable. These epic battles, fought over eons, ended up putting you at a card table. And you still hold all these fight-or-flight impulses. You should listen to them.

When all else fails, trust your instincts. If it just really *feels* like you're being trapped, you probably are. Fold.

If there's just something basically wrong with that lady's last big bet — it just doesn't feel right somehow — call it. This isn't math and it isn't science — it's instinct. Use it and you'll be right more than you're wrong.

Just fold already

Okay, what started all this was that you were confused by the tells you were seeing. Then you looked at the hand positionally and couldn't come up with any hints as to what that psycho on the other side of the table might have. Then you wanted to try your gut feeling, but the hot dog you had for lunch is burning a little too much to get the right kind of read.

In cases like this, especially as you're starting out, you should just fold. Sure, you'll lose some equity and occasionally be bluffed out of a hand. But one bad fold costs you a *lot* less than a string of bad calls (which is what happens if you're chasing an opponent who's actually trapping you).

You can always fold now and just play the next hand. The cards *will* be different there and you'll have a whole new set of possibilities. Don't let your impatience with a hand — or especially your current stack size — affect the quality of plays you're making at a table. If you think the quality of your play is suffering, take a break and evaluate your situation. Figure out if you should buy in for more or just call it quits for the day.

Zeroing In on Specifics

To *really* figure out a table, you should turn your beady little eyeballs into laser beams and heavily home in on the table around you. Here are a couple tricks you can use for help.

Figuring out the table in order

After a couple hours of play you should be able to mentally walk around the table and talk about every player you're playing against. You don't need to go into excruciating detail, but you should be able to lay down generalities. A sample might look like this:

Seat 1: Aggressive player who raises pre-flop only in later positions with no previous callers.

Seat 2: Passive/tight player. Only calls when he thinks he has the best hand.

Seat 3: Dangerous player. Varies betting sizes and styles. Hard to figure out.

Seat 4: Was playing well early, but got a bad beat and is now tilting.

Seat 5: Beautiful genius. (Oh, that's right, this seat is you.)

Seat 6: Inexperienced player. Tends to fold when raised.

Seat 7: Only calls with good hands. Only raises with the nuts.

Seat 8: Very loose player. Calls nearly every hand pre-flop. Almost never sees a turn card.

Seat 9: Uncertain. Player is either having a bad run of cards or is playing far too tight.

Seat 10: Aggressive. Likes to take control of the betting action every round.

As you go through this mental list in your head, as much as you can, make note of how the players interact with each other. For example, the player who was bad beat in Seat 4 almost certainly holds a grudge against the player who beat her. You want to make sure you're not interpreting something as a tell that is actually some other type of interaction. That doesn't mean that you can't exploit these types of situations to your benefit (you can and should), but make sure you're correct about the underlying reason behind the actions you're seeing.

Looking at individuals

By far the best way to figure out people at a table is to study them individually. If you pick one person and watch him *every* hand, through all of his moves — check, bet, call, fold, raise, win, lose, and ordering something to eat — you'll discover a tremendous amount.

Players expect to be watched when they're involved in a hand or farther down the line in the betting order. They aren't expecting it so much when their play is less consequential, and because of this you're more likely to see their true and/or real reactions to situations. You can use these real responses as a baseline to the other behavior you see at the table in a hand.

Whenever I'm having trouble figuring out an individual player — especially if I seem to be getting conflicting signals in recurring situations (like the way she behaves heads-up) — I drop everything else and just spend time studying her.

When you do, don't be belligerent about it, like giving her a continual icy stare-down. Instead, just make her a constant part of your attention for a few orbits of the dealer button — you might even try striking up a conversation. You'll find your chances of figuring her out will rise substantially.

 After your next poker session, come back and read this chapter again. It will give you deeper insight into the play you've just experienced and give one more reinforcement of the most valuable thing you can learn about playing poker.

Chapter 9

Bluffing: When Everything Isn't What It Appears to Be

*W*hen people first become acquainted with poker, they run quickly into the concept of *bluffing* — intentionally misrepresenting your hand in such a way that the other players are misled as to what you have (usually to make the other players fold).

Aside from luck of the draw, bluffing is *the* element that elevates poker from nearly all the other games of pure skill, such as chess.

To my mind, writing about bluffing is similar to writing about painting. Really the best way to actually do it is to go out and practice, but it's one heck of a lot easier to practice if you have at least a rough idea of the underlying concepts. In this chapter, I walk you through the hows, whens, and whys of bluffing.

Bluffing Basics

The most important thing in playing a poker hand is understanding the players at the table. Bluffs depend almost entirely on how other players will react to the information you're going to pretend to convey at the table.

 Before you head any farther, make sure you have a basic understanding of Chapter 8 and what it means to play the other players at the table — those concepts are the keys you need to understanding bluffs and making them work.

Your turn not to tell

In order for any bluff to work on your behalf, you first have to turn off all the other tells you normally broadcast in a game. For example, if you always riffle your poker chips on the table whenever you have a marginal hand, people are going to be one heck of a lot less likely to believe your big bet represents a good hand if you're shuffling your chips like a bored roulette dealer before you make it.

Of course, one of the problems of becoming overly stoic at the table is that all your small, and otherwise usually not noticeable, tells become much more pronounced. "Gee Mark, I never noticed that you rub your fingertips together for one second whenever you have a bad hand, but now that you don't shuffle those chips anymore it's a whole lot more obvious."

The best way to get a feel for the way you broadcast at a table is to either videotape yourself playing cards with your friends in a home game, or better yet, designate one of your pals as your poker watchdog and have him give you a rundown on the way you act and play. The only problem with assigning a watchdog is you essentially eliminate playing that person for money for the rest of your life — so if you do choose someone, it's probably better to pick the girl who beats you all the time rather than the guy who helps subsidize your rent every month.

If you can't shut off your emotional broadcasting system as you play, you should at least be aware of what your tells *are* such that you can mimic them in situations when you want to bluff.

When you first start playing poker, at least up through intermediate play, players will indicate the opposite of what they are. It's as though bluffing equates with "lying," so people will act the opposite — if their hands are weak they'll act strong, if their hands are strong they'll act weak. Don't fall into this same trap yourself. If you're not highly skilled, you're better off conveying no expression than trying to misdirect someone with an "act."

Don't bluff people worse than you

Okay, okay, the title isn't strictly true, but I've put it up there in headline bold to make a point and have you think about it. Bluffing people worse than you are, especially if they're *considerably* worse than you are, doesn't always work the way you want it to.

You're more likely to run across the types of people I'm talking about here early in your poker career. For *some* reason, they don't seem to end up playing the game for years on end. In the following sections, I tell you why *not* to bluff them.

Some people might call anyway

The killing phrase you want to listen for at a poker table is, "I just called to keep you honest." If you ever hear someone say that at a table, and you're convinced it's not a bigger part of some general poker ruse, that's a player you don't want to bluff. Essentially what he's saying is, "You know what? I'm a bonehead. I'm so stupid I'll actually call you with a hand that can't beat what you're representing, and yes, I *do* believe you have it. I'm just going to give my money away to you." And instead, he beats you.

If you do run across a player like that, you *can* beat him, sure. But the way to do it is to bet when you have a good hand, not a bad one.

Some people don't understand what "lucky" means

Many beginning players don't have a basic understanding of the mathematics behind poker (see Chapter 12), and may go ahead and call simply because they don't understand what's at stake.

For example, let's say the board shows a rainbow K-K-8-2 and the only hands you've shown all night have had Kings in them. You're sitting with A-Q in a No-Limit game and decide to push all-in to feign a set of Kings. To your dismay, your opponent says, "I know you have three Kings, but I've got pocket rockets here, and I'm going to call and hope for that Ace."

You've gone from having a person not understand what it means to draw to only two outs, to a much larger problem of drawing dead for all the marbles.

Assuming the river card wasn't an Ace, if you had waited to make this all-in bluff, you would have fared much better.

Now it's true that you may not have any idea just *how* far gone some of your "lesser" opponents may be, but if you're patient and let the game ride for a while, you'll get some idea.

For opponents who seem too dull (or just too weird) to successfully bluff, you're better off not relying on bluffing and instead taking advantage of other types of errors they may make — like playing too many hands or misjudging the relative strength of their hands to the rest of the table.

Making your bluff count

You only want to bluff where it matters, not where it doesn't.

To look at an extreme example, if you're sitting in the small blind with 4-2 off-suit, in a No-Limit ring game and bet all-in to gobble up the big blind, what have you proven?

If that player passes, you've won a single bet on the table by risking your entire stack. That's the upside.

The downside is that you've mildly aggravated the player with the big blind and, worse, you've drawn the attention of the table to you. Everyone saw the play; everyone has marked you as a potential bluffer. Slow-players (see Chapter 10) love to eat players alive who do that kind of stuff.

And if the player *does* call (slightly more likely than usual because everyone else at the table has folded), you're going to be behind in the race.

You're better off bluffing in situations in which:

- ✔ There are more chips in the pot (you actually get something if you're right).

- ✔ The bluff could make a difference in your tournament position/ standing (see Chapter 17 for more on tourneys).

- ✔ You have a reason to establish a stronger table image.

When to Bluff

One of the key elements to bluffing is knowing when to do it. If a bluff is well timed, it will mean more to your stack and it's more likely to succeed.

Bluffing based on your image of "predictability"

There are two polar-opposite philosophies about how opposing players should view you as a player at the card table. One is to have people think of you as an unknown-and-hard-to-classify player, the other is to be thought of as being *very* predictable. Both have their advantages and disadvantages.

Playing the part of the wild man

The advantage of being an unpredictable player at a table is that no one is sure what you have and what it means. Is he bluffing? Is he just over-betting? Does he have something but wants us to think he's bluffing?

There is certainly a kind of satisfaction in being thought of as the loose cannon at the poker table that can be had in few other ways (aside from doing something like standing up in the middle of a restaurant and starting to sing). The problem, however, is it will cause people to just stick closer to their pure game, and possibly think of your actions as static from the All Freak Network.

From a pure bluffing point of view, you're better off conveying a sense of predictability.

Playing the role of the predictable player

If you have a very predictable presence at the table — meaning players are always fairly certain they *think* they know what you have — a bluff is much easier to pull off.

To illustrate: If the only hands you've ever shown are very strong opening hands (like those I talk about in Chapter 4), people will start making predictions on what your hand is, based on the boards that they're seeing. Say a flop were to show a rainbow Q-J-10, someone bet in an early position, and you raised from a middle position (Chapter 4 also has more on the importance of position), you'd probably get players spinning into this type of thinking: "Let's see, she called pre-flop and now I'm looking at that board. . . . She's been playing only tight hands and very conservatively. . . . She's got something like a Broadway straight or trip Queens." Even though you may only have 7-7 for a pair lower than the board.

In fact, if someone *does* call a raise here, you're almost certainly behind and you need to see a 7 on the turn. Continuing to bet the hand to anyone calling the flop-raise on the turn and the river is probably suicidal, because if he's good enough to call you early on, he'll be good enough to check-call you throughout the entirety of the hand.

Looking at your hand from the outside

When you bluff, try to get inside your opponent's head, or at least take an objective view of the board. This can be harder than it sounds, because everyone has a natural bias toward his own play — people tend to think of themselves as better players than they actually are, and their opponents as worse than they actually are.

Boards that hint at the dangerous cards a player *could be* holding make the best bluffing opportunities. Here are some examples of "more bluffable" boards:

- **Flush draws:** A board with four clubs looks ominous. (More so if you don't actually hold any clubs in your hand, eh?) If you're up against only one other opponent, the chances are he doesn't have a club either. (If you're up against two opponents, odds are that one of them *does*.) You may want to take advantage of it.

- **Straight draws:** Any board showing a straight draw can be scary. Something like 6-7-8-9 is even scarier if people see you betting from a later position. If they know poker theory (or at least have been paying attention), they'll assume that you had a lower-quality hand and are overlapping the cards they are seeing.

- **Hidden trips:** Boards like 2-4-7 only get heavily bet one of two ways: Either someone has a big over pair, like pocket Kings, or someone has hit trips on the board. This bluff is harder to pull off against beginning players than it is against intermediates.

- **Overt trips:** A-A-2 is the type of board that's just screaming for someone to have tripped up (especially because people love to tag along into the game with Aces). Yet, half the Aces in the deck are gone, so acting as though you have one can potentially be a safer bet than it first appears.

You can never bluff a person who already has the best hand, or worse, holds the hand you're acting like *you* have. And you *will* run across these players sooner or later. Accept that as a risk, understand it will happen, and move on with your plans.

Bluffing in the right game

Some games are easier to bluff than others. In general Limit tends to be a much more difficult game to bluff. It's certainly not impossible, but the amount that a person can bet at any one time (and, therefore, lose at any one time) is limited. Typically, bluffing in Limit works best either in games with extremely advanced players or in games with beginners that don't fall into the "I never fold" category.

No-Limit is a much easier game to bluff because the stakes are higher, so the penalty of a bad call is more crushing. Obviously, it makes the bluffing risk that much higher, but that is both the beauty and horror of No-Limit.

The best bluff ever?

In my eyes, the best bluff in recent poker history came from Chris Moneymaker in the final two of the 2003 World Series of Poker (WSOP).

Moneymaker had gone into heads-up play against Sammy Farah with a 2-to-1 lead in chips, but over the course of the game he'd seen it erode to the point that they were nearly even.

Moneymaker was dealt 4-7 of Spades with Farah being dealt a K-9. A flop of 2-9-6 with one Spade gave Farah top pair and Moneymaker nothing more than a lot of hope. Farah made a large bet and Moneymaker (incorrectly) sensing weakness called.

The turn produced the 8♠, a card that was *finally* starting to make Moneymaker's hand look good, giving him a straight draw, a flush draw and a straight-flush draw. But Farah was still leading, and *all* of Moneymaker's plays were draws. Farah bet and Moneymaker made a sizeable raise — essentially a semi-bluff (more on these later in this chapter).

The river was the 3♥, a crushing card for Moneymaker. Sammy, with the winning hand, checked and Moneymaker pushed all-in. This play is nothing more than a pure bluff in a situation where Moneymaker knew he *had* to have the worst hand.

Farah sat and thought. Then he thought some more. Moneymaker's play meant that he would have to call with all his chips. He even felt something was funny about it, saying, "You missed your flush, huh?" but got no response from the stonewalling Moneymaker.

To Farah, it seemed like an amateur's play. Make a big bluff in a situation where it was *obvious* that the hand was broken. And yet, someone might make a play that *looked* like an amateur's play when he had a hand, intentionally to trip up the other player. That turn card was suspicious. Why the big raise right there? Had Moneymaker hit trip 8s and was now trying to back Sam off a perceived straight or flush draw?

After several agonizing minutes, he finally decided to pass.

This ended up being *the* pivotal hand of final table. The pot let Moneymaker spring back to being a 2-to-1 leader and he handily won the entire tournament a few short hands later.

Later, Chris Moneymaker said he noticed that Sammy tended to call when people answered his questions mid-hand. He figured that if he had answered, he *would* be called. So he just shut up.

Whether Chris's analysis is right or wrong, there's no way you can argue the outcome. It's the highest stakes and most successful bluff so far in the 21st century.

You can bet there'll be more.

Who to Bluff

Bluffing isn't something you do in a vacuum; you need to have a target. And the bigger and rounder you can paint that target, the easier it is to hit.

Preying on weak personalities

If the concept of picking on people when they're down just generally turns your stomach, poker may be a bad game for you. If you're not willing to just keep beating on an opponent — even when he's down — you better believe that that opponent is more than willing to come back and pound more than a little on you after he gets some footing.

Knowing weakness when you see it

Bluffing will always work the best on opponents who are willing to drop a hand, or those who can somehow be convinced that it's just easier to let this hand go for now and fight for a better one later.

TIP

Bluffing hands in the middle ground

Nearly all your successful bluffs will happen in the area I call "the middle ground." You can think of hands as being divided into three large categories:

- ✔ Good hands
- ✔ Bad hands
- ✔ In-between hands

When your opponent has a good hand, for the most part you're not going to be able to bluff her unless she thinks you have a *great* hand. So bluffing against a good hand is either rare, impractical, or foolish.

When your opponent has a bad hand, all you're really going to do is make her fold faster. Although it's true that semi-bluffs (later in this chapter) work against these hands, for the most part if you're even a *little* aggressive in your play, you'll win these.

The in-between hands, however, are the middle ground where it all happens. You want to be aware of, and probing for, the hands that your opponent has that she just isn't *that* committed to. *Those* are the hands you can bluff against *no matter what you have,* because, quite simply, your opponent would rather let them go than fight with 'em.

Think about how *you* feel about an in-between hand. Now fight that insecurity in your opponent.

The thing you want to look for in opponents are those who only play with the absolute best of hands, or better still, those who only call raises when they feel that they have something very close to the best hand possible on the table. These are the people you need to be turning your bluffing attention to because they will fold more than they should.

Playing against those who show no weakness

You'll run across people (especially early in your poker career) who simply refuse to fold a hand. The underlying theory is that they figure you're a pathological liar and try to bluff every hand. (Actually, it's more likely that they just don't want to be embarrassed by having been bluffed.)

If you run across these overly macho types, your best bet is to not bluff at all (it's not going to work because they won't fold) and instead only play hands of the highest quality. Unless you run into that awkward situation where your good hand is beaten by their great hand, you'll actually win money more quickly off these folks than you do off the ones you bluff.

Taking advantage of other situations

Bluffing may work to your advantage for other reasons. Those reasons run the gamut, but here are a few:

- ✔ **Some people, whether they win or lose, will set a definite limit of how far down they'll allow their chip stack to fall.** If you run across people with this proclivity, you can nearly always bluff them when they're getting close to whatever line that they draw because they don't want to cross a mental boundary.

- ✔ **It's easier to bluff people who are preoccupied.** If your opponent is taking a phone call from a nagging boyfriend (my editor made me change the gender), playing at another table simultaneously online, watching the grill at your poker game, or getting paged for dinner in the casino restaurant, it's *much* easier to convince her to let go of a hand with a big bet or raise.

- ✔ **Chip leaders in tournaments can bully the smaller stacks.** This is especially true when you get near the bubble that determines who will end up in the money and who won't. (See Chapter 17 for more on tournaments and strategies.)

- ✔ **Bluffing is cheaper on the hole cards and flop than it is in on the turn and river.** It's essentially half-price to bluff early on and may gain you an early pot win, or as you can see in Chapter 5, a free card.

> ✔ **Bluffing is easier with fewer players.** As a rule of thumb you
> want to be up against, at most, two other players when you
> bluff — and being up against only one other player is a consid-
> erably more favorable situation for you. ***Remember:*** When
> you're bluffing, you're trying to get people with intermediate
> hands to drop — if you try to push enough of them at one
> time, one of them will not be pushed.

The Semi-Bluff

A *semi-bluff* is where you bet a hand a little bit stronger than you
should, or make a bet implying a hand is a bit better than it is.
Usually the hope and prayer behind a semi-bluff is that if someone
calls you, you have a decent chance of outdrawing your opponent.

I think of a semi-bluff like having a pit bull puppy with a deeper-
than-normal bark. It sounds evil enough that most people will stay
away. And for those who venture into the yard? Well, maybe it'll
grow big enough that by the time my opponent opens the door to
my house, the dog can tear his leg off.

As I'm sure you can tell by the way I'm describing it, the semi-bluff
is one of my favorite plays in poker.

When to semi-bluff

The rules for semi-bluffing are nearly identical to those of regular
bluffing. The biggest difference is you're going to be playing more
heavily with the concept of drawing with a semi-bluff (whereas a
full-on bluff tends to deal more with the community cards that are
already dealt).

Here's an example: Imagine you have K♥ 10♥ and the flop is Q♦
Q♥ 9♥. You're sitting in later position and someone bets in front
of you. A raise here is a semi-bluff. You don't really have a hand yet
to speak of — just a straight draw, a flush draw, and a straight-flush
draw. The hidden beauty of a raise, however, is that it may make
people think you have trip Queens this instant and are trying to do
something like drive the flush draws away.

Here's another example: Say you have A♠ 3♠ playing from a late
position and the flop is a rainbow 9♠ 5♥ 3♣. That's a truly anemic
and shaky flop — so much so that there's a pretty good chance no
one's going to touch it with his hole cards. A raise post-flop isn't
that bad of play in and of itself, but considering that you can catch
an Ace, or have a freak shot at two running spades for a flush, a

raise there falls into the category of semi-bluff. (If you got a caller here and then saw another spade on the turn, it's probably worth following it with yet another semi-bluff. Your opponent almost certainly would put you on trips at that point, because he wouldn't think you'd be crazy enough to play for a running spade flush.)

Obviously, people who are more likely to fold to a flat-out bluff are also more likely to pass on a semi-bluff.

Why semi-bluff?

There are a couple of reasons to consider a semi-bluff:

- ✓ **When someone folds, you get their money 100 percent of the time.** There are no bad beats, no lucky draws — you just flat-out win. The more often you can make this happen on a poker table, the better your game will do in the long run. Semi-bluffing gives you chance at making that happen.

- ✓ **Semi-bluffing is also a nice toe into the water of the bluffing pool.** It's not a full-on bluff so you may not be as uncomfortable about doing it (either consciously or unconsciously), because you feel that you can actually make things better with a draw. This comfort, in turn, may make the play seem more "natural" to other players at the table and make them more likely to pass. Getting this kind of emotional support and security over your bluffing habits will do nothing but help your game.

- ✓ **Semi-bluffing is harder for opponents to read and figure out, even after they see your cards.** Unless you're playing in a home game, and *especially* if the people around the table are a little fatigued and the game has essentially dropped into autopilot, what happened is often not totally clear. You may get a mild taint as being either insane, or just a bad player, if people can't put rhyme or reason to it. But it's not as if a reputation like that is going to bother your game.

Getting Caught — Now What?

First of all, understand that you *will* get caught bluffing. It's all a part of the game. When you do, don't freak out or let it rattle you. Instead, it's time, once again, to step outside yourself and try to see the hand through your opponent's eyes. This turns out to be considerably less difficult than evaluating your pre-bluff strategy, because oftentimes your opponent will just sit and start crowing at you at length about how he just *knew* that you weren't telling the truth and that you never *were* a good bluffer and a whole bunch of other gibberish you'd rather not hear (but absolutely should listen to).

The immediate thing that your bluff tells other players is that, yes, you do in fact have the ability to bluff built into your character. This knowledge may cause a few players to immediately, completely reevaluate your play on the chance they thought you just weren't even capable of it.

You'll almost certainly be thought of as a looser player, no matter how tight or loose they thought you were before. This means you'll be more even more likely to be called, so tighten up on the hands you play a bit, but don't be afraid to go ahead and bet aggressively. Because players are more likely to call, you may well be able to recoup what you've lost in just a few large bets.

It may also indicate to other players that you're unable to read a tell on another player at the table if she happened to have a monster hand and you sort of missed that in your frenzy of trying to bluff against her. This, in turn, may cause the other players to be not quite as guarded toward you in their plays (because, after all, you're an idiot if you couldn't see *that* one coming) and you may find you're suddenly able to pick up *much* more information about other players (especially when playing only one other player heads-up in a pot).

Chapter 10

Maximizing Your Win: Check-Raising and Trapping

In This Chapter

▶ Checking out check-raising

▶ Setting a trap

▶ Getting the most you can

*I*n any investing situation, you want to maximize your wins and minimize your losses. When you've hit a great hand (you lucky dog, I can't believe you did it *again*), your next trick is to figure out how to make the most of it.

Check-Raising

A *check-raise* happens when you check in the betting action and then raise any player that bets after you. A check-raise indicates strength and *always* draws attention from even the most comatose of opponents.

Bluffing on a check-raise . . .

When you check-raise, you're automatically thought of as being tricky and potentially dangerous.

. . . and getting caught

If you check-raise on a bluff, and you're caught, you are immediately colored with the "idiot" crayon from everyone's box. Not necessarily a bad thing, but it will force you to only play better hands the next time you check-raise, because you're more likely to get callers in subsequent hands.

. . . and getting away with it

If you bluff and get away with it, it still ups your chances of being called the next time, because everyone has that nagging doubt in the back of their minds. "Did that guy really have a hand there, or not?" And until you've played a fair amount of poker, the odds are pretty high that you're sending out some weird vibe when you're bluffing — people think you are, they're just not willing to find out . . . yet.

Playing a good hand on a check-raise . . .

Until your skill increases quite a bit (and your opponents become much more wary of you), you're more likely to check-raise with a good hand.

. . . but getting no callers

If you check-raise, but don't get any callers you get a couple of side-effects:

- ✔ **The table becomes a bit more leery of you.** When you check in the future, people are less likely to bet behind you, especially with a lesser hand, because they're afraid you might be check-raising *again*. (This also means that when people *do* bet behind you in the future, they're more likely to have a good hand.)
- ✔ **People will wonder what you have and there will always be a nagging feeling that you may have been bluffing.** This makes people more likely to call your check-raise in the future.

. . . and getting called

If you check-raise and get called, in many ways this is the best possible of all worlds, because in one short action you:

- ✔ Got to show off your nasty, yet perfectly groomed, monster hand
- ✔ Proved to the table you weren't bluffing
- ✔ Helped to establish a table image of being a nasty bruiser that is not to be toyed with
- ✔ Got to line your pocketbook with extra cash

When the time seems right to check-raise, you absolutely should do it, but in the back of your mind you should keep in mind that check-raising and getting called is the most effective way to make the whole process work.

Considering a check-raise

There are a number of situations in which you may want to check-raise:

- ✔ You have top pair with top kicker on any board that is not overly threatening otherwise.

- ✔ You have two pair.

- ✔ You have trips.

- ✔ You suspect your opponent is bluffing and by check-raising, you might get him to fold.

- ✔ You have a good hand and think there's a good chance you can check, get a bet behind you, raise, and still get a call.

- ✔ You have a mediocre hand, but you believe that someone is likely to act behind you, and then might fold if you raise. Think about this particular bullet long and hard — this scenario is usually not *that* likely.

Check-raising round by round

In the following sections, I walk you through each of the possible places to check-raise.

Pre-flop

Uh, no. It *can't* happen here. The blinds force you to call, raise, or fold. There is no such thing as "check" pre-flop, which makes check-raise, well, *hard.* Really hard. As in impossible.

After the flop

This is the first place you can check-raise. The biggest advantage of doing it here is to thin the field if there are too many callers. People with marginal hands who have called a bet behind you, especially those in late positions, may well fold on a check-raise, because they may not like the idea of playing for twice the stakes on the turn and river.

Note: It's very unlikely that you'll get everyone to fold here. Unless you have a table image of being someone who only plays super-quality hands, almost anyone who bets behind you will call your check-raise after the flop.

Having said that, if someone does call you on a flop check-raise and you follow up by betting first on the turn, it's much more likely that your opponents will fold. (Anyone who calls you when you open betting on the turn has a very good hand, thinks you are bluffing, or has pot odds on some draw she's trying to make.)

Don't forget that if you force a fold from an opponent on a check-raise on the flop, you would have made more money if you'd waited for the turn (but you also would have exposed yourself to one more dangerous card).

After the turn

This is where check-raising starts working well, because the stakes are doubled.

Your best rule of thumb on the turn is to check-raise only if you're likely to get a bet *and* a call behind you.

If you have a good hand, and you have much doubt as to whether someone actually *will* bet behind you, you should just go ahead and bet rather than check-raise.

After the river

Because this is the last betting round, only check-raise if you're fairly certain you'll get a bet behind you *and* one of the following is true:

- ✔ You have a great hand.
- ✔ You think that, if you check, your opponent will bet and then also pass when you raise.

Trapping through Slow Play

Slow-playing is the half-brother of check-raising. A slow play is possible in any situation where you start off with a very good hand, but don't bet it hard in the early betting rounds in an effort to maximize the total return on the hand.

Timing a slow play

Slow-playing works well in a couple of situations:

- ✔ **When you're at a table with several players who are very aggressive:** In these cases, all you have to do is sit back and make what appear to be meager calls as everyone else bets, raises, and carouses through the poker neighborhood. Doing this keeps the quality of your hand camouflaged, as well as the general focus of the table off you.

✓ **When you're *so* far ahead in a hand that it's unlikely another player will catch up:** For example, if you were dealt A♣ 3♣ and the flop is K♣ 7♣ 2♣, you have the best possible hand at that moment. The only hands that *could* potentially beat you are the cases of someone flopping a set and then following *that* with a pair on the board (giving them a full house). There's also the super-fluke of drawing quads.

You should *not* slow-play in the following instances:

✓ **You flop a big hand, but bigger hands are threatening.** For example, say you're holding Q♥ J♦ and the flop is A♠ K♠ 10♣. The great news is that you have a Broadway straight. The bad news is that there are several attacking hands possible: If someone is holding two spades, she's on a flush draw; it's also very possible that someone is holding two pair (especially if a lot of players are still on the table), giving her immediate full house draws. In cases such as these, you should just come out firing. Anyone who wants to stick it out for either drawing her flush, or her full house, should have to pay for the privilege.

✓ **You're playing a fairly passive player who is not likely to bet.** *Remember:* Your big hand is only worth money if someone actually *bets* against it.

✓ **Your hand is big, but not *that* big.** For example, if you're holding A♣ 4♣ and the flop is A♦ Q♣ J♥, you have top pair, but no kicker. Other people at the table are definitely holding Queens or Jacks (there may even be another Ace sitting out there) and your weak kicker is leaving you vulnerable. You should just bet your hand now.

Slow playing works better in No-Limit than Limit because of your potential to take down *so* much more money at the end. Also, because the bets can be any size, you can wait until the river to make your betting play. The bigger the hand, the longer you should wait.

The Theory of Two and slow playing

All slow playing is governed by what I call the *Theory of Two,* namely:

✓ **To the best of your knowledge, is your opponent twice as likely to bet as he is to check if *you* check first?**

> ✓ **If you bet in front of your opponent, is he twice as likely to call as he is to fold?** This is especially important on the betting rounds that happen before the river because each round represents an opportunity to help relieve your opponent of some of his cash.

The act of slow-playing

Actually making the slow play is almost an art form in and of itself. Think of it as another form of bluffing. What you're trying to do is make your opponent think that you're calling *his* action with a hand that is much worse than your own; or if necessary, placing a bet that appears to be a bit more reluctant than you'd like.

Slow-playing usually involves check-calling, rather than check-raising. When you do your check, you should make it fairly fast, but without being suspicious. Your opponent will then bet and when you go to call, you shouldn't agonize over it for a long time (this looks too much like you're acting), but you also shouldn't call immediately. A rapid-fire check-call, especially on a beginning and low-intermediate Hold'em table, is a sure sign of someone trying to slow-play.

There is one exception to the don't-overpause rule: If you're calling with many more people waiting to call behind you, it's pretty easy to act like you're worried about them calling as well. When you pause, make it a point to look at the players and/or their stacks behind you. This "consideration" may also end up getting you a few extra callers. (Remember, though, more callers also increase the risk of your losing the hand.)

On intermediate tables (and up), you should try, as much as you possibly can, to *not* pause if you're first to act and you've hit a big flop. That millisecond pause, where you're gaining recognition of what your hand is before checking, is a dead giveaway — and it's almost impossible to fake.

It's very possible that if you check-call on the flop, when you check on the turn you won't get a bet behind you. (This is especially true if you're thought of as being a good player — or you've called a large flop bet in No-Limit without raising.) If your opponents seem to be cooling down their betting, make sure *you* put a bet out on the river, even if it's a small one — you don't want to let that betting opportunity walk by.

Maximizing Your Returns

Getting a big hand is a rare enough occurrence that you really want to milk every last cent possible out of it.

Deciding when to sit back

The decision of whether you bet a big hand or sit back is based on a few factors:

- **The aggressiveness of your opponent (see Chapter 8 for more about understanding your opponents at the table):** The more aggressive your opponent is, the more you want to lay back — especially in No-Limit. The less aggressive your opponent, the more you'll have to bet it along.

- **The excitability of your opponent:** There are many players, especially at upper skill levels in No-Limit, who will not become aggressive against an opponent who is checking, but *will* act up if that same opponent bets a minimum amount. To them, these little bets feel as though you're trying to steal a pot for cheap. Like a crazed pit bull, a little action is like the smell of blood to them, and they can't help but attack back. If you're a slow player, you learn to like these little doggies.

Rafting the river: Check or bet?

The Theory of Two has some implications on the river. I'm listing these in the order you should consider them:

- **If you are *certain* your opponent will check if you check, you should absolutely bet.** There is a whole category of mediocre hands that some people will call with but would never bet when checked to (like a medium pair versus your flush).

- **If you think that betting in front of your opponents will cause them to fold, and you have a *great* hand, you're better off checking to see if they'll try to snatch a pot from you.** This has the added benefit of mildly confusing your opponents because not all people (especially beginners) can understand why someone would check first action on the river with a great hand.

- **In No-Limit, bet the maximum amount that you think your opponent is twice as likely to call as they are to pass.** If you have absolutely no idea how much this amount might be, make the minimum bet you're allowed.

Chapter 11

Camouflaging Your Play and Dodging Traps

In This Chapter

▶ Creating an image for yourself

▶ Watching for trouble

After even a little exposure to poker it becomes obvious that you need to be fairly fast on your psychological feet to be adept at the game. Like a well-executed battle, you need to be stealthy as you attack and nimble when others start firing back at you.

Setting Expectations throughout a Game

There are many people who espouse keeping your opponents guessing throughout a Hold'em session. The good thing about general bewilderment at the table is obvious: People have no idea what you're playing. The bad news, however, is that if people don't know what you're doing, or how you're playing, they're bound to just play a bit tighter and then fire at you harder when they do decide to play in the hand. These are some of the very hardest people to beat.

Better, at least in the short and medium term of a game, is to present an image at the table that is very predictable and defined to the other players. After you do that, you can take advantage of the expectations you set, because there is a difference between what you appear to be and what you are.

Other people very rarely see your cards. All they're aware of is how many times you play your starting hole cards — if they see you in a lot, especially over a long period of time, they'll know you're loose. Aside from that, there isn't much indication. You need to concentrate on what they don't know and help influence the things they do.

Setting a style

Pick a style you're happy with displaying, as well as that is easy for you to portray, and then follow through with it.

Choosing a personality

Your choices are as different as there are personalities in a card room. Here are but a few possibilities:

- ✔ Businessperson just playing cards to kill time while in town
- ✔ Crazed sports fan
- ✔ Hard-core poker student
- ✔ Half-interested player

Feel free to bring props along with you — crossword puzzles, magazines, books, whatever. And don't forget to dress the part as well.

If people think you aren't completely absorbed in the game, you're setting a style and expectation from the other players that you can take advantage of as the game progresses.

Showing a playing style

Just because you don't *have* to show a hand doesn't mean you can't go ahead and do it anyway every now and then to reinforce whatever you're trying to convince people of at the table. So if you're:

- ✔ **The crazy person,** make sure to show the occasional set of bluff cards to your opponents. If you do this, though, be warned that people are more likely to call you in the future. This isn't necessarily a bad thing, but you *do* need to be aware of it.
- ✔ **The super-tight player,** show the occasional hand you win when there are no other callers and you have a good solid hand.

✔ **The player who will lay down a hand,** if you want more action pointed toward you in a poker game, show a hand to the table before you fold it. (Make sure to do this only if you're up against one opponent, or you're the last to act in a given round — you don't want to give a positional advantage to people who have yet to act.)

When you show a hand, you're removing all doubt about what your betting actions were relative to the hand you held. People are trying to figure out your tells, and because of this you should engage in the behavior *very* sparingly.

Also, if all you ever show are good hands, you still should show them only occasionally and not *every* time you have them. If you show every good hand and never show any of your bad ones, people will begin to figure it out. This, too, will play into their tell-bank on you.

Mark Harlan, kid

I began playing in card rooms at 21 (as soon as I was able to), back in the dark ages of poker. This was that nearly unthinkable time when poker was still looked upon as a vice, rather than prime-time TV material, and mastodons freely roamed the Earth.

At any given poker table it was *very* common for me to be less than half the age of the next youngest guy (and it was *always* a guy) seated there.

Instead of wigging out about being the young guy, and trying to figure out how to add to conversations about events that had happened before I was born, I quickly embraced it. Every time I'd play, I'd wear my Mickey Mouse T-shirt and I'd make it a point to take a comic book with me to the table.

Did it work?

Are you kidding me? People would line up to play at the kid's table. It became so common for me to be I.D.'d that I'd put my driver's license in my comic as a bookmark and when I won my first big pot, I'd put it on the table because I knew it'd be about two minutes before security was asking me questions. (For some reason, I found that people became much more concerned about whether I was of legal age if I was winning, but they didn't seem to care if I was losing.)

The age demographic of poker has changed so much that this strategy wouldn't work nearly as well today. (It's common for an entire table to be younger than I am — I'm in my 40s — so now I play the role of the "old guy.") But if you watch carefully and think about the dynamics of your local poker room (or even your home game), you can come up with something that'll work for you just as well.

If showing cards to enforce a table image seems too dangerous or difficult, *never* show a hand. It's the easiest and safest thing to do. (I only show a hand when I have to.)

Changing your style

Sometimes your best-laid plans can suddenly run amuck through nothing more than a turn of an unfriendly card or an unexpected call. You know how it goes: You were playing along just fine as Mr. Tight and suddenly — *boom!* — it gets exposed that you were actually trying to bluff a pot with your 2-7 off-suit.

When this happens, don't sweat it. Just get ready to drop into another playing style. As soon as your opponents see a gap, or difference, in your play from what they were expecting, they'll start treating you differently. This means you can start treating them differently as well and it's the perfect time to shift gears in both your strategy and your table image.

When you shift gears in playing styles like this, just make sure that you aren't playing *into* a style that they're starting to expect. For example, if you get caught bluffing, don't suddenly start bluffing *more* because that's what your opponents will be playing against from you. Instead, you should tighten up a bit, and consider doing something like becoming more aggressive with your bets when you *are* in a pot.

Avoiding Pitfalls

Setting your own style, and then exploiting it, is only half the battle. The other half is watching out when other players are doing it to you.

First and foremost, even though I talk about your visual table image earlier in this chapter, you need to ignore *all* of that in your opponent (unless she is really inebriated). Instead, you should focus exclusively on her betting actions. She can tell all the jokes she wants, wear a hula skirt, and whisper in your ear what her hole cards were every time, but it may all be one giant concoction. The betting is the real thing.

The one absolutely and positively true thing that your opponent expresses is his bet. He's saying definitively that he believes his hand has a chance to win and he's backing it up with his money. *This* is what you need to watch in your opponent. (And when he doesn't bet is nearly as important as when he does.)

When aggressive players merely call

Let's say you've been playing at a table with a demon woman for a few hours, and pretty much any time she enters a hand, she raises. All in all, she's a very aggressive and very tough player. On a turn card, you bet, expecting the usual raise — and instead you just get called. There are a few possibilities as to what this could mean — read the sections that follow, and think about the situation relative to your opponent's position on the table and her previous betting patterns and behaviors.

Waiting for a draw

The absolute pure play if you have pot odds for a flush or straight draw (see Chapter 12 for more on pot odds) is to merely call until you hit it. Different players will play differently (it's common for very aggressive No-Limit players to make a slight raise when they are on a draw — or push all-in if they have a pair and a draw), but the "right" play is to just call.

Look closely at the board and try to remember the types of cards you've seen that person play before — don't forget to factor in the position he's in. What you're looking for is three suited cards or three cards that a set of connectors (or gapped connectors) could play into.

An aggressive player will often raise on a draw on the flop but cool down if the turn card missed his hand.

Backing away from a possibly better hand

If an aggressive player suddenly backs off, another possibility is that the player is holding a big hand that has now become threatened. For example, if she seemed all too eager to cap the betting pre-flop, but the flop came out as a rainbow A-10-6, it's very possible that she's holding a high pocket pair — Queens or Kings. What was a great hand has now gone downhill with the exposure of the Ace.

Setting a trap

The other possibility when an aggressive player backs off is that a hand has been made and she's setting a trap for you. If you've established that you're a player who is willing to drop a hand, you'll often get a flat-call after the flop and a raise on the turn (because the bets are doubled there).

If you ever receive a flat-call in No-Limit, especially from an experienced player on a large bet, you've definitely fallen into a trap. Unfortunately, you can't reach into the pot and take your money back saying, "Sorry, I didn't mean that." That means you should do the next best thing: Check on the next card. And although it's true that checking will, in fact, get you a big bet on the end from your opponent, it will keep you from sending any more money her way in the meantime. Just be glad you didn't push all-in to begin with.

Raising and reraising after rounds of checking in Limit

In Limit, when you see raising and reraising after checking through the flop or the flop and the turn, you are *definitely* looking at opponents holding big hands. Unless you're playing against raising maniacs (which certainly *can* happen, but you'll always know well in advance if it is), you should be quick to drop a hand if you're in a pot with more than one player — unless you're holding a *very* big hand.

For example, say you have the 9♦ 8♦ on the button. There are three other callers in the hand. The flop and the turn both were checked through and on the river the board looks like this: J♥ 10♥ 3♣ Q♥ 4♦. By the time the river betting gets to you, it has already been bet, raised, and reraised. The good news is you have a strong hand, a Queen-high straight. The bad news is there are two other straight possibilities (9-K and A-K), as well as heart flushes.

 In the example, your hand is good, but it's still a loser. Yes, it's hard to let go of a five-card hand, but never forget that a second-best five-card hand is nothing more than a first-place loser. Panicked betting, especially in Limit, *always* means that someone has a good hand.

Judging when you're dominated

The biggest way to dodge a trap is both to recognize, and to admit, when you're dominated. As I said in the last section, the hardest time to admit you have a losing hand is when you're holding a very good hand yourself. Don't let your blinkered, eye-rolling reaction to your hand let you overlook bigger forces at play.

Here are some examples of situations to look out for:

✔ **You hold a big pocket pair, but larger cards appear on the board.** For example, you have Q-Q but the flop is A-K-8. Congratulations! Your great starting hole cards are now losers. You should probably fold in any circumstance, but definitely if you're up against two other players — *someone* there is holding an Ace or a King.

✔ **You have a big pair, but the board is screaming about other possible hands.** If you have A♠ A♣ and the board is Q♦ J♦ 10♦, you have a world of problems. Diamond flushes are possible here. Two pair is likely. K-9 is a straight. Any diamond gives a flush draw. In Limit you can check-call with a hand like this, in No-Limit you'll save a ton of money by checking and folding.

✔ **You have a tiny end of a straight that is easily made bigger.** If you're holding 7-7 and the first four cards are J-10-8-9, your hand has morphed from a pair to a straight; unfortunately, anyone with a Queen has a bigger straight. In Limit, you can check-call this hand. In No-Limit, you can try a small reraise on a small initial bet, but fold on anything large.

✔ **You hold the "tiny sides" of full houses.** If you were playing 9♠ 10♠ from the button and the first four cards are 10-10-A-A, you've officially got a problem. Although it's true you flopped trips and then went full, anyone holding a single Ace has an even bigger full house (Aces full of 10s seriously stomping your 10s full of Aces). In Limit, you can bet and then check-call. In No-Limit, you should bet minimum amounts to make it look as though you're trying to maximize an Aces-full full house. But *really* what you want to do in all cases is start thinking about dropping this hand if you get any hints of activity against it at all.

✔ **You hold a weak two pair on a board that is made for stronger two-pair versions.** J-Q looks pretty good against an A-Q-J flop until you stop and consider that A-Q or A-J is on top of you and K-10 gives a straight. Opponents who play dangling Aces can get punished here, for sure, but the risk is pretty high — especially in Limit where they get two shots at pairing their other card (or the added possibility of drawing a straight when holding A-K or A-10).

Chapter 12

Considering Mathematics

● ●

In This Chapter

▶ Putting math in perspective

▶ Using quickie math

▶ Making math your super-friend

● ●

Many math-o-phobes avoid the game of poker simply because they don't want to deal with the math involved, or they think they can't handle it. And although it's true that you do need *some* math, there's not as much as you might think — and you can cheat your way through a *lot* of it, either through some easy memorization, or just by remembering some of the basics you already know about a deck of cards (for example, there are four suits).

Many of your decisions on a poker table, especially when calling a bet in Limit, will have some mathematical basis. Pot odds crossed with the chances of making a hand, in particular, are worth knowing and using to your advantage.

Don't sweat the work, though. If you're able to memorize a multiplication table, you can handle all the math you need for poker. And if you want to get really rabid about it, you can get as good in mathematics as the best pros in just a few weeks — because there just isn't that much to master.

I'm not talking calculus here — it's really just multiplication and division. And you can always make things easier by approximating.

Delving Fact from Fiction in Math and Poker

Through the wonders of hidden "lipstick" cameras in modern poker events, television has taken to displaying the odds of any given player beating the others to an exact degree of precision as any hand in a poker tournament is played through. It makes for good viewing because you can ooh, ahh, and groan as the player you love to hate draws his 24.7 percent shot to beat everyone's favorite card player sitting at the same table. It's fun to watch — and if you have even a passing interest in probability, you can get a voyeuristic kick out of watching the numbers change as cards are dealt. It's cool in a geeky sort of way, because it gives you a deeper feel for what each card on the board means relative to the hand as a whole.

Unfortunately, it also gives the viewing public a warped suggestion that mathematics is the all-seeing, all-powerful force behind poker. It idealizes the card world as some sort of grand place where math is all, and *everything* else kneels at some elaborate, fractal-ized, numerical throne. The problem with this notion is that not only is it essentially untrue, but it also takes some of the importance away from the things that actually *do* matter.

Close enough is good enough

When you're playing at a poker table, especially in live action, don't get so enmeshed in the odds, statistics, and probabilities of what's going on that you lose track of the greater part of the game. The math in this chapter is important, yes, but it's rarely the over-riding way you will make a decision. There are many other factors to take into account as you play:

- The personality of the players still in the pot (see Chapter 8)

- In a tournament, your relative chip standing (see Chapter 17)

- In No-Limit, the likelihood of the action on the *next* card following the one that has just been exposed. (For example, if a player is just now pushing half of his stack, and you call, you better believe you'll be seeing the other half coming at you on the next betting round.)

If you get so bent out of shape on the math stuff that you lose track of the bigger picture, you've done yourself no good. In fact, in those cases, the math is actually hurting you.

All the math in the world isn't going to prevent a bad beat — it'll just give you justification for what you did as you wipe the tears from your cheeks and become aware that your wallet doesn't seem as thick. People can, and will, play cards that are mathematically "incorrect." Some of them will beat you as a result. Get used to it, accept it, and understand that in the long run these are your best customers. (In the short term you may want to get used to chewing on a towel.)

In the following sections, I walk you through enough math basics to make you a very competitive player. From a pure math point of view, the most important thing you should do is have a fairly good idea of the numbers that you're working with. They do *not* have to be exact — just close enough to know if you're making the right play.

In the online world, math becomes slightly more important. Because you can't get as good a feel for the players, poker is a little bit more of a pure mathematical game. See Chapter 15 for more on online play. If you find you're really interested in computer poker, you should pick up a copy of my other book *Winning at Internet Poker For Dummies,* co-authored by Chris Derossi (Wiley) — it dovetails almost perfectly with this book.

Understanding players is better than understanding numbers

Okay, so it's true that my degree is in applied mathematics, and yeah, I've always had a knack for numbers and calculation. That's not the reason I tend to talk down the importance of math in poker. The reason I do is you're not playing a table full of computers — you're playing human beings. They will fake, conceal, bluff, ignore, and misplay. They will also have tells, predictable patterns, and behavior that will take you far outside the mathematical world.

For an extreme example, say you're playing Johnny Rocket. All this guy ever plays is an Ace with some other card. If you're holding a pair of cowboys (K-K) and the flop is A-10-3, guess what? You have a losing hand. At this point, all math is going to do for you is let you know your likelihood of hitting another King. The reality is, right this very second, you're beaten. You're losing, and you're losing badly. Unless you have the pot odds to make a call (unlikely because you only have two outs) or you can convince Johnny he should fold with a bluff, you need to fold now.

This example is an unlikely scenario, but as you play, and as your perceptual skill grows, you will be amazed at how easy it is to read certain players. In your poker life, you'll definitely make calls that are not mathematically correct, but are absolutely right relative to the player you're up against.

If you have an extremely good idea of the way a certain player behaves, and you see a set of community cards that spell danger or death for the poker hand you're holding, ignoring the behavioral pattern of your opponent is a huge risk to your bankroll. *For mathematical reasons, do not ignore what you already know about the way a player plays any given hand or situation.*

Chapter 8 is all about playing the other players. At some point, either before or after you finish reading this chapter, you should go back and review Chapter 8. I have a large circle of (winning) poker playing friends who are also math guys. All of them say that playing the player is more important than the mathematics of the game. They don't say this because they know math — they say it because they know that playing your opponent is much more important. The psychologically astute player will beat the pure math geek every time.

Taking a Shortcut with Math

Now that I've spent enough time bending your mind about how unimportant math is to poker, I guess it's time for me to actually show you some.

Counting your "outs"

An *out* is a card (or sometimes a sequence of cards) that will turn a losing hand into a winner. People tend to make a big deal out of counting outs, but it's really pretty simple as long as you keep in mind the basics of a deck of 52 cards, namely:

- ✔ There are four suits in a deck.
- ✔ There are four of each rank in a deck (for example, four 2s).
- ✔ There are 13 cards of each suit.

You count one out for every card that will make your hand.

Looking at Figure 12-1, say you're dealt 8♣ 6♣ on the big blind with no raise — a good deal because you have a gapped suited connector and get to play "for free." There are three other players still in the hand and the flop is 5♥ 4♣ A♣.

Because there are three other players in the hand, it's a certainty that you are behind. All it takes is *one* other player having a card bigger than an 8 and you're currently losing. Because there are three other players, it's also pretty likely someone is now holding a pair of Aces (although probably not trips because that person probably would have raised pre-flop).

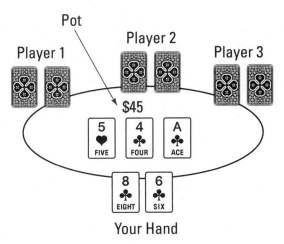

Your Hand

Figure 12-1: A hand with 12 outs.

Assuming you have to beat a pair of Aces here, you now have the following outs:

✔ Four 7s are outs that make the gut shot straight draw.

✔ Nine clubs are left in the deck, but one of them is the 7♣, so really there are only eight other clubs that count as outs to make the flush.

Add those two together and you have a total of 12 outs.

 There is a risk in calculating your outs: You *must* make an assumption on what the other player has. As a result, calculating your outs is an imperfect way to measure what's going on at the table. In Figure 12-1, if one of the players has pocket 4s, it means she's currently holding trips. If the turn card is the 5♣, you've made your flush, but your opponent is now sitting on a full house (4s full of 5s), essentially killing that out.

There are a couple of other disasters in waiting: someone holding two clubs with one larger than your 8♣ (meaning all the clubs are now fatal), or someone holding a 2-3 who has already made a wheel. You can see how this actually reduces the number of outs you have.

 Overvaluing your outs is balanced slightly by opponents who are bluffing (you're actually over them without knowing); as well as a series of freak draws that can make you a winner (for example, catching river 7♣ after the 5♣ in the preceding example gives you a straight flush).

Just keep it simple: Close enough is good enough. In Figure 12-1, you should assume you have 12 outs. And because you never see anyone else's cards, you never consider them in as you do your counting. From a pure numbers point of view, you should act as though they have never been dealt. Before the turn, you have 12 outs (7s and flush draws) and there are 47 cards left in the deck. (You have already seen five cards: your two hole cards and the three on the flop.)

Sometimes in professional card rooms you'll see a card inadvertently exposed at the start of a hand (either through a dealing mishap or an accidental exposure on mucking by a player). If that happens, be sure to work the cards that you see into the numbers you're counting on your outs.

Calculating your pot odds

Pot odds is a term used to describe the ratio of the pot size relative to the bet you have to make to call. For example, if you have to make a $5 call on a $20 pot, your pot odds are:

$$20 \div 5 = 4$$

This is expressed as a ratio: 4-to-1. In other words, if you call for $5 and win, you are paid four times what your call cost you.

Note that you do *not* count the calling bet you put in the pot as part of the pot odds. Again, in the example, you're making a $5 call on a $20 pot — 4-to-1 pot odds. You are *not* making a $5 call on a $25 pot.

Online you can easily calculate your pot odds because a running total is always kept for you. In live action it's a little harder because you have to keep track yourself. You can do quick pot addition in your head, but an easier trick is to just keep track of how many bets have been made in front of you. Looking back at Figure 12-1, for example, you already know the pot odds of any call, before anyone makes a bet: Three players in the pot with no raises, your big blind, and an uncalled small blind means that the pot odds will be a little better than 4-to-1. If someone makes a bet that you have to call, the pot odds will increase to 5-to-1 (because another bet has been added). If someone makes a bet and another player calls in front of you, those pot odds increase to 6-to-1.

Try to avoid using math as a tell at the table. If you sit and start babbling numbers under your breath, people can listen and figure out what you're drawing to. As much as possible, you want to *not* let people know that you're sitting and calculating odds — at the very least it encourages them to behave as though they're holding cards over yours, even if they may not be.

Taking a Shortcut with Math

After you know your outs and the pot odds, you can begin making mathematical decisions based on your play.

Combining outs and pot odds

 The number-one rule for calling a bet: *The odds of making your hand must be better than your pot odds.* This is *the* way you make mathematical money playing poker (and it's called *positive expectation* by math heads, *positive expected value [+EV]* by poker sharpies). In simple English, all this means is that your reward is greater than your risk when you're trying to pull a card you need out of the deck.

 If you ever get confused about which has to be bigger, just use an extreme example in your mind — for example, would you like to be paid 10-to-1 for an even-money bet? Of course you would. That means you want the pot odds bigger than the amount of your hand.

Using quick math tricks

When you go to do calculations in your head, you don't have to have the calculating accuracy of Rain Man. Use shortcuts whenever they present themselves.

For example, looking back at Figure 12-1, you know that you have 12 outs with 47 cards left in the deck. Your odds of making this hand, therefore, are slightly better than 1-in-4. How do you know? Forget about dividing 47 by 12 in your head — instead, just consider that 12 in 48 is *exactly* 1-in-4. Because 47 is one less than 48, that means your odds are a little bit better.

In Figure 12-1, this means any pot odds that are better than 4-to-1 make it correct for you to call.

Figure 12-2 shows the betting round after the flop. You checked, one player behind you bet, and there was one caller and one fold. Your pot odds are now better than 6-to-1 (four pre-flop bets, two post-flop bets, and the small blind), and you have a slightly better than 1-in-4 chance of making the hand, so you should call.

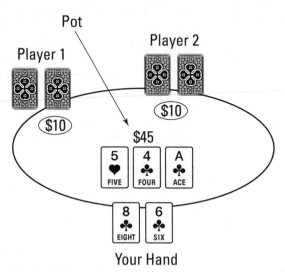

Figure 12-2: Your pot odds are better than 6-to-1. Call or fold?

When you need to do calculations quickly in your head, there are several tricks you can use. Again, the important thing is to just be in the right ballpark — you don't have to be numerically accurate to four decimal places.

The easiest thing to do when you're counting outs is assume 48 cards for both the turn (it's actually 47) and the river (it's actually 46) because it's very common to be dividing by even numbers. Doing this will slightly *under*estimate your odds of winning, but that's okay. What you don't want to do is *over*estimate and get it wrong.

Considering implied odds

Implied pot odds takes the pot odds concept one step farther. That is to say, you think about the ratio of what you *should* win if the betting follows an expected pattern.

For example, if you're getting ready to make a call on a turn bet and you can tell by the way the player behind you is acting that he's definitely going to make a call as well, you can include that money in the implied-odds calculation.

By their very nature, implied pot odds are making *large* assumptions about the betting and calling behavior of other people at the table. These assumptions are reflected not only in the current betting round, but also in all subsequent betting rounds for any given hand. Because implied pot odds imply more money, you'll end up calling more. And calling more can be a certain way to lose a bankroll. If you're ever uncertain as to what your opponents will do in subsequent betting rounds, you should make no assumption about implied pot odds.

Pot odds are a strong mathematical fact. Your bet will be paid a certain amount if you win. Implied pot odds are *not* a strong mathematical fact — they're guesswork and, by their very nature, a tad questionable.

To give you an example of how implied pot odds might work, if you're playing at a table with a *calling station* (someone who plays every hand, and always calls), you can go ahead and assume that her money will be in the pot on every betting round and just add it in to your calculations.

Typically, unless your opponents are extremely predictable, implied pot odds won't come into play much in Limit Hold'em. No-Limit, however, is another story. Any time you see a player pushing half a stack as part of a bet, you can be fairly certain you'll see the other half in the next betting round. In a similar vein, any player who makes a gigantic call on a bet (say, 80 percent of his stack), will almost always put the remaining 20 percent of his stack in the pot before the hand is over (either as a bet or as a call). Be sure to include the facts of these betting patterns in your calculations.

Flipping a coin

There's one common face-off that happens on a Hold'em table that is worth talking about in its own right, and that is an under pair versus two over cards. (The classic face-off is 2-2, the worst pair, versus A-K, the best set of over cards.) Partially due to television, people often refer to these as *coin-flipping* situations.

Before any community cards hit the table, the under pair has a very slight edge. The exact percentages depend on a few factors:

- ✔ **The suits involved:** It's better for the pair if one or both of the over cards aren't in the same suit. That way they have a shot at flushing on any four-suited community board, no matter how the over cards are faring as cards are drawn.

- ✔ **Interference with straights:** If the pairs interfere with straights of the over cards, they remove more of their outs. For example, 10-10 is a more dangerous hand to A-K than 7-7 is because it takes two cards away that make the Broadway straight.

- ✔ **How small the pair is:** A hand like 2-2 gets counterfeited by a board of 3-3-4-4-5. Any opponent holding a card with a rank greater than 5 win the hand. The bigger the pair, the harder it is to get counterfeited.

- ✔ **Gaps in the over cards:** The bigger the gap in the over cards, the harder it is for them to make a straight. Technically 10-J is better to hold than A-K against 2-2 because it can work the Broadway straight on the high side and 7-8-9-10-J on the low side. (A-K can only work two cards to the straight on the low side, and the A-2-3-4-5 wheel is missing a couple of possible deuces to draw.)

These differences, though, are slight. If you think of the proposition as something like 55 percent to the pair and 45 percent to the over cards, you're going to be in the right ballpark. This is pre-flop, of course, and assumes that the hand will be dealt to completion.

Post-flop, the over cards become desperate it they haven't paired, with the pair becoming dominant. If the over cards do hit on the flop, the under pair the opponent holds can typically only be saved by making a set of trips on fourth or fifth street.

Playing the coin flip in Limit

It's rarely clear in Limit if you're in a coin-flipping situation because of the way the betting works (there's not that obvious and immediate threat of all-in in your face). However, if you believe you're in a coin-flipping situation, you *definitely* have a call with either the pair or the over cards (because your pot odds will almost always be better than 1-to-1, thanks to the blinds and other callers).

Holding the small pair

If you're holding the small pair, playing Limit, you can continue to bet (even if you're the first to bet), keeping a careful eye on how your opponent reacts as she sees the up cards exposed.

If your pair is higher in rank than the board, you can bet (and raise) with impunity. Really your only threat is if someone is slow-playing an over pair, if an under pair managed to hit trips, or if something truly skanky happened like a big blind with 2-6 managed to hit two pair.

Holding the over cards

If you're playing the over cards in Limit and the flop hits blank, you should consider dropping the hand unless your outs and pot odds are telling you that you have a reasonable call.

The one exception here is if you think you can get your opponent to fold with a bluff. Roughly speaking, if you think she's twice as likely to fold as she is to call, you should try it. Never forget: The more you try bluffing, the more likely you are to be called.

Coin flipping in No-Limit

No-Limit is the place where you see, or at least suspect, coin-flipping as coming into play. Pushing all-in pre-flop is a common move for small pairs, especially:

- ✔ Early in a tournament, in an attempt to build a stack for later

- ✔ When short stacked, as an effort to double up

- ✔ As a semi-bluff, to back down bigger hands

As a general rule of thumb, in No-Limit if you think you're up against a better player, you should be eager to coin-flip with him (especially if you're holding the pair, which has a mathematical edge). Random chance will boost your odds of beating him over what your chances would be if you played for hours on end. If you're playing against someone you think is worse, you should avoid the coin flip and instead battle with him through skill.

Playing the over cards in No-Limit

If you're early in the action, I don't recommend pushing all-in immediately with something like A-K. You're better off making a sizeable raise (anything from three times the big blind, on up) and then watching the action and behavior behind you.

Several callers, *especially* those who flat-call you, can help you spot the Aces around the table. Every person holding an Ace or a King is reducing your number of outs if you're up against a pair.

When a short stack pushes, you can call or lay a big raise on top of the bet to try to isolate that single player. As much as possible, you want the action to just be between you and one other player. If you see an all-in fest in front of you where multiple people are pushing stacks that could significantly hurt you if you called, you should pass — almost certainly you're looking at a big pair (A-A and K-K are both taking cards from the deck that you need), and with multiple callers, there's going to be an Ace or two in there as well.

However, A-K seriously dominates any other player holding an Ace and trying to make a play for the pot. If you have even an inkling that you're up against Ace-anything, you should call.

Holding the small pair in No-Limit

If you hold a pair, you should coin-flip if you're short stacked and if:

- ✔ **You think your opponents will fold.**

- ✔ **You haven't made many all-in plays.** You don't want multiple callers to increase your chances of losing.

- ✔ **Your pair is big.** The bigger the pair, the more likely your opponent will only have one over card rather than two, in which case you'll dominate him. Anything Jacks or better is a potential fire-breathing monster for an opponent.

Consider just folding for now if:

- ✔ You can survive for several more hands.

- ✔ You've made several all-in plays and may get called by multiple players.

- ✔ You have early action in the betting order.

- ✔ You have an exceptionally tiny hand (5-5 or less).

The big danger of playing all-in with a pair is that someone else will call you with an over pair. If she does, you're essentially doomed because you only have two outs and you need one of them to keep away from death. For this reason, if nothing else, just consider folding small pairs.

If you put nothing in the pot, you lose nothing by folding those small pairs.

Using Math to Your Advantage

Because I've already got my numerical hard hat on, I'm going to dig just a little deeper on the math vein here.

Memorizing a little goes a long way

The math in this chapter may seem like a hill that's a little too steep to climb at first, but if you go back and read it a couple of times, you may well find that it starts making sense.

If not, you can still arm yourself with basic defenses. Table 12-1 is a poor-man's way to remember odds of any given occurrence.

Table 12-1 Quick-and-Dirty (Approximate) Poker Odds		
What You Want to Know or Do	*Quick-and-Dirty Odds of It Happening on a Single Card Draw*	*How the Given Chance Is Wrong*
Draw a fifth card for a flush after holding four suited cards	1-in-5	True odds are slightly worse.
Draw an outside straight after holding four in order	1-in-5	True odds are slightly worse.
Draw an inside straight after holding four with a gap	1-in-12	True odds are slightly better.
Make trips from a pocket pair	1-in-25	True odds are slightly better.
Draw a specific single card (for example, A♠)	1-in-50	True odds are slightly better.

If you want to know the odds of something happening on the turn *or* the river, you can cheat and just divide the odds number in half. For example, drawing a fifth card for a flush on either the turn or the river happens once in two and a half times. Again, the true odds are slightly worse (and because you're fudging it twice, the error becomes greater) at about 1-in-3, but saying 1-in-2½ is good enough to give you an idea.

In Table 12-1, every column represents wanting to draw to *one* specific hand. If you want to consider multiple possibilities, like drawing a straight *or* a flush (and you nearly always will), you're better off just counting up the outs. That way you won't accidentally count up cards in the intersecting scenarios (like a card that both makes your flush *and* your straight) twice.

For the truly curious, Table 12-2 has some other probabilities you might find interesting. No need to memorize, but the figures there *do* give you a good feel for how likely certain things are to happen at a poker table.

Table 12-2	Mathematical Hold'em Oddities
Thing That Can Occur	*Rough Odds of It Happening*
No player at a ten-handed table has been dealt an Ace or a King.	1-in-100
You flop a flush holding two suited hole cards.	1-in-100
You make a flush holding two suited hole cards in five community cards.	1-in-20
You're dealt a pocket pair.	1-in-20
You make a trips-or-better hand after pairing the flop.	1-in-12
You flop trips after holding a pocket pair.	1-in-8
Five community cards make trips or better of your pocket pair.	1-in-5
You pair one of your (no-pocket pair) hole cards on the flop.	1-in-3
You make a full house or better after having trips on the flop.	1-in-3
You make a flush on the turn or the river after having four flush cards on the flop.	1-in-3

Calculating deeper

It's worth saying a bit more about the concept of expectation. You do *not* have to know or memorize this to be able to play, but it will give you a glimpse as to the Big Math that's lying under the hood of your poker cruiser.

The expected value of a hand — that is to say, what it's worth in the long run — can be thought of this way:

Expected Value = [(How Much You Can Win) × (The Odds of Winning)] − [(How Much You Can Lose) × (The Odds of Losing)]

Here's an example of that equation, put into action. Imagine a magical world where you already know your opponent's hole cards. You're holding A♠ K♥, and your opponent has K♠ J♠. The board, before the river, shows Q♠ 4♠ 2♠ 5♥.

In this scenario, your opponent holds a spade flush. You *must* draw a spade, and if you do, you'll have the best hand. There is $80 in pot and your opponent has just bet $10, making the pot $90.

If you fold here, the expectation is easy to figure out. You lose $0, 100 percent of the time, because if you fold, you can't win and you can't lose. In math terms, this would be an expected value of $0.

If you call, it gets just a little more complicated. **Remember:** You'll be throwing $10 into the pot if you call, so the pot you're winning or losing would now be $100.

Because you can see your opponent's cards, you know you have the seven spades here as outs. There are 44 cards left in the deck, which also means that the other 37 cards do you no good whatsoever. Using the equation for expected value, you get:

$$\text{Expected Value} = [\$100 \times (7 \div 44)] - [\$0 \times (37 \div 44)]$$

$$= \$16$$

$$= \$16$$

This means that if you call, with $10 here, in the long run, you'll win an average pot of $16. If you fold, you don't win anything, so the right answer is to call.

For the mathematically hard core, you can also go back and check your work another way. Your true pot odds of winning are:

$$7 \div 44$$

or a little more than 5-to-1. The pot is offering 9-to-1, so you call.

Again, this isn't the kind of math you're expected to work at a poker table (although many pros can and do). I just put it here to give you an idea — and I make reference to this concept in Chapter 13.

Chapter 13

Advancing Your Knowledge

In This Chapter

▶ Getting hip to game theory (bring your own mind)

▶ Playing poker by equity

*E*ven if you master all the basics of poker and can play "perfectly," like a robot would, that actually only takes you so far. Setting aside the debate of whether there even *is* a "perfect" strategy, if everyone played exactly the same way, poker would become nothing more than a kind of complicated and sort of glorified game of chance.

The big question, then, is how do you move ahead from *there?*

After you have down the basics, in order to really advance you need to step back and think about how games themselves are played. This level of thinking is different from worrying about details like how to tell if a person is bluffing. Instead, you start considering that person's play as a whole — and how you can beat her because of the specific way that she plays.

Welcome to the world where you'll now reexamine, and possibly even question, everything you've learned. In this slightly surreal world, don't be too surprised if you go to look at the time and find that your watch is melting — it's probably also a good idea to have an extinguisher handy in case your giraffe catches on fire.

I absolutely believe you should at least be aware of the underlying concepts in this chapter — even if you never plan on actually practicing them — but this is a far cry from "I've never played poker before, please teach me" stuff. Starting your poker career with this chapter would definitely be detrimental to your poker health.

Playing with Game Theory

Game theory is a snooty phrase that mathematicians use to describe the concepts behind strategy in a game, or in other words, how you should think about the *way* you play a game. In this section, I tell you what it means and how to use it.

What game theory means

The tack here is different because I start talking about overall playing strategies as a whole, rather than the little tiny pieces that make up the parts of any *one* strategy. Or looking at it another way, everything in the first 12 chapters of this book can be thought of as one theory. Call it whatever you want, but I just call it *basic poker theory.*

If it helps, you can also think of basic poker theory as being a house on a street. Everything you use in basic poker theory — the hands you play, the way you bet from position, and so on — is just stuff in that one house. The obvious interesting question is, "What do the other houses look like?"

Understanding how to use it

Aside from geeky math heads, it turns out that kids are probably the best people in the world at understanding game theory — not because they're born with an uncanny mathematical sense of what it all means, but because they play games with reckless abandon and joy (unless you were a chess player at my house, in which case you always cried when you lost). And because you were a kid once, you've got a chance at actually knowing some of this stuff.

You probably still remember the thrill in learning how to never lose in tic-tac-toe (if you didn't, please send me a check for $10 and I'll send you my one-paragraph publication *Winning at Tic-Tac-Toe For Dummies by Playing in the Center Square First or Tying by Playing in the Corner if the Other Guy Has Played in the Center First*). And you probably also remember playing Rock, Paper, Scissors (a game that also goes by the snooty mathematical phrase, *roshambo*).

Roshambo, in case you've forgotten the fine points, was a game with two players where you make a fist, shake it up and down twice, and on the third shake made a hand signal for one of three shapes:

- **Rock:** A fist
- **Paper:** A flat hand
- **Scissors:** Two fingers (*not* raised up, for you Brits)

The two opponents compare shapes. For the winners: rock smashes scissors, scissors cut paper, paper covers rock. Whoever wins typically gets to do something unreasonable to the other person, like slap him or take his drink. Ties just try again. Like poker, it's a fun game — unless, of course, you lose.

Now I ask you this question: In roshambo, what is the best shape to play — rock, scissors, or paper?

Aha!

That's right. There isn't one because really it depends on what shape your opponent is playing. If you're up against Edward Scissorhands, you could play as The Thing, always using your rock fists, and you'd be a cinch winner. But The Thing wouldn't stand a chance against a book full of paper dolls in roshambo. And to close the loop, the paper dolls would take a shredding by Mr. Scissorhands.

This leads to very key element of game theory. In games that are *indeterminate by strategy* — meaning Strategy A beats Strategy B beats Strategy C, which in turn beats Strategy A — the most important thing to figure out is what strategy the other person is using and then to attack and exploit that strategy. So very cool.

But this is *supposed* to be a book about poker and not a crawl through childhood memories, right? As you've already guessed, this concept has huge poker ramifications. . . .

Poker is a complex enough game that you can pick any number of theories, ranging from "I always fold and never play a hand," to "I'm all-in all the time," to basic poker theory. Needless to say, there are *many* more ways to play (including exactly the way that you play the game of poker today). All these strategies have strengths (even "fold all the time," which will never give you the heartbreak of a really bad beat), but they also all have weaknesses.

In fact, *any* poker theory or style (call it *Style I*) can be beaten by another theory or style *(Style II),* if in some way you're privy to the secrets of how Style I worked. In roshambo, if you knew that your opponent was going to show paper, you could beat it.

Likewise, in poker, if you know your opponent is likely to bluff on any last hand at a table just because he likes to place one last bet before he leaves, you'll beat him. Taking it a step farther, if you knew precisely how multitime world champion Doyle Brunson played every hand and every situation, all the time, you could beat him. He's one of the best players in the world and yet if you knew how he played, you could shake him by the poker throat like a cheap carnival doll. (If you've read Chapter 8, you can see we're right back in the concept of playing the players again, but just looking at it from a slightly different angle.)

Basic poker theory will give you what you need to play a very competitive (and, once sharpened, winning) strategy at a poker table. The techniques and ideas in basic poker theory are based on years of practical human play and computer simulation. To keep your bankroll healthy, happy, and warm you should *never* stray from it without extremely good cause or reason — especially as a lame excuse for a bad play.

Cashing In on Equity Theory

Equity theory is not a "normal poker expression." It's a phrase I use to describe using knowledge of basic poker theory along with a little psychology mixed with mathematics (in the form of equity calculations). I like using the phrase *equity theory* because it reminds you that the emphasis of your play is on equity calculations or concepts. If you're not familiar with the mathematical concepts of poker, or if you could use some review, read Chapter 12 before marching on here.

The remainder of this chapter assumes you have a very thorough grasp of basic poker theory and that you've played it, used it, and understand what it means in application. If you've never played poker before, or if you aren't familiar with the underpinnings of general poker thought, do *not* start with this chapter and apply these concepts. Without basic poker knowledge and experience, this chapter could very well damage a developing poker game. If you're new to the game, skip over this chapter and go on to any other in the book.

Cross-breeding the animal of psychology with the beast of mathematics

There's a new trend in music you may have heard in the last few years called a *mash,* where two songs, or samples of two songs, are played at the same time on top of one another. The result is noisy sometimes, cool sometimes, and, every now and then, eerie.

Hunting for new poker theories and styles is similar. Coolness is definitely out there somewhere, but if you're not careful, you'll find yourself getting involved in situations that leave you with a suffering bank account.

Using what you know against (people just like) you

Now that you understand basic poker theory, if you stop and think about it you'll realize that you know several things about your opponents who use it, including:

- ✔ The kinds of hands they play
- ✔ The positions that they play those hands from
- ✔ The way they bet in different situations

The thing that is going to vary amongst your opponents, even if they all use basic poker theory, is how aggressive or passive they are. Using the tricks and techniques from Chapter 8, you can get some idea.

The basic poker theory and the psychology of your opponent are two of the pieces you need in the equity-theory puzzle. Math is the other piece.

Bring on the players, bring on the math!

Consider this scenario: You're playing in a No-Limit tournament (more on these in Chapter 17), you're in the final two (way to go, see, I *told* you this book would work), and chips are evenly stacked at 100,000 each. Blinds are getting pretty high at 5,000 and 10,000. You're on the big blind.

Louella in the small blind started the tournament very tight but has been getting looser and more aggressive as the tournament has progressed. You've been using more or less the same tactic, maybe just a tad more conservative, and keeping a watchful eye on her.

On this hand she opens with a raise to 30,000, and now it's your turn to act. It's going to be 20,000 for you to call — about a third of your stack will be on the table.

Freeze.

Fold, call or . . .

First take a look from the outside and forget all about what cards you're dealt. This should be easy to do because I haven't mentioned them yet, but remember, Louella can't see them either, so it's not *that* far-fetched of a concept.

There's a broad generality in poker, especially at the upper levels, that calling is the weakest play you can do. You either raise to take control of the hand or fold to play something better.

If you fold here, you give away 10 percent of your stack 100 percent of the time. You just give it away. No fight.

You *could* just call, but if you don't improve on the flop (and odds are you won't), you'll either have to bluff your way through or fold then, only to have lost more. What's worse: You're giving bullets to a person who is getting more and more openly hostile.

What about raising? Well, the minimum raise here would be 20,000 more (you have to raise at least what she raised) and then you're in for half your stack. At that point it's just going to be a coin toss, because if she flat-calls you, half of all the chips on the table are in the pot. It's going to be a difficult proposition for either player to drop the hand at that point, because as soon as she does, she's a 3-to-1 underdog in chips.

. . . All-in?

How about the *big* raise? How about pushing all-in?

The question to ask yourself is what do you think the chances of Louella dropping this hand are if you push her all-in? She's been playing more and more aggressively. You know that she plays basic poker theory and there are only two players left here at the table.

If she had a somewhat sturdy hand, say two cards greater than 8, she might make a raise to take a shot simply to snatch the blind. In fact, she may do that anyway. In the old basic poker theory days, you might have let her do that — but here in Equity Theory Land you might not.

You'd guess that 3 out of 4 times (or 75 percent of the time) she'd fold in this exact position, right now, if you pushed her all-in. You haven't made any big moves and, although you're getting more aggressive, you haven't banged heads with her. From the way she's acting at the table, her hand just doesn't seem *that* strong. Her hands tremored slightly earlier in the tourney when she had pocket Aces and they're not shaking now. She might respect you and just back off. If she's bluffing, she'll almost certainly drop.

On the other hand, if she calls, she'll probably only do that with a pretty good hand and you'll be playing this hand for the tournament.

Writing the equity equation

If I write out the expectation (see Chapter 12 if you need to brush up) as a couple of sentences, I say this:

> 75 percent of the time, you win 45,000 flat out. You're guessing she folds that often and you win. Simple.

In Hold'em, any two cards have roughly a 25 percent chance of beating any two other over cards on the table. So in the one-quarter of the time that Louella doesn't fold but instead calls, you'll have a 25 percent sliver of the time that you win 100,000 through pure luck. The bad news is you'll lose 100,000 in the 75 percent sliver of the time because you were bested pre-flop.

As an equation it looks like this:

$$\text{Expectation} = (0.75 \times 45,000) + (0.25 \times [(0.25 \times 100,000) - (0.75 \times 100,000)])$$

$$= 33,750 + (0.25 \times [25,000 - 75,000])$$

$$= 33,750 + (0.25 \times -50,000)$$

$$= 33,750 - 12,500$$

$$= 21,250$$

Whoa. That's a *positive* expectation of over 20,000. That's huge when you consider that something like folding right now gives you an expectation of 0 (you can't win and you can't lose).

That means pushing all-in right here, right now, is the right move!

But be aware of the ramifications of your actions. When you push all-in, if Louella *does* pass, she'll remember vividly and know what you're capable of. Every time you push all-in and someone passes, it makes it more likely that person will call you in the future. As that likelihood rises, the equation you're working against changes.

The fine print

There are a lot of assumptions here, and irrespective of my whippy equation in the preceding section, some of this is much less than the hard science I'm making it look like. The big question, really, is how likely is Louella to pass? The more likely she is to drop, the better an all-in play is.

Getting in Louella's dress

Whenever you play an opponent in any game of skill, it's worth taking a hard look at the situation from her side, which means it's time to jump into the skin of Louella and imagine the scenario that's been described here.

If she has a monster starting hand, like Q-Q, K-K, or A-A, she's going to be pleased (especially after she's seen your cards), because she's going to be sitting heavily over you with something like an 85 percent edge (assuming you have a relatively normal hand). Unless there's a lightning bolt of luck, you're most likely going to experience the tinny taste of loss.

If she has a somewhat anemic pair, like 6-6, she now has a very sweaty call to make. She's mildly ahead in the coin toss if you're unpaired, *but* she's crushed if you have a pair over the top of her. And she has no idea what you have. It's true that she's walking away from about a third of her stack if she folds, but that's going to trump a near-certain death if she thinks you're sitting over her with a large pair.

If she's holding a set of larger connectors, say J-Q, it's very possible she will pass, interpreting that you're playing an Ace or a King sitting above her.

If she's playing an Ace, she'll probably call but not like it. The exception might be if she's playing an Ace with a low kicker — this would be easier to pass.

If she's bluffing, she'll almost certainly pass. People don't like taking a shot at the big money on a crying call that started out as a bluff.

As you can see, there are *lots* of ways for her to say *no mas* to this hand . . . and all you need is *one*.

You can play with the equation if you want, but the break-even point with the betting set up as described is as low as 27 percent for Louella folding. If Louella is more likely to fold than 27 percent, then from a pure equity-theory point of view, the right play is push all-in. If her odds of folding are less than that, the right play is to, well, at least look at your cards.

Don't expect, or even try, to do these kinds of calculations at the table. This is a *For Dummies* book, not an admissions test for the Rocket Science Academy of the Universe. Just play with the idea in your mind and get a rough feeling of what it might take to win in situations such as these.

Don't assume that all raising situations in all circumstances come down to a 27 percent chance of the other player folding. That just happens to be the number for the example shown here.

The important concept in this chapter is not these numbers, or even how they're derived, but the fact that there are other ways to look at poker. A deeper form of the game, if you will.

Playing the cards

Do note that if you were to do something like not look at your cards and just push all-in, Louella would be far more likely to call if she had a hand. The *instant* she makes a decision to call, your odds of winning drop considerably (assuming, of course, you're behind in the hand).

As you can tell, we're out in a different land here. Is this bluffing? Sort of. You could argue that it's a mathematical basis for bluffing. But it's important to remember that moving all-in is the right play here, even if you only have a one-in-four chance of winning the hand straight out.

But really, it's more just testing a person's resolution with her hand and the way she plays relative to basic poker theory. What you're really starting to do is pry under the floorboards of the basic poker theory mansion to see where the weak spots are in the foundation. (Actually, it's more akin to ringing the doorbell and running away.)

When you do actually look at your hand, and you discover it's a good one, you can play it as you normally would: raise, slow-play, or all-in — whatever seems most appropriate for this opponent at this time. But if you don't have a hand, you still shouldn't be afraid of pushing if her odds of passing are as high as you've guessed (as long as *you* don't give away a tell that you have a bad hand, of course).

Going back to square one

The catch in equity theory that I described in this chapter, if you haven't figured it out already, is that if someone knows you're playing that way, she can take counteractions to put you down. This includes such evil activities as *not* folding 75 percent of the time and instead calling, or only making a run at you when she has a seriously crippling hand and taking you out with a quick, deadly jab.

Just like roshambo, when this starts to happen, you need to move to yet another theory, yet another style, searching for the inevitable gaps in the way she plays. If you have a rock and your opponent grabs paper, it's time for you to switch to scissors.

Doyle Brunson: Equity theorist

Doyle Brunson has won more World Series of Poker bracelets than any other person in the history of poker (with the exception of Johnny Chan, whom he's tied with). Considering how much that tournament field is growing year over year, that's a record that could potentially stick in the record books for some time.

He's famous for saying that he could beat most players without even looking at his two cards (assuming that the other player didn't know he wasn't looking), based entirely on that person's play and demeanor on any given hand.

This concept lies right in the very heart of equity theory. If you look at the example in this chapter, I talk about the hand being dealt and played without looking at the cards.

Now Doyle may not think of himself as an equity theorist, but from a mathematical schooling point of view, he'd be the dean of that department.

Any time you make changes or adjustments in the philosophy of how you play, your bankroll will suffer for a bit. It takes a while to fully try on, and adapt to, a new style, theory, philosophy, or thought. In some senses it's like being a beginner again. Don't expect to instantly become greater. But keep an eye on how and what you're doing — if you don't see improvements, you're trying to bark up the wrong tree.

And don't sweat it. This chapter is the gnarliest one in the book. *Everything* before and after this chapter is "easier." I just want to make sure you got your money's worth when you bought this book. You can (and should) refer to this chapter in the future as your game improves.

Part IV

Casinos, Card Rooms, and the Internet: Places to Play Hold'em

The 5th Wave   By Rich Tennant

"I still don't understand why they would ask if we wanted to bring our accordion to a poker party."

In this part . . .

Poker is *so* popular these days that you can play almost anywhere in the world. The chapters in this section are dedicated to the nuances of each: home games, professional card rooms, and online.

You can also find a chapter dedicated to tournaments if you'd like to take that first step to putting a World Series bracelet on your wrist in a few years (or days).

Chapter 14

There's No Place Like Home: Playing in Private Games

*E*veryone starts his poker "career" at a home game. Maybe your favorite uncle asked you to pull up a chair to the nickel-ante game when you were a kid, or perhaps your dorm mates seemed sloshed enough from the kegger that you figured you could learn the rules and *still* beat them (turns out you were wrong, but that's another story).

Whatever the situation, home games are worth looking at because they're both the most fun and, in many ways, the most potentially dangerous ones to play.

Determining the Level and Type of Play

Of any way you can play poker, home games have the biggest variation and variety. They can range anywhere from getting together with a few pals with a roll of quarters and knocking down a few cold ones, to extremely serious affairs with multi-thousand-dollar buy-ins and professional dealers.

Home games are the roaming dog on the poker streets. Some are cuddly and nice. Others are rabid and should be avoided at all costs. Just like when you were a kid, before you try to pet the nice doggy, it's worth figuring out which type is in front of you.

Identifying stakes and games

When you play in any home game, you need to get an idea of the stakes and games that you're going to be playing before you go. And for your bankroll's sake, you need to get this as accurately as you possibly can.

Gleaning the stakes

For some reason many people like to be a little coy about buy-ins — especially when larger stakes are involved. I guess they think it just sounds cool to be cavalier when you're talking about a bunch of money. If you're getting answers that sound evasive, you can ask a small battery of questions that will give you a better idea:

- ✔ What's the buy-in?

- ✔ Are there rebuys of some type allowed?

- ✔ How much do people tend to win or lose in a session?

Knowing the games

Just as important as the stakes are the types of games that are played.

- ✔ Do they play straight Hold'em or are other poker variants (for example, Five-Card Draw, Omaha, Seven-Card Stud, Dealer's Choice) played as well?

- ✔ Do they play tournaments, ring games, or both?

- ✔ Are the games Limit, Spread-Limit, No-Limit, or a mix?

The Limit/No-Limit question is exceptionally important. Because of the vicious swings in No-Limit, you can easily bust out (especially if you're playing in a rebuy tournament format — see Chapter 17 for more). You want to be sure to bring a wad of cash that will support your play (while also being sure to not play an amount that's hazardous to your bankroll as a whole — see Chapter 3).

Playing with friends

All my favorite games, and the vast majority of my best times playing poker, have been with my pals. (These games aren't my most profitable, though — I think it's because I just don't pay as close of attention, or care as much, as I do in a professional environment.)

Those goofy venture capitalists

To give you an example of how important it is to determine a buy-in, there's a group of venture capitalists in the Silicon Valley, where I live, who have a monthly home game. When they got wind that I was writing my last book (*Winning at Internet Poker For Dummies,* with Chris Derossi), I miraculously received an invitation.

"What's the buy-in?" I asked, as I could hear the odd sound of shears being sharpened in the background.

"Oh, just a few bills," the Italian-loafer-wearing lad assured me.

In gambling parlance this would mean a few hundred dollars. But I knew this was a circle of folks who pay more than that to have the wheels polished on their sports cars every week. Some more pushing and prodding brought out the truth: Typical wins and losses in the game would run around $10,000. In the recent past, people had dropped as much as $60,000 — and more than one person in the last year had made $100,000 in a single sitting.

To answer your question, no, as tempting as it was, I did not play — probably forever making it impossible to raise any venture capital for future start-ups.

Playing with friends is easy and fun. It's a great way to unwind and gives you an interaction that's a considerable step above watching whatever game is on the tube.

There are a couple of things you need to watch out for, or at least be aware of.

Watching out for the hotheads

There are some people who take many things in their lives, but especially poker, a little too seriously. There's something about poker and the way it affects certain psyches that's just a little *too* caustic. I've seen a couple of different real-life friendships explode over nothing more than an interaction at an otherwise "friendly" Friday-night card game.

Poker is an interesting and fun game, but when it starts getting in the way of real-life interaction, that's just too much. Don't ever be afraid to leave a game early if the vibe just doesn't seem right, or if you find that you yourself are getting too hot under the collar. It's not worth it.

Dealing with demigods

Some home games have people who are either so wrapped up in the game or so bent out of shape on their own ego trips that they control nearly every action. They're easy to spot because they sit and bark out commands on what to do when. All that matters to them is the poker game and the action going on surrounding it.

These kinds of guys (and they are *always* guys) are surprisingly common in home games. I used to play in one home game where the "poker room coach" drove me insane enough that I simply quit playing. There's another where I tolerate the guy only because the game is *really* loose and they always have good food.

The best piece of advice I can give you is to find your points of tolerance and play within them. You can always find a game *somewhere* (especially these days), so if you're playing in one you don't like, quit it and look for one elsewhere.

Meeting strangers

Usually the way you meet someone new in a home game is through a mutual acquaintance. Maybe your work pal's cousin is in town, or a couple of old friends hook up after a few years apart. Those are the easy and obvious situations.

There is a new breed of home game that is becoming more common, mostly through the wonders of the Internet, and that is groups of people playing together who don't really know each other outside the game. Maybe it's a bunch of people who read the same newsgroup, people who all go to the same school, or people who get to talking over an Internet poker table and decide to get together and play live-action.

These sorts of feral card games vary widely. The majority are just a bunch of people who like the game and want to get together for a good time, but it's still worth watching your back for the few individuals who aren't on the level. Make sure to find out the stakes and the games played before you show up. You might even want to stop by and say "hi" once before you play, just to get a lay of the land (it also can keep you from getting rolled for your cash if the people involved are less than savory).

What You Should Give

People running home games will tend to expect different things for running the game. Most will probably want nothing more than help in cleaning up the room after it's been trashed over a few hours of poker (which of course you'll do, right? *right?*). Some hosts may want more.

Skimming the pot

Some houses will want to take their own version of raking the pot, known in gambling parlance as a *skim*. Skimming is where things start to get dicey, so you need to know about it in more detail.

Good skimming

At some home games, the host provides all the refreshments and then takes a dollar or two out of the biggest pots until he's paid himself back. I have no problem with this; it's a very equitable way to pay the expenses — the winner doesn't mind throwing a chip or two out of a big pot, and the losers are watching their money walk away anyway.

The skim, of course, should be limited to the actual food cost. (I used to play at a home game where the proprietor would skim a little *more* if he was losing — typically it's not the kind of thing I would tolerate, but the game was *so* lucrative for me that I didn't mind.)

If you're going to be playing in a game with a skim, you don't need to bring your own food. Or, if you do, have the people running the game throw you a buck or two to cover it.

Bad skimming

In the other kind of skimming, a home-game host takes the equivalent of a rake — a chip or two out of every pot (or every pot of size).

The problem is that now this "home game" is acting like a professional card room and, depending on the state the game is happening in, that means your gentle host is either operating a card room without a license or just flat-out breaking the law. Setting aside what the rake does to your money on the table, when you play in a game like this you're at a certain amount of legal risk. If this game gets busted while you're playing in it, you'll likely have to make an uncomfortable call to someone from jail.

Although it's unlikely that any given government would come after *you* for being in the game (the people they *really* want are the folks running the game), it's very possible that your cash could be held as evidence. If you're a college student, you could risk expulsion from school. (There's also the more diabolical thing that can happen playing in a game like this, which is a *fake bust,* where someone who isn't actually a cop comes in and takes the cash.)

In case you haven't figured it out by now, you should *not* play in a home game that is skimmed. Your personal risk is too high, and for some reason places that condone this kind of behavior also tend to be dens of other types of iniquity (drugs, prostitution, weapons, and so on). It may look cool when you see something like this in the movies, but the phrase you *should* be thinking about is what it would feel like to hear the phrase, "Could you please tell the court. . . ."

Bringing on the refreshments

Any time you play in a home game, especially as a new member to the game, you should always bring enough food and drink to share. For snacks, you want to bring anything that's *not* greasy (like potato chips) or sticky (like fruit or Gummy Bears), because those kinds of items tend to spoil cards over time. It's also better to get something you can easily reseal and take back home if you end up with leftovers.

If your main goal for the evening is to win some cash, stay away from alcohol but consider dosing up on caffeine to keep alert.

What You Can Get

Especially in a home game, you want to make sure you get what you want out of the game. As I mention in Chapter 1, consider what you want: Good times? To make a little money? To sharpen your poker skills? Whatever it is, make sure you know what you want and get it from your home game.

Enjoying the situation

Have a good time. You're not playing in the World Series, so that means you can leave your shades and your bad-ass go-ahead-and-call-my-bluff looks at *your* home (unless, of course, that's part of what gets you off).

Don't get so wound up in the games, or the beats, that you lose track of the bigger picture of just having fun. And if you play in a home game you just don't like, bag it and play somewhere else. You can *always* find another game somewhere.

Watching the action

The best learning tool that a home game can give you, particularly if you're playing against people you know away from the card table, is a dictionary (that you'll build from scratch) for reading players. Really study the other players at the table and see how they react as they win and lose. Watch how their play changes over time (particularly in respect to their bankroll and fatigue).

Everything you learn here isn't designed so you can keep track of these particular players (although that is a nice side effect, especially if you end up playing with them many times); instead, this is your first step into a deeper study in general poker psychology.

Focus the majority of your concentration on the hands where you're just sitting out. This gives you a chance to examine players without the filter of your own personal prejudices and without emotions being involved. Lots of times, especially if you're with your buds, they'll show you their hole cards, giving you a rare chance to tie personal reactions to very specific situations.

Before you play in a home game, have another look at Chapter 8 for the kinds of things to look for.

If you ever wander into a professional card room, the knowledge and experience you gain from studying the reactions at home games will give you a tremendous step up in what can be an otherwise intimidating experience. The edge this will give you over an online-only player is enormous.

Looking for the unusual

One of the things professional card rooms have that home games are lacking is the concept of surveillance. No one is really watching what's going on with the game as a whole, and this can lead to problems.

Mistakes

If you're playing with your pals, cheating is pretty unlikely (if it *is* likely, man, you need a new set of pals). More common are hazards and mishaps:

- ✔ **Cards getting damaged during play:** This is easily the most common thing I see happen at home games, especially those that are using cardboard-based cards rather than plastics (see Chapter 20 for more). Aces, in particular, tend to get warped because people hold and play them more than the other cards in the deck. If you notice the cards starting to show noticeable bends (the corners will start lifting up), ask for a change of deck.

- ✔ **A card getting dropped on the floor:** This tends to happen more with Stud than it does with Hold'em (because more cards are dealt in more crazy positions in Stud), but it definitely *can* happen. Make sure to count the deck occasionally.

- ✔ **Owners forgetting how much they buy in for:** Lots of times whoever is acting as the house will just give herself chips, instead of putting cash in the box for the house. If the house player is losing, she may dip in multiple times and forget how often she does. To keep this from causing problems, on any home game, all players at the table should be cashed out first, before the house player takes any remaining money.

- ✔ **Players getting cashed in or out for the wrong amount:** When you buy chips, make sure you're given the right amount (watch everyone else, too, to make sure they're given the right amount as well). When cashing out, count your money, especially if it's a large number of small bills. People who don't deal with cash on a day-to-day basis often make mistakes.

Cheating

Unfortunately, *any* time money is involved in any transaction, cheating is a possibility. It should go without saying that if you're playing in a home game where you have a strong suspicion that there's cheating, you need to permanently quit playing that game. My experience in home games has been that people are *far* more likely to make an honest mistake than they are to cheat, so if you find something awry, don't automatically assume you're being cheated.

However, due to a general lack of surveillance, home-game cheating can happen. (I've seen it twice — I wish I could say I hadn't — and have suspected it strongly a third time.)

Here's a list of things to be on the watch for:

- ✔ **People withholding cards from the deck (also known as** *the ace up the sleeve*): What you want to be suspicious of is people who seem to be showing down the same card (or cards) too often. Deck counting will help keep this to a minimum.

- ✔ **Chip stealing or swapping:** Know your stack any time you leave the table and keep an eye on those of your opponents. Any time you see unaccounted chips showing up in an opponent's stack, *something* is going on. In a ring game, the added chips don't matter (assuming the player isn't stealing them from the house and then slipping them in — if so, it will put the accounting off at the end of the night), but in a tournament, someone may be grabbing the chips from the chip stock and slipping them to his stack. In tournaments, the house rule should be that *all* chips are kept *on* the tournament table at *all times.*

- ✔ **Unusual dealing habits:** What you're looking for is someone who deals cards in a very unusual or awkward manner — particularly if he deals off the front of a deck rather than from the corner. Another possibility is a thing known as *flashing,* where a dealer gets a peek at a card sometimes before it's dealt. Do note: If someone is an extremely good deck mechanic, you won't be able to tell he's cheating you. And whatever you do, don't confuse someone's lack of familiarity with handling a deck of cards with an inability to deal. That 3-year-old sitting across from you isn't a card shark — he just can't shuffle a deck of cards.

- ✔ **Collusion:** You want to be aware of some players signaling others, either to the quality of your hand or theirs. This isn't as important in Hold'em as it is some other poker games, but it's still worth watching for.

- ✔ **Marked cards:** This almost never happens anymore, although there is a thing known as *smudging,* where a player will intentionally deface a card (or series of cards) so she can recognize them facedown around the table in later hands. This one is easy to watch for — all cards should look the same, always.

If you're pretty sure that cheating is going on in a home game, quit playing — and never go back.

Chapter 15

Opting for the Internet: Online Games

*T*he world's largest poker parlor is no farther away than your computer. You can plug in, log on, and go, go, go!

Even though getting an account and playing is simple, there are some things you should be aware of first — namely, the differences, hazards, and glories of online play.

And now for my (nearly) shameless plug: If you find the online poker bug biting you after reading this book, or after dabbling a bit in online play, pick up a copy of my other book, *Winning at Internet Poker For Dummies*. It goes into *much* more detail than this chapter and what's great is that you'll get your full money's worth because there is very little overlap with what I cover in this book (because *Winning at Internet Poker For Dummies* was originally written to dovetail with *Poker For Dummies,* it doesn't cover the general strategy and play sections that you find in these pages).

Choosing a Site

There are, literally, hundreds of poker sites to choose from. All of them offer Hold'em, Seven-Card Stud, and Omaha — some go even farther, with things like Razz (Seven-Card Stud low), Pineapple (a variation of Hold'em where you're dealt *three* hole cards), and Draw.

Picking a site

Online sites make their money the same way brick-and-mortar places do — either by raking the pot or through a tournament registration fee. And they make that cash by the bucketful.

Because you're going to be putting a little water in their money buckets, you need to pick a place that you're satisfied with and a place that's safe.

To find a possible site, just use your favorite search engine to search on something like "poker room reviews" and read as much about the different sites as you can. Make sure that the review site you're looking at isn't sponsored, or owned by, the site that it's reviewing. (You can pretty easily tell, because no other sites will be discussed.) At their very heart, all the poker rooms are the same — I mean, come on, poker is poker — but the sites *do* vary in the way you interact with them (known as the *user interface*), the way they look, and the kinds of perks they give to the players.

Here's a series of questions to ask when you're considering a poker site:

- ✔ **Does it support the large transfer agents (NETeller and/or FirePay)?** If so, that's a good thing, because only legitimate sites can have accounts with those folks. (The transfer agents have to protect their integrity as well.)

- ✔ **Is the site located in a gaming jurisdiction that takes licensing seriously?** Malta, Gibraltar, Alderney, Isle of Man, Australia, and Guernsey are all examples of locales with stringent gambling laws — you want your site to be sitting in places like these. The Kahnawake reservation in Canada and Costa Rica are both a little less stringent (they tend to grant licenses to poker sites because the sites have paid the money, as opposed to being investigative, making sure that the sites are legit), although there are several big and reputable sites there. If a site is based in Kahnawake but has everything else on this list, you're most likely okay. Avoid anything in Africa or any of the former Soviet jurisdictions; at the time of this writing, I'm not aware of any legitimate site functioning in those locales.

- ✔ **Does it play limits that you're comfortable with?** If not, move along.

- ✔ **Does it have enough players that you can find a game when you want to?** This factor is also important just for the site's financial well-being.

- ✔ **Does the site pick up the transfer fees from your third-party holding company?** Because most do, it doesn't make any sense for *you* to do it. If you can't figure it out from the poker Web site, you can always write and ask the support people.

✔ **Does the site use a securing function (a company such as Thawte)?** This gives you a level of security in the transaction, and again, Thawte only works with people *it* trusts.

✔ **Does it have a bonus you can earn?** For more on this, turn to "Exploring the bonuses," later in this chapter.

Whatever site you choose, be sure to play several orbits on their free play tables first to get used to the way the site acts and behaves. If there's nothing that bugs you, go with it. If you find something about a site that you don't like — even just a little bit — keep looking. With the kind of money you'll ultimately spend, you deserve to get an experience you like.

One thing to watch out for on a site is overlapping action buttons. By that, I mean that the *future action* buttons (the ones that say what you're going to do when it's your turn), don't have the same intent as the *present action* buttons. So something semi-evil can happen, like you go to click on the Check button, and just when it gets to be your turn, it becomes a Call button instead.

Do not assume that free chip play is like playing for real money. It's not. You should play on the free chip tables merely to get a feel for the way a site acts. Playing at length on a free table will actually *damage* your poker game because soon you'll find yourself raising on things like a gut-shot straight draw — just like everyone else at your table.

Transferring money

You get your money into the poker site of your choice by using a third-party transfer agent. If you're familiar with using something like PayPal for an eBay transaction, the process in the poker world is identical. The rub is that PayPal doesn't support gaming sites, which, as you might guess, has opened a multimillion-dollar industry for companies that *do* support gaming. The big boys in the transfer league are NETeller and FirePay — both are reliable and can be trusted as much as any corporation that you give your banking information to.

Like visiting the parents of your latest flame (or worse, your in-laws), it can all seem a little scary and spooky at first. But after you've done it once or twice, it all becomes second nature. From a pure security point of view, by far the biggest thing you need to worry about is keeping your account information (the account number and password) safe.

Don't *ever* access your poker account or your transfer agent from a public computer (such as one that is in your local library). If anyone is storing keystrokes, he can look the information up later and you can lose as much money as you transferred to a site. You *do* get a warning in that you'll get an e-mail saying a transfer is in process, but it's still much better to be a problem you never have to deal with at all.

Exploring the bonuses

One way the online world trumps the brick-and-mortar operations is in the ability to get bonuses. You'll see claims such as "100% sign-up bonus," meaning if you deposit $100, you can earn a $100 bonus.

Are the bonuses too good to be true? Well, kinda yes and sorta no.

Like the real world, online sites make their money through the rake. (In fact, they tend to rake less: Web sites typically rake at 5 percent — real-world card rooms usually do 10 percent.) But the online card rooms' operating expenses aren't very high. Really they only have to cover customer support, gaming license fees, and the cost of maintaining a large bank of computers — they don't have to pay valets, cleaning staff, cashiers, cooks, bathroom attendants, security guards, light-bulb changers, and so on. As a result, they can rebate some of this rake back to the player and still make a tidy profit.

If you read the fine print of a bonus (and you *definitely* should read the fine print) you'll see it's not as easy as depositing $100, getting $100 to match it, and cashing right back out again.

These are the things you need to look for on bonuses:

- **Is it an "all-or-nothing" bonus?** In other words can you only be paid your bonus if you earn it in full? You want a bonus that's paid piecemeal over time. That way, if you leave a site early, or you have a bad run of luck and lose all your cash, you'll still get a little kickback.

- **Is there a minimum amount of necessary playtime necessary to make the bonus?** It's not bad in and of itself if there is — you just have to figure out if you can make it.

- **Roughly how much bonus will you make over a certain period of time?** This can be tough to figure out sometimes, so the best thing to do is look at the tables, figure out how many hands per hour they're playing (this is usually listed in a column in the lobby), get a feel for the average, and see how long it will take. If you're comparing multiple sites, run the figures a couple of times. What you're looking for is a *big* difference in how quickly you're earning your bonus. If the sites that you're comparing are about the same, choose the site you want to play based on some other preference (ease of game play, number of opponents, other perks the site offers, and so on).

✔ **How big are the "chunks" of payout?** For example, some sites pay $20 worth of bonus at a time — this isn't as good for you, the player, as $1 at a time because you'll leave some bonus on the table when your time period expires.

 If you keep track of your wins and losses (see Chapter 22), remember to put the bonus in a separate column. You certainly can still count it as your money (because it *is* your money), but over the long run, if you aren't constantly paid bonus, it won't give you an idea whether you are *truly* beating the game.

Checking up on Two-Fisted Karpov

In *Winning at Internet Poker For Dummies* I made reference to my pal, Two-Fisted Karpov. He's an actuary by trade (the people who figure out what your odds of dying are) and the best applied mathematician I know. He's also a fanatical record keeper and plays about ten hours of online poker a week (he plays single-table tournaments only, always two at a time Pot-Limit Hold'em and Omaha High/Low).

Even if he plays like a lunatic with two hands at once, he's a winning player and I asked him to send his data along for this chapter.

Two-and-a-half years ago, Karpov deposited (with both hands, I'm sure) $400 to a major online poker site.

As of today his account stands at $1,633. He has also withdrawn $1,350 and at one point won a $9,000 prize package (it was a poker cruise with a $7,500 tournament seat and $1,500 in cruise fees/spending money). Which is to say that in 30 months, he has won $12,000.

In that time, he's played in 2,538 tournaments, representing over $68,000 in tournament entry fees. Because all the tournaments he plays are of the pay-$10-+-$1-to-play type, this means his poker site has made $6,800 off him.

Looking at this another way, Karpov has averaged more than $4 winning in every tournament he's played. It's a spectacular result, but when looked at through the average-filter, it sounds like very little.

And here's something that will send shivers down your spine: At the low point (and this was after many months of play), Karpov's account was at $11. He explains, "It was a bad combination of my starting to play higher limits in tournaments, while simultaneously taking a series of bad beats. I cut back and things got better."

Many sites give player referral bonuses — giving a piece of the rake to any player who recommends a site to another player. When you recommend a pal, make sure she lists you as a referrer. If you're going to play at a site where no one has referred you, you can contact their customer support staff and see if you can refer yourself. Sounds strange, yes, but some places will let you do it, and it may give you yet another sliver of money back.

The vast majority of people who play poker in a situation where it's raked, lose money *because* of the rake. *Any* bonus you get is better than none — and the more you can get, the better. I've seen the accounting books of online gambling sites, and I would guess that bonuses probably double the number of winners a site has. A bonus *is* worth seeking out and using.

Watching Your Back

The online world is not without its treacherous spots. I help you avoid them in the following sections.

Being wary of robots

In the sense being used here, a *robot* isn't something that protects Will Robinson from Dr. Smith. Instead, it's a program that is designed to play poker automatically.

When I wrote *Winning at Internet Poker For Dummies* three years ago, robots online were merely a rumor — today, they are a well-known fact. Some sites actively look for them and seize accounts that are associated with them. Others claim they are on the lookout for robots, but do nothing. A few don't even try to fight the battle and welcome them (because after all, a robot pays rake, just as everyone else does).

There are a few things to be aware of about robots upfront:

- ✔ They can still lose, just as anyone else can.

- ✔ They don't have the ability to see the cards you're holding.

- ✔ To be the most effective, they need to play at higher limits (because that's the way you maximize your return and minimize the ratio of your win to the rake taken).

Because they're programs at their very heart, robots have predictable behavior. Anything that can be predicted, *can* be beaten (see Chapter 13 for more on the concepts of game theory).

Especially at lower limits, I honestly don't think robots are a problem for a player. But as a general rule, if you ever have your doubts about a table you're playing at, move to another. And if just the *idea* of playing against robots is creeping you out, don't play online at all.

 All the robots I know of are Limit ring-game players. If you're a No-Limit player — and especially a No-Limit tournament player — you have nothing to worry about as far as robots are concerned. (But playing No-Limit, you may have a whole lot to worry about as far as your *bankroll* is concerned.)

Spotting collusion

Collusion is what happens when multiple players share their knowledge of a hand with each other in an effort to beat another player. The best example of this would be two people talking on a cellphone or instant messaging (IMing), and telling each other what their hole cards are. In theory this could give one player an edge over another.

There's also a more advanced possibility of this where one player actually sits at multiple seats around the *same* table — essentially seeing the cards for multiple players and picking and choosing what to play from there. On the surface, this sounds pretty bad, but the reality is a little bit different. For one thing, the operating poker sites already know what all the hole cards are, so they can see when one player backs away from another in a situation that normally wouldn't warrant it. They also keep a *very* close eye on which players commonly play together as well as the Internet address that all players log on from. Large-moneyed cash games go one step farther and have humans on the back end who actually sit and monitor the play as it happens.

The reality is that collusion just doesn't happen that frequently, and the host sites can very easily spot it and stop it when it does happen.

If you sit and think about it for a second, imagine two players at your table who are sharing their hole-card information with each other. That, in and of itself, is of limited use. If they both get in big raising battles to try to force you out, and then they quit betting, well, that's a certain tip-off to the site. If they always transfer money back and forth when not at the tables, this is also a tip-off. If they try to pick on people only sporadically to throw the monitors off, they're starting to open themselves up to other people pounding *them* with big raises, because other players will think the colluders are actually bluffers.

"This site is rigged" and other lies

The number-one thing you'll hear about online poker is a claim that the site is rigged. Every poker site in the world has someone whining about how some beat he's just taken could *never* happen in the real world.

First and foremost, a poker site makes its money off of action. Unlike a game like blackjack or roulette, the poker site doesn't have a vested interest in who wins or loses — they just want a lot of people to play the game.

Also, if you're using a site in a good jurisdiction (see "Picking a site," earlier in this chapter), the software the site is running has already gone through a significant auditing process.

There are several factors at work here:

✔ **You are seeing *many* more hands than you do in a physical card room.** The more hands you see, the more chances you get to hit low-odds possibilities.

✔ **A mathematical edge doesn't mean mathematical *certainty.*** If one card on the river will make someone a winner when she should have lost, and 52 tables are playing, one table is going to have what appears to be a miraculous card.

✔ **You tend to remember bad beats and freak cards.** No one is surprised or comments when the hand that is mathematically likely to win does.

✔ **People don't complain when they win.**

✔ **Losing players will often focus on *anything* aside from the fact that they're losing and either need to quit poker altogether, or need to improve their game dramatically.**

Never forget the fundamental mantra of a skeptic: Extraordinary claims require extraordinary proof. If someone claims that a site is intentionally promoting *action cards* (that is, cards that turn losing hands into winning ones), he needs to show you a statistically significant number of *consecutive* hands that prove it.

But, of course, the people who claim this won't be able to provide such evidence — they won't even know what "statistically significant" means in the first place. And *that* is part of the *real* problem.

As I said, it's not that big of a deal.

If you play in tournaments, collusion is never a problem. If you play in ring games, you're better off playing at full tables rather than short-handed ones (because if there *is* collusion, it's more diluted that way), and in general it's probably a good idea to avoid tables where everyone seems to know each other.

Chapter 16

Harrah's, Here I Come: Playing in Card Rooms

In This Chapter

▶ Starting up in Casino Land

▶ Sidestepping beginners' land mines

▶ Taking down a jackpot

As far as flash, glitter, and "importance" go, you can't beat a professional card room as a place to play poker. With nice tables, comfortable seating, professional dealers, and government oversight, they're the nicest places to play in the world.

Playing in a Professional Card Room

All professionally run card rooms essentially operate the same way, and as you'd guess, they are all expedited such that you can get playing as quickly as possible.

Card rooms always have a set of rules of play, usually posted somewhere or available as a handout. It's always a good idea to ask for them and take a quick glance, looking for anything unusual — especially relative to their jackpots (see "Trying to Score a Jackpot," later in this chapter, for more on those).

Introducing the staff

Here's a virtual tour of who-does-what in a card room.

The board person

The *board person* stays at the main podium for the card room and keeps track of the waiting lists for the tables. If you already know what limit you want to play, tell him and he'll either immediately direct you to a seat or put you on the list. You can sign up for multiple different limits and you'll get called for the first one that's open.

If the waiting lists are long but there are still obviously poker tables that are not being used, don't despair. Often what a casino will do is open a new table if it has an idle dealer and enough players to fill it.

When you get called, the board person will always refer you to a specific table number. The table numbers are always either on a placard on the table (next to the chip tray, where the dealer drops the rake), or hanging from signs above the table. If you can't find your seat, ask the floorperson where you should go (see the following section for more on the floorperson).

The floorperson

The *floorperson* (sometimes just called *the floor*) keeps track of everything that happens at the card tables. In very small card rooms, the floorperson and the board person are the same guy. (Don't ask me why they all have moustaches.)

The dealer

Yep, it's exactly who you think it is. The dealer doesn't play in the game — she just acts as a card-and-chip distribution mechanism. If you ever have a problem in a hand, you should always start by asking the dealer (not the other players at the table). If you don't get an answer to your liking, you can always ask for the floorperson.

Sometimes a dealer will give you your chips. Just put your money on the table and the house personnel will tell you what to do.

The chip runner

This *chip runner* is the person who takes your cash and gives you your chips (assuming the chip runner actually works for the casino — if not, it's the person who takes your cash and then runs from security).

The cashier

Also known as *the cage,* the *cashier* is the place where you cash your chips when you go to leave the game. In a large casino, there is always a special cashier for the poker room that is separate from the main game. (If they do have a special cashier, use it — the lines are always shorter than the main casino's.)

If something slightly unusual happens — like you win some huge amount of money, you have an altercation with another player, or you just want to get a little closer to a man in uniform — you can always ask the cashier to have security escort you from the card-room property.

Proposition players, or props

Proposition players — more commonly known as *props* — are people who are paid a small hourly rate by the card room to play in the games. They have to use their own money — wins are theirs to keep, losses are theirs to bear. Nearly all card rooms have a rule that props either have to wear identification, or at least be identified by casino staff when asked.

Being up against a "professional" paid card player may feel a little daunting at first, but in reality they're just normal people like anyone else. My experience with props has been that their games are very solid but not flamboyant. They can be beaten, just like anyone else, but they'll probably be some of the tougher people you'll run up against.

Typically, you'll only find props at short-handed games or starting up new tables — there's no reason for the house to play them on full tables.

As you know, poker is on a huge upsurge (that's part of the reason you're reading this book, after all), and as it grows in popularity, houses aren't having to employ as many props. In fact, props are becoming a bit of a rarity, but they're still worth asking about if you're curious.

Shills

Shills are similar to props except they play with house money and do not keep their winnings. Because of this, they often play by what are known as *shill rules* — a predefined set of rules defining what they can and cannot do during betting rounds.

Shills are essentially the dinosaurs of the poker rooms and now are all but extinct. In the last ten years, the only time I've seen them is in games to assure that the bad-beat jackpot conditions are met — they get dealt a hand and then automatically fold (turn to "Trying to Score a Jackpot," later in this chapter, for more on jackpots).

Off-duty employees

Some card rooms allow their employees to play when they aren't working their shift. Gaming regulations nearly always require that these people be badged. Why someone would sit working in a poker room for eight hours, only to turn around and sit at the other side of the table is beyond me. My experience has been that these people are a threat at the higher limits and no problem at all at the lower limits.

Getting started

When you decide to finally take the dive and play in a professional card room, follow these steps:

1. **Make sure you have your cash and a government-issued photo ID before you enter.**

   If you need cash and want to save a buck, use an ATM outside the casino — casino ATM rates tend to be a little pricey.

   Nearly all professional card rooms require that all players carry an ID in order to play, although you'll probably never be asked for it. (I've only been asked for mine at very major tournaments.)

2. **Go to the board person to find out the limits the card house has.**

   The floorperson will either direct you to a seat or he'll add you to a list. (You may ask to be added to multiple lists.)

3. **When the floorperson directs you to a seat, tell the floorperson (or your dealer) how much you would like to buy in for.**

   Put your money on the table before you sit down. In some houses, the dealer will give you your chips, in others the chip runner will get them for you. Don't worry about how it works, though — you'll be told.

4. **If the dealer tells you that you have to post a blind to get cards, do so.**

   In some card rooms (those in California, for example), you must post an amount equal to the big blind, regardless of position, to get your first hand. In others (like those in Vegas), you're dealt in to the hand "for free."

   Theoretically, you're better off waiting until it's your turn to post the big blind (because your automatic posting also counts as the big blind), but it doesn't make *that* much difference.

5. **Cross your fingers and start playing.**

Exploring your possibilities

Here are a few of the things to be aware of while you're in a card room. Take advantage of any or all of them.

Picking up a free magazine

Nearly all card houses carry *Card Player* magazine or the *Poker Player* broadsheet. Those publications, and any others you might see, are free to players (even if they list a cover price). You should *always* pick up a copy. The articles tend to be great and sometimes the very card room you're playing in will run special promotions for readers.

Taking a break

Any time you want to take a break from the game, you can just leave the table with your chips sitting. It's mildly polite, but not strictly necessary, to tell the dealer, "Deal me out" before you do.

In some houses — especially extremely busy ones — they'll put a clear plastic box over the top of your chips. That lets another player play from your spot, setting their chips on top (sometimes called *piggybacking*). Yes, it's as weird as it sounds.

The rules for how long you can be gone from your seat vary by casino. It's usually about an hour, but be sure to ask a dealer what the house rule is before you're gone for an extended time. If you happen to be gone longer than you should be, your chips are picked up and can be collected by the floorperson.

Ring-game absence

In a ring game, the dealer will often put a small orange marker in front of your seat that says something like "Player Absent." If you miss a blind they'll put markers in front of your seat that say "Missed Small Blind" and "Missed Big Blind." The dealer will *not* deal cards to an absent player's spot while that person is away from the table.

When you return, you can either:

- ✔ **Wait until it's your big blind.** At that point, the dealer will take all the old markers from you, and you'll post and play as normal.

- ✔ **Rejoin immediately.** To do so, you need to pay for the blinds that you've missed. Most likely, you'll have missed both the small and large blinds so the big blind acts exactly like an out-of-position big-blind bet (you're automatically in the hand), and the small blind goes into the pot as dead money. Believe me, no one will argue when you do this.

Tourney absence

In tournaments, the dealer will continue dealing cards to the vacant seat (which are automatically mucked in turn) and the absent player is blinded off until he returns. At extremely large tourneys, the bathrooms tend to fill up heavily during the breaks, so you may want to consider ducking out a hand early before the break if things are becoming "urgent." (There's always a clock somewhere to let you know when the next break is due.)

Don't sweat it if you miss the beginning of a tournament that you're signed up for, especially a large one. It takes a long time for the blinds to become serious — in fact, many pros intentionally miss the very start of games such as the World Series Main Event just so they won't have to compete against the early maniacs who will be taken out over time.

Switching your seat

If you don't like the particular seat at your table, you can tell the dealer that you want to move whenever another player leaves the table.

If the seat you move to is counterclockwise (toward the blinds), you may continue playing with no penalty. If the seat you move to is clockwise (away from the blinds), you'll have to repost to get a hand immediately, or wait for the number of hands that equals the number of positions you moved (this ensures that you're paying blinds at the same rate as everyone else at the table).

Changing your table

If the table you're playing at is just too tough, too grumpy, or you simply want a better view of the TV, you can ask the floorperson for a table change. He'll put you on a list and grant you the change when a player leaves another table of the same limit.

Chowing on cheap food and grog

Card rooms very often will have bargain (or sometimes even free) food for the players. Ask any dealer or floorperson for the situation at the house you're playing. Often, the attached restaurant will have a special bargain menu for seated players, complete with cool little rolling stands to serve you right at the table. Dig that two times.

In Nevada card rooms, the house will pay for all your drinks. (And I'm sure all your tablemates will appreciate it if you down a six-pack while you're playing.)

Validating your parking ticket

Some of the parking lots attached to the Nevada casinos have parking that is free if, and only if, you validate your parking. Give your ticket to the floorperson or dealer — if you're playing, he'll validate you for eternity.

Getting a good room rate

Most card houses attached to hotels have a special rate for poker players. Ask before you go or ask any floorperson when you're there. The strip in Las Vegas is becoming expensive — it's a good way to stay cheaper in a town that's getting more pricey by the day.

Watching your favorite team

Sports — especially sports *betting* — and poker go hand in hand. There isn't a card room in the country that won't be playing six different sports channels, horse tracks, dog tracks, and sumo-midget wrestling on some bank of TV monitors within eyesight. Watching your favorite team is a great way to break from the monotony of the card tables — or to cool down if things get steamy after too many beats. You can even have the house hold your seat at the card table while you do it, if you want.

Avoiding Common Mistakes

New players in card rooms seem to make the same smattering of mistakes.

All actions at a professional card table are being monitored by the "eye in the sky." You want to do everything in such a way that the surveillance can obviously and clearly see what you're doing.

Here's some advice to help you steer clear of the Newbie Rocks.

Betting properly

When you place a bet in a professional card room, put it in front of you in one movement. If you're betting more than four chips, divide things down into stacks that are countable (for example, if you're making an $8 bet at a $4/$8 table, bet a stack of four and another stack of four next to it).

Do *not* place your bet into the middle pot — even if you did see it in *Rounders*. That's a technique known as *splashing* and is definitely uncool.

Playing in turn

The order of play is clockwise, by person. I don't know what it is about a card room, but for some reason a *lot* (if not most) of the new players try playing out of turn — *especially* when they have a hot hand.

The easiest thing to do is to just wait until the person in front of you acts. If the person in front of you does nothing, you do nothing.

Raising properly

Start by saying "raise" to the dealer. In Limit you now can take your own sweet time putting the chips out that you want, because it's well defined that you have to add one unit amount to the bet. If you say "raise" to a turn bet at a $3/$6 table, you have to put out $12.

In No-Limit, you should arrange whatever amount you want to move very close to the rail of the table, and then move the entire set of chips forward with one motion.

What you want to avoid is what's known as a *string raise:* putting some money into the pot, and then putting out more, in two actions.

Your oral action at a table is binding. If you say "raise," then you *must* raise. Be very careful what you say during the course of a hand — it's easy to have a side conversation misunderstood as action in a hand.

Minding your own money

Do not, under any circumstances, touch anyone else's chips. Similarly, do not make change for yourself out of the pot if you don't have the right chip amount. That means if you're going to call a $5 bet and all you have is a $25 chip, say "call" and put the chip in front of you like a normal bet. The dealer will make sure you get the proper change.

The one-chip rule

When you're playing in a professional card room and you throw a single chip out that is bigger than the bet you need to call — for example, throwing out a $25 chip for a $2 bet — that bet is considered to be a call and *not* a raise.

In order to raise with a single chip, you must say raise *first,* before you place the chip on the felt.

Playing only your hand

There is a common phrase in card rooms: *Only one player to a hand.* This means several things:

- ✔ **Do not show your hand to other players still in the hand at the table.** Doing so gives an unfair advantage to one player by giving her additional knowledge of the deck.

- ✔ **Never give advice to people still in the hand (for example, "Call that loser!"), and do not take any advice from other people.** Again, this has to do with knowledge of the deck that not everyone has. If you see this kind of behavior from other players at the table, feel free to tell your dealer about it (actually, your dealer should jump on top of it without your saying anything). If the dealer is unresponsive, call for the floorperson.

- ✔ **Don't show your cards before you muck them.** In general, this is bad form, but if you do, make sure you show them to the whole table (or at least everyone who is still in the hand).

Any time you get asked about your hand — or asked for advice — while the hand is in play (even if your hand is already mucked), your standard response should be, "We can talk about it as soon as the hand is over."

Trying to Score a Jackpot

One of the ways that a few of the brick-and-mortar sites beat the online world — from a pure cash point of view, at least — is by offering players money in addition to what is being bet in the hand. This money is known as a *jackpot*.

There tend to be a few different kinds of jackpots, and I cover them in the following sections.

High-hand jackpots

A *high-hand jackpot* is a bonus amount given to the highest hand in the card room over a given period of time — typically, something like four hours, but sometimes as long as a day or a week. You might be surprised at what it takes to win something like this; over a period of time as short as four hours, it nearly always will take quads or better to pull down a jackpot.

Specific-hand jackpots

Similar to high-hand jackpots, some houses pay a bonus for royal flushes, or, in more liberal cases, jackpots are set for any hand that is quads or better. In houses with specific jackpots for given hands, there's always a large display touting what you *could* win.

Bad-beat jackpots

This jackpot is the granddaddy of them all. A *bad-beat jackpot* is always defined by some ridiculously great hand being beaten by an even *more* ridiculously great hand. It's very common for the rule to be "quads or better, beaten," meaning you have to have four-of-a-kind and then have it beat.

Minting the bad-beat cash

Casinos that have bad-beat jackpots will very often rake an extra quarter out of every pot for the jackpot. Because the hands involved are based on such long-shot odds, it takes forever to pay them out. The resulting jackpots can be massive. (Here's one example: A card room that I visit occasionally in Northern California had a bad-beat jackpot of $85,000 last time I was there.)

Like everything else having to do with the rake, you don't really notice the extra quarter leaving the pot. But over time it's very corrosive — and at the lower limits even more so (because 25¢ represents a bigger portion of the total pot).

Paying the bad beat

The payout structure for a bad beat varies from house to house, but it's usually something similar to this:

- ✔ 80 percent to the hand that is bad beat
- ✔ 10 percent to the winning hand
- ✔ 10 percent to everyone else who was dealt a hand at the table

In some cases, the payout is even larger and spread to everyone in the card room. (In fact, my co-author of *Winning at Internet Poker For Dummies*, Chris Derossi, received a bad-beat payment for playing poker in the same casino *chain* that had a bad beat — the table where it actually happened wasn't even in the same casino. And still he took home an extra $400!)

Believe me, if you take down a bad beat, you'll have friends for life.

Improving your chances

If you want a better shot at winning a bad-beat (or high-hand) jackpot, you should change the starting cards you choose from Chapter 4. Consider playing *all* pocket pairs and all suited connectors (with no gaps). This strategy makes you more likely to hit quads (which can beat other quads, or more hopefully, be beaten), or it gives you a chance to catch a straight flush on one end while someone else is working the other.

When you've hit a bad beat condition (quads or a straight flush), do *not* bet your hand. Yes, you want to win the pot, but you want even more to drag down that jackpot for yourself and you don't want some measly bet to scare someone off from making the single-card draw he needs to win.

Qualifying for jackpots

Okay, this part is *super important* (if I had a Super Important icon, I'd repeat it on every bullet below). If you're going to be eligible for either high hands or bad beats, you *must* follow the eligibility requirements. Casinos tend to be fairly stringent about this (as you can imagine, they don't *enjoy* paying out extra thousands of dollars), so be sure that you're playing by the casino's rules and qualifications to win:

- ✔ **You are not allowed to talk about a jackpot during the progress of a hand.** That means you can't say things like "Hey man, I've got quad sixes! Now someone else beat it!"

- ✔ **If you're playing in a card room with a bad-beat jackpot and you don't have the minimum number of people (usually six) at your table, ask the floorperson to waive the rule, or have the floorperson send a shill over to take a hand.** (I've never seen this request refused — often the floorperson will just take a hand himself and then immediately muck it.)

- ✔ **In most card rooms, you must use both cards in your hand.** That means if you're holding A♥ 2♥ and the flop is 2-2-2, if your quads are beaten, they do *not* count toward the jackpot.

- ✔ **If the pot doesn't have enough money to qualify (often $10), but you have a necessary bad-beat hand, hold off on your betting until the river (assuming the bet and the call will hit the minimum), so you don't scare off a drawing opponent.**

- ✔ **Make sure you are dealt in.** You can only get paid if you were physically dealt cards in the hand, not if you were just sitting there gaping at the wonders of the world.

Houses always have their jackpot rules printed out and in plain sight. Always ask to see them before you start playing. Nothing in the bad-beat poker world would be worse than actually hitting your bad beat but not getting paid because of some freakish wrinkle in that particular card room's rules.

Chapter 17

Competing in Tournaments

· ·

In This Chapter

▶ Looking at the differences among tournaments

▶ Checking out your chip stack

▶ Working your way to the top

▶ Cashing your checks

· ·

*T*ournaments are an interesting form of the game — more so now that television focuses almost exclusively on tournaments and tournament play.

Fifteen years ago, the majority of Hold'em tournaments were Limit affairs with No-Limit relegated mostly to those who were either serious or insane. The explosion of televised events has driven the Limit form of tournaments into the shadows — with the vast majority of play now being No-Limit.

If you assume tournament play and ring-game play are the same, you'll find yourself standing outside the money winner's circle of the tourneys you play in — even if you're a regular ring-game money winner.

 If you have a burning interest in the single-table tournaments you find online, you'll find a much more extensive write-up than what I have in this chapter in my other book, *Winning at Internet Poker For Dummies,* which I co-wrote with Chris Derossi (published by Wiley).

Coming to Grips with the Differences

In some ways, tournaments are the purest form of Texas Hold'em. In ring-game play, you can bash heads with a table full of people all night, come out roughly even, and argue for the following week about who's really the best.

In tournaments, prizes are given out in a very specific order. And yes, you can still *argue* about who is best, but the tournament board at the end will definitely display all winners, best to worst. Nothing quite says, "You lose," like seeing your name on the bottom. Time to do the work necessary to get you on top.

Tourney basics

In a tournament, you get a specific and predefined number of chips. When you lose them all, you're *bust* and removed from the tournament. Man, does *that* ever hurt.

Getting something for nothing with freerolls

A *freeroll* is the exact spot on the freeway of life that the big rig of the American Dream crashes into the sexy sports car that is Texas Hold'em (and it's every bit as pretty). In freerolls you can, truly, get something for nothing.

In the brick-and-mortar world, you typically see freerolls as a perk to players who play a certain number of hands, or during specific hours of the day. "Play a total of 20 hours any time during the month and get an entry in our $1,000 freeroll," that type of thing. Although qualification isn't too difficult, the tournaments themselves tend to be extremely competitive and difficult to win, because they're filled with card-room regulars.

In the online world, it's more common to see freerolls as a come-on to get players onto the site. Unknown poker sites may get less than a hundred players vying for something like $100. The very large and well-known sites may get several thousand players competing over multiple days for the same amount.

Especially in the online case, you should never judge tournament play by what you see in a freeroll. Because it costs nothing to enter, there's nothing to lose, and you'll see an unbelievable number of plays — such as people calling all-in with nothing more than an inside straight draw.

From a pure *mathematical* point of view, freerolls are the best deal going. Nothing to pay with prizes to win.

From a *practical* point of view, they're both maddening because of the amount of time they take to play and dangerous because you get too much exposure to how you should *not* play poker, especially as a beginner.

Play 'em to get a feel for tournaments, and you can keep playin' 'em if they really turn your crank, but otherwise you should move into money play to truly sharpen your game.

All tournaments have a unique structure in the form of entry fees you pay, the chips you get for that money, and the speed at which those chips will be blinded off.

Entry fees

In the world of tournaments, you pay an *entry fee,* which goes directly into the prize pool. On top of this, you fork over a *registration fee* (typically 10 percent of the entry fee), which goes to the house.

If you see tournaments talked about in writing or online, the entry fee and registration fee are usually represented by something like "$50 + $5," meaning $50 to the prize pool and 5 bucks to the house.

A tournament with no entry fee "$1 + $0" means that all the money goes directly to the prize pool. From a mathematical point of view, aside from freerolls (see the nearby sidebar), these are the best deal going in a poker room because you're never leaking any money to the house.

Unless the tournament says something like "+ $0," "No registration fee," or "All monies go to prizes," you should assume that you'll have to pay a registration fee and you need to read the fine print to find out what it is.

Chip-stack sizes

For your fees, you're handed a predetermined amount of chips. The quick, small, and dirty tournaments — like single-table sit-and-goes online (see Chapter 15 for more on online play) — will typically start you off with something like 1,000 or 1,500 in chips. Any tournaments with starting stacks less than this are called *short-stack tournaments* — a peculiar subset of the tourney world where you have to start improving your stack size almost immediately or you'll find yourself scratching your head and wondering what happened all too soon from the rail.

Big monster tournaments — like the main event at the World Series of Poker — may start with stacks of 10,000. These are known as *deep-stack tournaments.*

Sometimes tournaments will give you the ability to start with bonus chips — usually by playing extra time in the same card room's ring games. Be sure to find out if the tourney you want to play in has something like that on offer. As a general rule, the more chips you can start with, the better off you are.

Conventional wisdom (correctly) has it that the deeper the stacks are in a tournament, the more favorable it is to the better players — the longer you can play, the more the vagaries of luck of the draw wear off, letting pure skill shine through.

Blind dynamics

In tournaments, the blinds start small and escalate over time. (See Chapter 3 for blind basics if you're not familiar with them.) The exact timing of the escalation depends on the tournament, but they're usually based on either a set number of hands (for example, "blinds increase every ten hands"), or a set time period ("blinds increase every 15 minutes"). Deep-stack tourneys typically have slower blind escalation (this, again, favors the better players).

As you can see in my theoretical example in Table 17-1, blinds in Hold'em tourneys start small but ramp up to the point where they have a significant influence on the play. And don't let the end of the chart fool you, they continue to escalate — as long as there is play left in the tourney, the blinds continue to march right on up.

Check it out: If you were given 1,000 chips to start in the tourney, and you lasted 90 minutes, by the table's schedule, every orbit of the dealer button at that point would be taking 1,200 chips (small blind + large blind) — more than you were given to start with.

"Hey, what happened to the '$?!'"

Throughout this chapter, you see that I don't use $ to denote the amount of money the players have in chips. That's because, technically, the chips don't actually represent dollars (you certainly can't leave a tournament in the middle and cash them), it's just a form of playing scrip that is batted around between players.

In fact, in most tournaments, there's no correlation between the amount you pay to play and the stack of chips they hand you. For example, a $10 + $1 online tournament may hand you something like 1,500 chips.

In professional card rooms, you'll find the physical poker chips used in ring games, which represent real money, to be very elaborate. The elaborateness of the chips makes them not only attractive but also much harder to counterfeit.

These same card rooms may well have an old grungy set of tournament chips, so worn that their faces are no longer legible and you can identify their value only by color. Although it's true that they're not pretty to look at, all the wear sure makes 'em easy to shuffle with one hand. . . .

Table 17-1	Theoretical Blind Structure for a Tourney		
Level #	*Time*	*Small Blind*	*Large Blind*
1	10 minutes	10	20
2	20 minutes	20	40
3	30 minutes	30	60
4	40 minutes	50	100
5	50 minutes	100	200
6	1 hour	150	300
7	1 hour, 10 minutes	200	400
8	1 hour, 20 minutes	300	600
9	1 hour, 30 minutes	400	800

Some tourneys also add the concept of an *ante* (pronounced *an*-tee) after several levels. The ante is a bet that *all* players are required to pay *every* hand before the start of play, but it's significantly less than the blind amounts. For example, at blind levels of 400/800, the ante would be something like 25. You can think of it like a mini-blind for everyone.

Rebuying and adding on

Some tournaments are single buy-in affairs. You pay a flat amount, you get a stack of chips, and you play until you lose what you have or win every chip in the tournament. In others, you're allowed to get more chips by rebuying and/or adding on. Read on for more info.

Rebuying

Some tournaments have a feature known as a *rebuy.* The rules of when you can rebuy vary a bit (ask your dealer or read the rules for your tourney), but typically you're allowed to rebuy any time you dip below the number of starting chips you're given in a tournament — including if you bust out.

You're only allowed to rebuy before the start of a deal of a hand, and if you bust out, you must *immediately* rebuy to be dealt in the next hand. If you don't rebuy at that time, you're out.

It's worth talking about how rebuys work and when you should do them.

Breaks and blinds

In tournaments, all players must post their blinds and antes in turn, even if the players aren't at the table. This process is known as being *blinded off.*

In ring games, you're allowed to leave the table at any time — the blinds just skip over you when you do. You are, however, required to post any blinds for a round you've missed when you return to the table (you never owe more than one small and large blind, regardless of how long you were away). In a professional card house, the dealer will put markers in front of your seat ("Missed small blind," "Missed big blind," "Missed blinds") indicating that you still owe money for that orbit of the dealer button.

In ring-game play, you can avoid having to pay the blinds for that particular orbit by sitting out until what would normally be your turn to post the big blind and just start playing then. Ask your dealer before you leave how long you're allowed to be gone from the table — after a certain period of time, the floorperson will pick up your chips and you have to retrieve them from him or her if you're playing hooky from the table for too long.

In extremely busy casinos, they'll sometimes put a clear plastic box over the absent player's chips and let another player sit in the seat with their chips on top of the clear box. The squatter has to leave when the original owner comes back. Yes, it's kind of weird.

All tournaments schedule breaks, so you're better off waiting to leave the table until a scheduled break time for the tourney than wandering off mid-round.

The dynamics of rebuys

Sometimes the number of times you can rebuy is limited, but more commonly, you're allowed to rebuy as many times as you want (as long as your current stack is under the starting chip amount), up until the first tournament break.

A rebuy will typically give you the same amount of starting chips for the same amount of cash (but this time without a registration fee). For example, if you were playing in a $20 + $2 tournament and given 1,500 starting chips, another $20 + $0 will gain you another 1,500 chips. (And don't squander them *this* time, okay?)

In tournaments with rebuys, most players plan on rebuying, and you should give it serious consideration yourself. For this reason, a $10 + $1 tournament may well end up costing you $31 (the $10 entry, two rebuys for $10, and the $1 registration fee), so don't see the $10 price tag and assume that will carry you through the tournament. A good rule of thumb is to think that any tournament will cost you a buy-in and two rebuys.

To rebuy or not to rebuy?

Rebuying in a tournament is an option exclusive to some multi-table tournaments. Whether to rebuy depends almost wholly on what the situation is at your table. In most rebuy tournaments, people *will* rebuy (usually several times), so for the most part the tables tend to hold the same players until rebuys are no longer available. You can use this table-stability factor to your advantage and to help make a decision on whether to rebuy.

If you're at a table with a lot of sloppy play, or folks who are overeager to continually rebuy as they bust hand after hand, you're playing at a table that's essentially a chip factory, and you should strongly consider rebuying. In a No-Limit tournament, any player with especially sloppy play should be thought of as an unguarded stagecoach waiting for an unscheduled delivery to you.

If, however, you're at a table that is playing extremely tight, and *especially* if there hasn't been a lot of rebuying at your table, but there has been at the others (keep an eye and ear open around you to see what's happening), you should skip it. As people are eliminated, and tables are consolidated, you'll be at too great a disadvantage to the chip giants who start getting mixed onto your table.

Adding on

In many rebuy tournaments, you have the option to *add on* to your stack at the first break. An add-on typically is for the same dollar amount as your buy-in, but with get a slight discount on the price per chip (and you don't have to pay that annoying registration fee). So a $20 + 2 rebuy tournament that gave you 1,500 starting chips might offer you an add-on of something like 2,000 more chips for another $20 + $0.

Of course, just like with rebuys, you have to know when you should, and should not, add on.

When adding on makes sense

As you get to the add-on break, look around your table and as much of the rest of the tournament as you can (very big tournaments will display average chip standings on a large screen in the casino) to get a feel for your relative stack size. If you're roughly even with everyone else, you should definitely add on — nearly all players will, and you need to keep up with them.

Saving your money by not adding on

If you're way down, say 25 percent less than the average stack, adding on isn't going to give you the firepower you need to advance (because everyone else will add on as well and you'll still be down). You're better off just holding that money for another day.

Likewise, if you've been striking fear into the hearts of mere mortals during the early part of the tournament and you find you'll be *way* up after the add-on break, say in the top 20 percent of the tournament, you also should *not* rebuy. The marginal value from the extra chips simply doesn't justify the purchase. Why throw more money into the purse when you have an extremely good shot of winning it all right now?

Prize structures

With the exception of the registration fee, all the money you pay into a tournament goes into the prize pool and is divided unevenly into prizes.

In *single-table tournaments* (tourneys that consist of only one table — you typically will only find these online), the prizes are usually broken up something close to the following: 50 percent to first place, 30 percent to second place, 20 percent to third place.

There is a form of single-table tournament found in professional card rooms known as a *satellite*. Satellites are qualifying tournaments that win you a seat into a "larger" event and are often used in cases where entry fees are astronomically high or for special qualifications. For example, the World Series of Poker Main Event has a $10,000 entry, but you can play in a satellite for a mere $1,000, where the winner gets a seat in the main event. (You can even play in a super satellite, where winning a $100-entry event gets you a seat in the $1,000 satellite.)

Satellites sometimes have multiple qualifications prizes (for example, "Top two players get seats in the Main Event of the World Series of Poker"). In these types of events, it doesn't matter who finishes first or second — as long as you're in the top two, you're a winner.

Multi-table tournaments will typically pay out prizes to about 10 percent of the places — so a tournament with 250 players will pay something on the order of 25 prizes. Here, too, the prizes will tend to be heavily weighted to first place.

In *heads-up tournaments* (found almost exclusively online, where only two players are pitted against each other), the winner takes the prize pool. The loser gets to wonder what's for dinner. (These tourneys typically have a 5 percent registration fee rather than 10 percent — something like $20 + $1.)

Why Mike Caro hates tournaments

Mike Caro, the "Mad Genius of Poker," is one of poker's foremost theoreticians. He made a name for himself originally by contributing to the technical portions of the seminal poker book *Super/System* and followed that with the definitive work on the outer psychology of the game, *Caro's Book of Poker Tells.* For these reasons alone, he should be listened to pretty much any time he talks about poker.

And guess what: He hates tournaments.

Mike rightly points out that there is inequity in poker tournaments, essentially saying, "Why am I given only a portion of the prize pool at the end of a tournament if I've won all the chips?"

From a pure equity point of view, he's right on. The person who wins all the chips has essentially given some of his equity away (in the form of prize money) to the other places along the way. And for this reason, he doesn't play tourneys.

I'm a math guy, and I play in tournaments. In fact, I consider them to be my specialty. I like tournaments because of the dynamic and the game theory involved — I also win more money in the long run in tournament play than ring-game play (probably because I focus on them more and find them less boring than playing in ring games for hours on end).

But from a purist's point of view, Mike's right. I shouldn't be playing tourneys.

Good thing I'm not a purist.

Understanding Your Chip Position

Your *chip position* is where you stand relative to the rest of the tournament (for example, first, second, and so on). You should always think of your chip position in two different ways: your relative position to the table you're playing at, and (in multi-tables) your overall position in the tournament.

Your position at your table

A player's chip position at the table will often influence her play. You can expect to see chip leaders (especially if they have overwhelming chip stacks) bully other players on the table by putting sizeable raises down, stealing blinds, and otherwise distributing general forms of misery.

Those who are short-stacked, especially those with the very tiny stacks (say only about five big blinds' worth of stack or less), will typically pick a hand they think looks fairly good and push it all-in. Any time you have a very short stack that is waiting to act behind you, be aware that person may well act all-in on you. You shouldn't consider bluffing these people because when they find a hand they like, they're going to push it all-in and they don't really care what your betting action has been.

In general, especially early in the tournament, you just want to be more or less in the middle of the chip standings. Bigger is better here, of course, but there's no cause for alarm if you don't find yourself rising, or you find yourself moving back a bit in the ranks from folding hand after hand.

Your position in the tourney as a whole

Large multi-table tournaments (and all online ones) will project the overall tournament standings. Keep a close eye on these listings.

The big figure you want to watch here is the *average* chip stack. It really doesn't matter if there's some gigantic chip gorilla around (unless, of course, he's sitting at your table and raising you all-in every time you bet). Your aim, at least for the first half of the tournament, is to be no more than 20 percent below that average figure, because it shows you're staying with the pack.

The crowd as a whole is too big to move ahead of in the early phases. You need to wait and bide your time.

Playing Your Way Through

The one thing that makes a tournament unique is the way players are eliminated. Like the shark that you're trying to emulate, you need to keep moving (up in the flow of chips) in order to survive.

Shifting tables

As the tournament advances, people are eliminated and the remaining players are continually balanced between the remaining tables to make sure the same number of people are sitting everywhere.

Especially in large multi-table tournaments, the vast majority of your play will be at full tables, or those with just one player missing. For this reason, in order to make it to the final table, you need to master playing at a table that is full.

In order to win the whole thing, you need to come to grips with playing against a table of competitors that's shrinking in size.

Maneuvering relative to the herd

You can think of a tournament as having three stages: early, middle and late.

Getting it on from the start

Early in a tournament, especially in multi-table affairs, your best strategy is to sit back and get a feel for the other players. Be very careful to not overplay or over-bet your hands, because to win you have to survive — and survival isn't an option if you don't have any chips. "Slow and steady" is the rule of the day.

In tournaments that are deeply stacked or have especially large fields of players, keep an eye out for players that seem antsy or anxious. These types of tournaments take *forever* to play, and if you have an opponent who's showing open signs of wanting things to move along, almost certainly he'll make a bad, aggressive move at some point. Although they're dangerous to play against, in early and middle stages you'll find that a disproportionate share of your chips come from these jitterbugs.

If you find yourself with a nut hand, make sure not to over-bet it. You're better off winning a small pot than making a large bet that isn't called, because you'll need those chips later — it will also give you a reputation at the table for being someone who plays very solidly and tends to under-raise. This rep will be helpful if and when you try to pull off a bluff later.

The golden rule of any gaming situation is to maximize your wins and minimize your losses. In the early rounds of a tourney, you maximize your wins by making sure winning bets are called and readily folding on hands that seem uncertain or a little too dear.

In the early stages, if you see a player make an obvious or taunting bluff (like showing his cards when he's bluffed a small pot), just ignore this behavior. When tournaments are getting started, especially when the blinds are still tiny relative to the table stacks, players commonly try to establish a table image that is essentially a lie, with the idea of exploiting it later. This trick tends to be far more common at low-entry fee tournaments and freerolls. Don't fall for it.

Muddling through the middle

When the tournament has lost about a third of its players, it begins to change its character. You'll notice that the madmen, the misfits, and the terminally impatient are starting to get culled out, leaving a more calculating and quiet type of player in the tournament.

Blinds may start coming into play at this point, and you need to keep your eye on that 10-to-1 ratio.

You want to start getting just a tad more aggressive with your betting and still be quick to drop marginal hands — especially when multiple players are competing for the same pot.

From the middle of a tournament forward, make sure that any time you bring in the betting on a pot pre-flop, you raise for at least three times the big blind. You don't want to let anyone at the table, including the big blind, see cards "for free." (This includes if you're playing on the big blind and the table folds to the small blind, and the small blind merely calls your big blind. Again, if you're going to play the hand, and you have good cards, you should raise the small blind to at least three times the bet.)

Watching your stack relative to the blinds

There are two key moments in playing a tournament: when your stack is roughly equal to about ten big blinds, and when your stack is less than five big blinds.

The 10-to-1 rule for your tourney play

Throughout a tournament, keep an eye on the size of your stack as a multiple of the number of big blinds. For example, when you have 1,000 starting chips, and the starting big blind is 20, you have 50 times the number of big blinds.

Don't worry, you don't have to be a math wizard — you're really only worried about one multiple: 10-to-1. Take the big blind and multiply it by 10. If you have more than that in chips, you're fine. If you don't have more than that, especially if you're still a fair way out from winning a prize, you need to tighten up your play and get more aggressive when you *do* bet. You're behind and need to raise your chip count.

As you make this adjustment, the table will probably notice your play becoming more aggressive and may assume that you're panicking (and, in turn, bluffing). By tightening what you play as you get more aggressive, those people who *do* call you are more likely to fall, and this is the very trick you'll use to help climb back out of the hole.

The 5-to-1 rule for your tourney play

You should think of this as the fraternal twin of the 10-to-1 rule. Take the big blind and multiply it by 5. If your stack is smaller than that, you're in a situation known in poker slang as "big frickin' trouble."

At this point, your stack won't be enough of a threat to make anyone back off when you push all-in, so don't even *think* about bluffing. Instead, find a hand you like and push it hard (maybe all-in pre-flop).

Worthy hands for playing to the hilt:

- ✔ Any Ace with a complimentary suited card
- ✔ Any pocket pair 8 or greater
- ✔ Any two cards 10 or greater

Fold anything else. You want that one shot to be a good one.

If you find yourself in a blind and you've seen a flop for free, push all-in if you have the semi-bluff hands of four cards to a straight or four cards to a flush (see Chapter 9 for more on semi-bluffs); or if you've managed to make a pair with the board. Don't forget to pray lots when you do.

Going for the gold at the end

As the field is winnowed down, you'll find the play getting tougher and tougher. Betting will be more aggressive and blinds will become a serious threat to your stack.

Also, for the first time in the tourney, you'll start playing on short-handed tables. If you played in a tournament with 1,000 players and only 11 are left (way to go, you're in the money!), assuming there are 10 seats to a table there'll be 6 players on one table and 5 at the other.

No matter where you're seated, this will be the first time in the tourney that you've played against this few players. That means you need to start playing a little more loose because:

- ✔ The blinds will be coming around on top of you more frequently (and they'll be huge).
- ✔ With fewer players at the table, you don't need as strong of a hand to win a pot.

Seating adjustments

Throughout the tournament, players (including yourself) will be moved from table to table to keep the number of players at each table balanced. If you get transferred, make sure to get a good feel for the sizes of the chip stacks around the table relative to your position.

Make sure to keep your eyes open for new players arriving at your table. In brick-and-mortar card rooms, noticing new players is easy to do because confusing the biker who just sat down with the grandma who just got eliminated isn't likely. But online, sometimes it's just a name placard change and it's easy to overlook.

Each player has a different stack size and a different playing style — watch each new player and find out all you can. Ignore new players at the risk of your stack.

Bursting the bubble

The *bubble* is the spot in a tournament where the losers stop and the money starts. For example, if there are 19 players left in a tournament that pays 18 spots, the tournament is said to be *on the bubble*.

Bubble play is interesting because nearly all players tighten up approaching that moment. And no wonder — it's possible they've been playing for hours (or in the super-huge tournaments, days), and they want to get paid.

The bubble can be a prime time to get a little more aggressive. Blind stealing is easier near the bubble than any other time in a tournament. Raise when you have a good opening hand and get a little more aggressive with the opening hands you'll play in later position (especially if the table has folded to you). You don't have to collect many sets of blinds before it's the equivalent of winning a fairly large pot.

When most tournaments near the bubble, they drop into *hand-for-hand play.* All tables must wait until the hand is finished *everywhere* in the tournament before the next hand is dealt. This keeps the terminally low-stacked from just sitting, sitting, sitting until someone *else* gets eliminated, so they're not forced to choke down a debilitating blind.

After the bubble has burst, you'll find that players loosen up and start playing more hands. This is a good time for you to tighten up your play — not only because every step on the prize ladder can mean considerably more dough but also because there may well be a few steaming people at the table that would like to get even for your little blind-stealing stunts just before the bubble.

 Let the people with high testosterone counts slug it out — play your cards when you have good ones, or obvious opportunities present themselves.

Adjusting Your Play for Prizes

All right! You've made it so far that you actually have to worry about money.

Keeping your eyes on the prize

If you've played an extremely long tournament, losing track of what's going on, either relative to your hand or relative to the position, can be easy to do.

 Make sure to remember what you're playing for and the relative importance of your stack to it. In a tournament, even one chip can make you eligible for a prize. Zero chips always qualifies you for the rail.

Splitting the prize money

If you play a tourney all the way to the prizes, it's not unusual to see someone offer you a *deal* (an offer to split the prize money with you).

For example, you might play in a tournament where top prize is $45,000 and second is $27,000 (that's $72,000 in prizes total). You and another player are evenly stacked, and the other player offers to split for $36,000 each. Basically, it's a lot of money and the other fellow just wants to be assured of some bucks.

Whether or not you split prizes is entirely up to the players in the tournament. Brick-and-mortar card rooms will always enforce a split if asked to do so by the players (and those requests are common enough that they won't be surprised if you ask for one). Most of the top online sites will split prizes as well.

What happens when you don't pay attention

I'll give you an example from my past that ranks right up there with the most humiliating things I've ever done on a poker table.

I had been playing online for six hours in a qualifier where the top two players would win seats to the Main Event in the World Series of Poker. After fighting through a field of thousands of players it was down to the last three players: myself with 225,000, Tiny Tim with 10,000, and Action Monkey with 235,000.

I was on the dealer button, Tiny Tim had a 2,000 small blind and the Monkey was on a 4,000 big blind. I was dealt A-A and brought in the action at 12,000, hoping to maybe catch the little one.

No luck. Tiny Tim immediately folded. The Action Monkey paused and then pushed all-in.

Now, the Action Monkey was a guy whom I'd grown to hate over the course of the game. I'd been unfortunate enough to be forced to sit with him for about three of the hours I'd played. He was loudmouthed and rude, but worse, he was an extremely good poker player. I had to make a repeated conscious effort to avoid him and his great play.

But this was sweet. I had the best starting hand and I could clock him dead right now. Without thinking twice I called.

He had an off-suit A-K and proceeded to flop K-K-7. I never caught up to his trip Kings. I was eliminated (he openly taunted me, of course) and he and Tiny Tim got their all-expense-paid ticket to Vegas. I got to chew on my hand.

Is it a bad beat? Sure. But it's also a serious error on my part.

The big mistake I made was not keeping my eyes on the prize. Two players qualify, and the order doesn't matter. Even though I had A-A, a heavy favorite to nearly any hand, it's not a certain winner. In just a few orbits of the button, Tiny Tim would have been forced all-in — if both the Action Monkey and I had called his all-in, and then didn't bet against each other, he would've had to beat two hands. (And even if he pulled this off, he would've had to do it again. And again. And again.)

No matter what the Monkey had, my odds of getting the trip were better by just folding and waiting for Tiny Tim to get blinded off or forced to play out of a very bad situation.

I still don't like to think about this hand. Don't let it happen to you.

Although I'm never the first person to offer a split, I've always been mildly in favor of taking it because it gets me some prize amount that's above the lowest left in the prize ladder and just generally sends a shot of good karma to the players you do it with.

I've passed on offers to split, always either in cases with players I've disliked for what I considered general ungentlemanly behavior (in my experience it's *always* been men and never women who act like beasts at a card table), or if I felt I was just flat-out better than they were.

Here are some factors to consider before splitting:

- ✔ **Your level of fatigue or how pressed you are for time:** If you feel really tired, you should seriously consider splitting.

- ✔ **The general poker skills of the people offering to split:** If you think your opponents are considerably better than you, you should do it. If you feel your abilities are above theirs, play on (but just make *certain* in the pit of your soul that you can accept a bad beat if it happens).

- ✔ **The mathematical fairness of the offer:** Prize money should be split roughly according to the chip stacks of the various players. Don't accept an offer that is grossly out of step to where your relative chip standing is. Having said that, don't sweat tiny discrepancies — for example, if you have 250,000 and two other people have 240,000 in chips it seems overly picky to insist on something more clever than a flat three-way split if you're offered it.

- ✔ **The likelihood of running across your opponents again:** Refusing a reasonable and equitable split will be mildly frowned upon. You'll get minor bad attitude from anyone whom you refuse. At a local card room, this may not be the kind of attention you want.

- ✔ **Taxes:** According to the U.S. government, as well as any state you live in, you must report your poker winnings as income (you usually can write off losses against those winnings — ask a tax professional for more information). In some states, they immediately take taxes for prizes above a certain dollar figure. You may be able to avoid immediate confiscation with a split that doesn't lap over the top of whatever this magic tax number is. Ask your floorperson — he'll know what that figure is.

Part V
The Part of Tens

The 5th Wave   By Rich Tennant

EDWARD SCISSORHANDS AT A CARD PARTY.

"Actually Ed, if any of us had been thinking, we'd have asked someone else to shuffle."

In this part . . .

The Part of Tens is where I've assembled the Mother of all Poker Lists. Here you'll find a variety of ways to enhance your game (both physically and mentally), as well as pitfalls to avoid.

And if you think the bad beat *you* took last week was bad, wait until you see what happened to a few other folks.

Chapter 18

Ten Differences between Online and Real-World Play

*O*nline and brick-and-mortar play are different enough that mastery of one doesn't necessarily mean success in another. The rules are the same, yes, but the differences between the two games are enough to turn a normal winner in one situation into a loser in the other — if you aren't careful.

In this chapter, I focus on *switching* from one version of the game to the other. I'm assuming you're comfortable with the game being played in one venue, but not as much in the other.

If you're completely new to Hold'em in all forms, you can save this as an intellectual morsel for later. Hey, you paid good money for this book — it's my duty to let you get your money's worth a little farther down the road, right?

Not Telling in Live Action

By far the most common mistake I see online players make when they play in the brick-and-mortar world is physical tells. The worst are those people who simply have no poker face — you can almost see what cards they're holding, just by their expression. Only slightly better are those who automatically drop into acting exactly opposite of the way that their hands are.

The opening days of the World Series Main Event are a true spectacle — not only for the sheer size, but for how truly bad some of the online players are in handling live action. I can only imagine what it must be like being a pro and looking at all those $10,000 entry fees sitting with all those people who have never actually handled a clay poker chip.

If you're new to live action, you should go back and have a look at Chapter 8 for more about tells, and think about the way people will try to read *you*.

Adjusting to Speed

The differences go both ways here:

- **If you come from the real world, online play can be dizzyingly fast at first.** It's worth playing with free chips for a while, not to sharpen your poker expertise (you won't — free-chip play will do nothing but damage your poker theory), but to get used to the way the controls work and the raw speed involved.

  When you start playing for real money, keep your other computer distractions to a minimum (no e-mail or insane BitTorrent work) and buy in for half your normal amount. That way if you lose, you're losing half as much — but if you win, you're still winning.

- **When you come out of the online world — especially if you're a crazy two-fisted player — live action will seem slow at a level that is beyond painful.** The biggest problem you'll have is keeping your mind from wandering as you chant, "Okay, I've folded, where's the next hand," under your breath. Because of this, here too, you should play half the limits you're used to, just to make sure you're not leaking money like a sieve due to your own personal form of molasses insanity.

  If you're finding live action just too hard to concentrate on, but you still want to play, consider taking a book or newspaper with you to the tables. It'll give you something to focus on as time passes.

Understanding Position

One of the great things about online poker is that it gives you a deeper understanding of what it means to play positionally. Because you aren't being inundated with real-world ticks and tells, you get a "purer" view of the game.

My pal Konstantin Othmer, author of the superb (but hard-to-find) *Seven Card Stud Poker,* said that more than anything, online poker has taught him the importance of position. This, in turn, has given him insight into how to incorporate those concepts into his bluffing strategies.

If you're a big fan of live action, you should dabble a little in the online world — even if it's just at low limits — to get a better feel for what Kon means.

Taking Up Space

If you play online all the time, and then venture into the real world, you may be surprised by how cramped the quarters are. You sit remarkably close to a *lot* of people for a long time — that in itself may put you off playing live.

If you feel cramped, there's an easy way to check if you're not getting the space you deserve. Look at the dealer, and then look straight across. In a nine-seat table, Player 5 should be immediately across; in a ten-seat table, the dealer should perfectly split Player 5 and Player 6. Divide up the rest evenly from there.

Lighting varies widely in brick-and-mortar card rooms. Make sure you have lighting you like — if you don't, ask for a seat change.

Getting at Your Cash

In the online world it typically takes a little while to get set up and going. To get your money into the poker site, you have to go through a third-party holding company (similar to PayPal) and sometimes it can take a couple of days to clear.

Getting your money out can take time, too. First, it has to be okayed by the site, and then it has to be transferred from your holding company. Simply put, it all takes a while.

In a physical card room, you bring in cash, you play, and when you're done, you walk out with what you have (with any luck, more than you came in with).

The advantage of the online world is it truly forces you to put aside some gambling stake and leave it in one place. It's clearly earmarked for poker and poker only. But the vast majority of people never bring that money back out, so it can languish — and money that just sits around *anywhere* has a strange habit of eventually going away.

Becoming "Serious" in the Real World

Playing poker in the real world is more of an ordeal than playing online. You have to pick up and go with the express purpose of playing poker. It's why you're reading this book, it's why you left the safe confines of your house, and it's why you wait for an hour ogling at the cute dealers while you're waiting for a seat.

Because of this, both the competition and the environment are more focused on card playing. This is a good thing, because it *really* gets you thinking "poker" — of course, the disadvantage is that it focuses your opponents as well.

Although I don't have any strong numbers to back it up, to me online opponents have always seemed a little sloppier because they have more distractions both wherever their computers are, and on the computers themselves (not to mention playing multiple tables at once).

Nothing will sharpen your play like live action, but your bankroll may appreciate the online world more.

Adding Up Online Mathematics

Mathematics is more important to online play than it is in the brick-and-mortar world. Because you see fewer indications of what your opponents are thinking or doing, the game comes at you in a somewhat "purer" form. This means that math will play a bigger role online. (Turn to Chapter 22 for a reference on a good online poker-odds calculator.)

But don't let that keep you from using math in the real world, too. You should absolutely understand pot odds (see Chapter 12). And any time you run across a hand in live action that you wonder about, jot it down on a cocktail napkin and go run the numbers the next time you're around a computer.

Tipping the Dealer

Don't forget, in live action it's customary to tip the dealer a buck or two when you win a hand. (They typically get paid minimum wage and live off their tips.) Don't worry about tipping when you've only won the blinds — nobody expects that.

Changing Your Venue

In the online world, the next card room is just one click away; in the real world, it may be miles.

Because of this reality, you should take advantage of changing tables, or even card rooms, online much more frequently. Don't forget: If you're playing at a table that's too much for you, you can always move to another one online.

In the brick-and-mortar world, if you find yourself struggling, you should just call it a night. You can always find another game some other time (unless you don't have any money to play in it).

Keeping Track of Your Online Cash

In the real world, keeping track of your poker money is easy: It's either whatever's written in your ledger (see Chapter 22), or it's what's in your jeans pocket that day.

In the online world, you can easily lose track of your money. First, you move some money into your transfer agent (for example, NETeller), and then you move it to the site you play. If you're playing multiple sites, you may have multiple accounts, and as you move money back and forth through your transfer agent, you may leave some bread crumbs there as well.

Every month or so, if you're playing multiple sites, drive around and be sure you know where your cash is. This gives you the ability to check out any new promotions, helps you get a feel for what the play is like at varying sites, and most importantly, lets *you* keep track of where your money is.

Poker sites make enough money — they don't need to be picking up your orphaned currency as well.

Chapter 19

Ten (Or So) Common Mistakes

. . . .

In This Chapter

▶ Watching yourself physically

▶ Keeping track of your mental state

▶ Trying not to get ground up by mathematics

. . . .

*E*verybody makes mistakes as they play cards. The wise learn and get better. The rest pull out another bill and feed everyone else at the table.

Playing Too Many Starting Hands

This is, by far, the biggest mistake that beginning and intermediate Hold'em players make. Sometimes there's a sense of passion behind it: like being on a losing streak so you start steaming and play more hands; or maybe you're on a winning streak and just want to rack up even more chips. There may even be a vendetta involved — you hate that idiot at the end of the table, so you start playing whenever you can to beat him.

Whatever the reason, the more hands you play, the more money you're putting on the table. And this ultimately means that you need to win more (or bigger) hands. The law of averages will tell you that you will hit your limit of how much you should expect to win *way* before you play a huge number of starting hands.

If you start getting desperate, don't play so many hands. Instead, concentrate on putting more firepower behind the hands that are legitimately *good*.

Playing Tired

Don't underestimate the raw toll that fatigue takes on your game. Poker — especially in professional card rooms — can put you in this strange zombielike state where you play for hours on end. If you find that you're having trouble thinking about *anything* inside or outside of the game, you're too tired. Stop and play later. There's always another game somewhere at some other time.

Playing Too Low or Too High of a Limit

If you play too low of a limit, your currency is just going to feel like play money. You don't need to bet so much that you feel a sting when you lose, but the money *should* make a difference to you — or you can at least understand what it means.

If you play too high of a limit, you threaten your bankroll (see Chapter 3 for more on that).

Coin-Flipping Too Often in Tournaments

The problem with pushing all-in and repeatedly coin-flipping is that every one of those plays is roughly a 50/50 proposition. Just like you can only call a coin the right way so many times before you miss, there is a limit to how many times you can push all-in and hit your side.

Over the long haul, repeatedly pushing all-in in coin-flip situations (especially if you have smaller pairs) is a guaranteed way to keep yourself away from making the money.

If you aren't familiar with the concept of coin-flipping in a tournament, turn back to Chapter 12.

Ignoring What You Know about Players at Your Table

You should be keeping a close eye on all your opponents (see Chapter 8 for more on that) and as you do, you'll pick up tricks, hints, and characteristics about them.

If you know something about an opponent that's warning you that the hand you have is a loser, you should fold. Make sure to consider any or all of the following:

- ✔ The way he is betting in a given situation
- ✔ The types of cards he tends to play at his current table position
- ✔ The way the board will interact with the cards he tends to play

Yes, it's hard to drop a good hand, but I always find that it's much harder watching my money walk over and sit in front of someone else.

Becoming Impatient

I see something along these lines happen repeatedly at card tables: In Limit games when a player goes card dead, he may sit for several orbits before he plays a hand. This makes the little demon on his shoulder say something like, "Hey man, you're here to play poker not to *watch* everyone else play," and the next thing you know he's in a hand that he shouldn't be playing.

In tournaments, the impatient spell often begins when someone loses a couple of fairly big hands — maybe even as much as 80 percent of her stack. This puts her into heavy-duty fight mode and the next time she sees *any* hand of value (even something as weak as gapped-suited connectors), she just pushes all-in. The problem with doing this is twofold:

- ✔ Being short-stacked makes you easy to be called.
- ✔ If you are called, you're probably dominated.

You don't have to panic and start pushing all-in all the time until you have less than five big blinds in your stack. And even *then* you should only pick a hand of value.

There's an added impatience problem these days, too, and that is that a lot of players learn and play on the Internet where games are *extremely* fast (possibly even upping their speed quotient by playing turbo versions or multiple games simultaneously). When they fall into the brick-and-mortar world, it feels like playing in a swimming pool filled with molasses to them. Action, action, action is what they want, want, want.

Don't always try to make the big plays happen. Let the cards come to you first.

Staying Too Long in a Tough Game

You are not the best poker player in the world and you probably never will be. When you buy that, it shouldn't take you too long to agree that some of the better players in the world may be sitting at your very poker table.

If you're up against a hard table, or a particularly bad combination of players, find a better game. In a professional card room, you can always ask for a table change (it won't weird them out — people do this all the time); online you can always just click on another table (or go to another site). If you're playing at a single-table joint, just pack it in for the day.

Losses are hard on your bankroll as well as your poker playing self-esteem. Don't torture yourself.

Letting Your Emotions Get the Best of You

Q: How can you make a bad beat even worse?

A: By letting it get the best of you psychologically, going on tilt, and destroying your bankroll hand after hand.

Yes, you *will* lose poker hands by someone drawing their highly unlikely outs. Yes, someone will call with some hand he should have dropped and flop some monster five-card hand. It can, does, and will happen. (And no, it doesn't mean the online poker site you're playing at is rigged.)

When you hit a big loser like that, you have to psychologically *let it go.* A bad beat is hard enough on your bankroll for that single hand; don't let it carry you through the rest of a session.

If you don't have the personality that will let you just shrug it off and play the next hand, just take a quick walk around the card room. It'll help you adjust and deal with what's happened, and then you can sit back down, settle back down, and play your best game.

Treating Your Internet Money Like It's Fake

When you buy in online, you lose the association you have with your money. It's very different from a brick-and-mortar card room where you pull out a roll of greenbacks and hand 'em over. In the online world, you fill out a couple of electronic forms, type in a couple of passwords and you're off and running.

Lose a little here? No problem. Buy in again over there? "Sure, why not, I already transferred the money from my bank account anyway."

Stop.

That money you're playing is real, honest-to-goodness cash that could be going to taking your sweetheart out to dinner, buying you that jacket you always wanted, or investing for the down payment on a house. The moment you get cavalier about the cash you spend online is the very point that your bankroll gets in danger.

Go back and have another gander at Chapter 3 to see what your bankroll should be if you're planning to play — and win — online.

Chapter 20

Ten Ways to Improve Your Home Game

*Y*ou don't need a pair of ruby slippers to know that there's no place like home. Home is not only where your heart is, it's also the roost for all your tunes and the haunt of your significant other (assuming he or she is still talking to you after all the poker you've been playing). Home games mean that you get to see your pals *and* you don't have to get chewed up by the rake.

If you're considering blowing some cash over a card table anyway, you may as well pony up a little bit for the game itself. If you have a bunch of pals who are regulars, you can all chip in — just a few bucks each can get you a *nice* setup.

Upgrading Your Deck

By far the best thing you can do for your game is getting rid of those wax-and-cardboard playing cards and moving to a deck made entirely of plastic. This is what casinos use at their poker tables and you should, too. All plastic cards last longer, are less prone to warping, and are even *washable* (for when your Cheetos fingers stain the cards orange). There are several brands, and I've played 'em all — by far my favorites are Kems.

Paying $30 for a setup of two decks may make you gasp, but believe me, you play one night with these babies and you'll wonder why you ever played with anything else.

All plastics have an odd form of fragility and that is that they're prone to cracking if you play them on a hard surface. If you play on something like a kitchen table, put a doubled-up sheet or a blanket down first. Your deck will last longer. (Oh yeah, and don't leave them sitting in the sun either.)

Chipping Up

One of the great things about the poker boom is that you can buy complete poker-chip setups for a home game in a nearly infinite number of places. Top-of-the-line poker chips are made of clay (this is what casinos use) and come in a cool aluminum case. Sets will usually also include a dealer button (and maybe blind and kill buttons).

The best chips are known as *clay composite* and are weighed by the gram (heavier is better). A nice 15-gram set will run you around $75; 11.5 grams (which are very playable and nice if you've been using bingo markers up until now) run around $40.

Chowing Down

Come on, if you're gonna take the time to get together with your friends, you need to upgrade your food and grog. Seriously, get out of the generic aisle of your grocery store and quit serving that beer you stole from your parents in the '80s. If money is an object, have your pals chip in and bring something.

Poker/barbecue is a surprisingly good combo. Ordering (good) pizza is *never* wrong.

Lighting Up

Before you host a game, set up the table the way want to use it, complete with chairs. Deal a hand around to every spot, and then play your own version of musical chairs, where you sit in each seat looking at hole cards to check out the lighting.

I've played at a lot of home games that have been heavily lit from above, but there isn't enough other ambient light to see the hole cards. An extra lamp here and there will make all the difference.

Venting It All

Home games get hot. Be sure you're playing in a place that has air-conditioning or windows that you can throw open to vent nicely (even more necessary if you're having a poker smoker and all the players are breaking out the stogies).

Your basement may seem like a cool place most of your life, but put ten sweaty bodies in there, and stir in a few bad beats, and the walls will be sweating in no time. Your living room or the kitchen are probably better choices if you don't have good ventilation downstairs.

Trashing the Place

The amount of raw waste that can be spawned by a poker game is truly amazing. (In fact, it seems like the quality of the game and the amount of garbage it generates are directly proportional.) Trash bags: Buy 'em, use 'em, leave 'em lying around while the game is in play.

Wiping Out the Badness

You want a wet washcloth, a towel, and maybe even a set of baby wipes, at the ready. Card tables and spilled drinks go together like kids around your car's fresh paint job — leave the two together long enough and you *know* there's going to be trouble.

Be ready in advance, catch it when it happens. (And don't forget, you can always use the towel for those *really* bad beats — for chewing on or crying into.)

Standardizing Chairs

Home games tend to have a problem in that not all the chairs are the same, almost always forcing a few players to crane their necks as they play.

If you're going to start playing a *lot,* it's worth the time and effort to go out and get a set of common chairs for the table so everyone's sitting in the same thing. Foldables work well (especially with cushions). The funky, college-student-budget alternative is to buy white plastic patio furniture.

When you get poker chairs, you want ones without arms — this lets you pack people in closer at the table (everyone rests his arms on the table anyway).

Getting Tabled

A folding card table is a great buy because it gives you the soft surface you need for your all-plastic cards and you can store it away when you're not pretending to be a budding poker professional. You can put two bridge tables end to end. Good ones will run you about $100 each.

If you want to get even more serious, you could think about buying a table that is professionally padded and liquid resistant with a low-friction surface (in the casino world, this is known as *speed-cloth*). One with built-in drink holders and detachable legs makes more sense, unless you want to just dedicate an area to poker in an extra room or basement. To get a feel for the type of table I'm talking about, you can see excellent examples at www.bvpokertables.com. A nice, and somewhat custom, table of this caliber will run between $500 and $1,000, depending on the bells and whistles you want on it.

Renting Your Game

Sounds crazy, yes, but you can hire anything and everything for a poker game. If you're going to get serious about it all, or maybe want to set up a poker night for your school or work, the things that you can get are only limited by your pocketbook. From the little to the big, here goes:

- ✔ **A table and chairs:** Keeps you from having to use grandma's rocker at the poker table and is an excellent way to try stuff you're considering buying later. These can be had for something on the order of a buck apiece a night.

- ✔ **A professional dealer:** A game goes more smoothly with a pro dealer, and it lets you focus more on the game. Typically, you can get one for anything from $15 to $35 an hour.

✔ **The whole shebang:** If you live near any large metropolitan area, you can find entertainment companies that specialize in poker events. They have dealers, tables, and complete poker setups. Good setups run on the order of about $50 an hour, complete with speaking dealer (who may or may not be cute).

✔ **Maybe even a casino:** The ultimate home game is to leave your home altogether and take everyone to your local card room (or better yet, really knock yourselves out and fly everyone to Vegas). Get the staff to set up a private table and room for you — it's remarkably easy to do and most places don't charge *that* much (because they don't have to do anything much out of the ordinary). Call your favorite card room for rates, and don't be too surprised if the response is, "All you have to do is pay the rake."

Chapter 21

Ten Bad Beats

. . . .

In This Chapter

▶ Taking a beating from chance

▶ When bad play gets rewarded

▶ Looking for a silver lining

. . . .

*O*ne of the ways to tell the lesser mortals from the greater ones at a poker table is to listen to who moans the loudest about being bad beaten. Bad beats are a part of all poker games, but they scream at you a bit louder in Hold'em (especially in No-Limit) because of the dynamic of the action. Unfortunately for your ears, not everyone understands this dynamic.

I've listed the following ten beats to help console you in your times of pain — or at least let you know that other people in the world are crying with you.

Red versus Spudnut

Might as well start the list with one that happened to me as I was writing this book.

I'd been playing in an online tournament for four hours, there were 135 people left, and the payouts started at 99. I was sitting in the top 15, and with a top prize of $45,000, my mouth was starting to water.

On the small blind, I was dealt A♣ K♥, only one player was in — a guy (I'll call him Spudnut) who I felt had been playing *way* too loose and had flat-called with a hand under the gun. He was 17th in the tourney, just slightly below me. I gave him a 5x raise, which he readily called.

The flop was K♠ 10♥ 4♦. With first action, I put down a pot-sized bet, which he readily called. A call here is both interesting and important: Any time he had a good hand, he was raising; any time he was behind (or thought he was behind), he called. The Spudnut had never slow-played a hand. I *have* to be ahead — top pair, top kicker, looks good.

The turn is a 7♣. I push all-in — it's about half of a pot-size bet. Spudnut waits, waits, and calls.

He's holding A♠ J♣. Unbelievably, he's called all the way through without a pair or even a flush draw. All he has is a gut-shot straight, which he summarily hits. My stack is damaged enough that I can't even take the next set of blinds.

Woman Beaten by Madness

In 1995 Barbara Enright became the only woman to ever have made the final table of the World Series Main Event. On the big blind with five players left (and a fairly large stack), Barbara was dealt pocket 8s. Brent Carter was dealt a 6-3 on the small blind and limped in, getting an immediate all-in push from Brenda.

For reasons still not completely clear in this galaxy, he called and flopped both a 6 *and* a 3 — winning a hand that had been a 15-85 underdog.

Hellmuth Yanks His Hair Out

At the World Series in 2002, bad boy Phil Hellmuth was dealt A♥ K♥ and quickly double-raised Robert Varkonyi holding Q♣ 10♣. Varkonyi pushed all-in, Hellmuth went into the tank and finally called. Varkonyi hit a pair; Hellmuth didn't and was sent to the rail.

Fuming, Hellmuth later stated on TV that he would shave his head if Varkonyi won the event. Varkonyi did (his final hand was another Q-10) and Hellmuth became Mr. Clean.

Nuts about Flushes

A friend of mine, Dr. Diamonds, was playing in a No-Limit ring game online. He was dealt K♦ 5♦ on the big blind and with three other players in, he checked.

The flop was 10♦ 6♦ 9♠, and the Dr. bet the pot with his second-nut flush draw. One person passed, the other two (both of whom had been playing fairly loose), called.

A J♦ on the turn gave my pal the second nut flush and, surprisingly, *both* people called. One held the indescribably bad Q-J off-suit (calling with only top pair and a straight draw); the other held Q♦ 7♦ for the third nut flush — it *was* third nut until the river of 8♦ gave the other player his one-outer and a straight flush.

Moneymaker

Chris Moneymaker was up against Costa Rican Humberto Brenes in the 2003 Main Event of the World Series. The action pre-flop hadn't been *too* hostile when a flop of K-9-2 hit. Brenes laid down a big bet. After some thought, Moneymaker pushed Brenes all-in — which he quickly (and gladly) accepted.

Moneymaker was showing pocket 8s and was visibly shaken to see he was up against Brenes's pocket Aces. The world whirled on its axis, though, when a turn brought another 8, giving Moneymaker trips and sending Brenes South of the border.

Moneymaker, Part Deux

Like most sequels, this one isn't that different from the original — it was just shot with a much bigger budget and much bigger names.

Not 12 hours after the previous bad beat (see the preceding section), Moneymaker was up against Phil Ivey. Ten players were left; nine would sit at the final table of the Main Event.

Phil was dealt pocket 9s, Moneymaker A-Q. Moneymaker raised pre-flop and got a flat call from Ivey. The flop was a Q-Q-6 — Moneymaker held trips, but held Ivey in the hand.

The turn was a diabolical 9, filling up Ivey. It was here that Moneymaker put down a large bet, getting an immediate all-in from Ivey. Moneymaker had no concept of the impending doom and called, immediately becoming a 15-85 underdog.

The Ace on the river was a bullet through the heart of Ivey and sent Moneymaker to the final table as chip leader.

When Wheels Go Flat

I was watching a single-table tournament online that had one of the strangest forms of counterfeiting I'd ever seen. Five players were left when the player under the gun raised — everyone folded except for the big blind, who called.

The flop was 4♣ 2♣ 3♥. Immediately, the big blind pushed all-in, as did the original under-the-gun raiser.

The big blind had 9-9 and played his over pair hard. The caller had A♦ 5♦ for a wheel.

The turn and river both produced 2s, and when the pot was pushed toward the guy holding the pocket 9s, I was so blinkered by what had happened that I had to go back and look to see that the trip deuces on the board had given him a full house.

Spooky.

No-Limit Means No-Money

I was playing in a casino in Las Vegas a couple years ago when there was a sudden commotion behind me. I walked over to witness the aftermath of a heinous card exchange.

It was a larger No-Limit game. One player had been dealt A♦ Q♦ and had managed to get his opponent to eventually commit all his money to the pot on board cards of K♦ J♥ 10♦ 9♥ — a very sweet setup because the A-Q player is holding the nut straight and the nut flush draw.

His opponent had been suckered into committing on a K-10, two pair.

Seems like a winner until you see the 10♠ surface on the river for a full house. This was a 4-outer that cost one player about two grand.

Mr. Aggressive versus Johnny Conservative

I watched this one from the rail at the Main Event of the 2005 World Series. Two players had been occasionally bashing each other: One played conservatively but strong, the other was so aggressive I thought he was going to have to be chained down. With about 125 players left in the tournament, the stakes are high, and every few positions you can climb is worth several thousand dollars.

Pre-flop, Mr. Aggressive put down a sizeable raise, which Johnny Conservative merely called. The flop was 4-4-2. Johnny Conservative placed the minimum bet, which made Mr. Aggressive quickly push all-in. Surprisingly, Mr. Conservative called instantly.

I knew the fast call from the conservative player meant that he had a big hand, and when he turned them over, I could see just *how* big: His pocket 4s had become quads. Mr. Aggressive turned as green as the felt when he showed his pocket 5s. Having seen the lowball flop, he had incorrectly assumed that Mr. Conservative had missed it altogether and was merely playing over cards.

And although we'd seen the truth of the hand, there would be no justice. Both the turn *and* the river were 5s, giving Mr. Aggressive quad 5s and a winner. Mathematically speaking, this is the longest possible beat in Hold'em — the odds of making this hand, after the flop, are 1-in-990.

Not All Beats Are Bad

With a chapter this evil, I simply can't leave it on a bad note, so I'll leave you this instead. . . .

Chris Derossi, my co-author on *Winning at Internet Poker For Dummies* (Wiley), was playing poker at one of the Station Casinos in Nevada. The floor man came over and handed every player at the table $147.

"What's this?"

"One of the players at another Station Casino was just bad beaten: quads-over-quads. Everyone playing anywhere gets a cut of the bad-beat jackpot."

Chapter 22

Ten Things You Can Do to Improve Your Hold'em Game

In This Chapter

▶ Thinking better

▶ Feeling better

▶ Being better

*W*hen you start playing seriously, your next goal is to get better — and there is *always* room to get better. In this chapter, I give you some places to start and some ideas to try.

Studying Your Way Up

There are two seminal poker works you should get your hands on and read. One is David Sklansky's *Theory of Poker,* and the other is Doyle Brunson's *Super System.* (From a Hold'em point of view, the differences between *Super/System* and *Super System II* are slight enough that either edition is fine.)

Both of these works helped define the theory of modern poker. Just as important, though: The more hard core you are in poker, the more likely it is that your opponents have read and studied these works. Understanding the concepts in these books will not only let you get a peek at a more technical explanation of poker than what I provide here, but also give you a deeper understanding of your opponents — even if you never adopt the playing styles or theories the books espouse.

Showing Off Your Game

When I was writing *Winning at Internet Poker For Dummies,* I spent several hours playing online with my co-author, Chris Derossi, standing over my shoulder and commenting. I was truly amazed at how much his commentary sharpened my game.

Find a friend you know and trust and start talking poker with him. Play one account together online and talk about the situations you run across as you play through the hands. When you play live action, take notes on your play and interesting hands and come back and talk with your pal.

Poker can be so incredibly emotional that having someone standing just outside your bubble of warped perception can be infinitely valuable. I still use this trick and I continue to be amazed at how much it improves my game.

Keeping Track of Your Bankroll

Every time you play you should record your wins and losses. Just a simple spreadsheet on a computer, or even a small hardback ledger (spiral notebooks lose pages over time), will do the trick. The steps are simple:

1. **When you sit down at a table, or launch your poker application, write down how much you buy in for.**

2. **Write down anytime you buy in for more during the session.**

3. **Write down what you have at the end of the night when you leave.**

Keeping track of records is the *only* way to know if you're winning or losing. And make sure not to lie to yourself or not record a session because "it didn't really count." **Remember:** From your money's point of view, *everything* counts — so everything should count in your ledger, too. (Review Chapter 3 if you seem to be winning all the time — or losing too much.)

Exercising

At the height of the Soviet chess system, all of their top players had personal trainers. This was an ancient and primitive time well before the concept of aerobics, back when Muhammad Ali was being taunted by some opponents as being "girlie" for skipping rope. The Soviets (rightly) believed that the better your physical conditioning, the longer you could endure the madness of an extended chess match.

You should put your body to work for you, too. You don't have to get all Arnold Schwarzenegger about it. Even if you've never done a lick of exercise, and you're what is known in medical terms as a *couch potato grande,* something as simple as walking 20 minutes a day, every day, will increase your stamina during long sessions and give you a nice little chunk of time where you can think about the game without being in it.

If you want a good starting place, pick up a copy of *Fitness For Dummies,* 3rd Edition (Wiley), and if you get the exercise bug, you can always move up from there.

Digging into the Math

From a poker point of view, one of the great inventions of the last ten years is the Hold'em odds calculator. What these calculators do is take any hand you feed it (at pre-flop, flop, or turn) and grind out thousands of random outcomes, giving you a percentage likelihood of each hand winning from that point. You can use a calculator either to figure out sticky hands you're unsure of or to prove that you really *did* make the right play when that idiot called you all-in and sucked out.

My favorite calculator is on the Card Player Web site (http:// tinyurl.com/3jb3j). And while you're there, you can look at a hand I was wondering about several months ago: Q♦ Q♠ versus A♣ K♣ with a flop of J♥ 5♣ 4♣. Which hand do you think is the favorite here, and by how much? The answer may surprise you.

Reading Poker Web Sites

There are several good Web sites with poker forums and discussions. I used to be a fan of recpoker.com (commonly called *RGP*), but it's not moderated and seems to be more and more filled with insult and ego than it is hard fact.

These days I'm a fan of Two Plus Two (www.twoplustwo.com). Any aspect of the game that you're interested in, and at any level of detail, can be found there. Better still, they use a moderator to keep the spam and truly vile stuff to a minimum.

Scoring a Free Magazine

Card Player can be had for free in nearly any brick-and-mortar card room. It's worth picking up, not only for the writing, but also for the super-great ads. You'll find lots of specials, tournament info, and other freebies that are available only to readers. (You can visit Card Player online at www.cardplayer.com.)

Throwing in the Towel

Several years ago, I took a horrific string of bad beats. It was *so* bad that it really started to rattle me. If I was playing No-Limit, I would go all-in, see the my opponent's under cards on the table, and start "knowing" that the next cards off the deck were going to beat me. If I had an extremely good hand in Limit, I would sit and look at the community cards, trying to imagine the cards my opponents held that would beat me.

Whenever my "insight" was correct, I became ever more convinced that I was cursed. It was starting to bother me at a very deep, and very real, level. I was even *dreaming* of opponents outdrawing me. Not being satisfied with this level of mental torture, I would dig even deeper and calculate the odds of taking the beats that I was seeing as a series.

I finally said, "Enough!" and tore the page off my calendar. I circled the day I decided I was finally fed up, swearing to myself that I wouldn't play cards for a year. Every morning, when I'd go to get the milk for my cereal, I'd look at the page on the refrigerator and remind myself to just let it all go. Although I kept reading and studying, I didn't play a single hand.

A year later, I returned renewed and reinvigorated. I enjoyed the game, I didn't psyche myself out anymore, and I was eating my opponents alive. Aside from studying and talking to friends, taking that year off is *easily* the best thing I've ever done for my game.

If you're finding yourself getting more and more tweaked over the game, take time off. The game is hard enough without having to fight the added monster within you. When you come back to the game, Redstradamus predicts that you'll be pleasantly amazed at how much better your game has become.

Varying Your Opponents

If you always play the same opponents — even if you're consistently beating them — you're not improving your game as a whole. Playing other players will get you used to other strategies, techniques, and ideas. And no matter how good you are, you'll occasionally run across the better player. Watch, listen, and learn.

Playing Other Games

I find that playing a sprinkling of other games actually improves my pure Hold'em record. I think the effect is twofold:

✔ It makes me less bored with the redundancy of Hold'em.

✔ I discover other, deeper idiosyncrasies about the game.

Omaha is good because it teaches you some variations of flop dynamics and helps reinforce just *how* important it is that your cards work together. Stud is good because it helps you focus on the intentions of other players.

Glossary

action: Bets made on a poker hand.

add on: To buy more chips in a rebuy tournament at the first break.

all-in: The phrase used to describe when all of a player's money at a table is in the pot. Once all-in, a player is not eligible for any additional bets made — these go into a side pot.

basic poker theory: The ideas of how poker "should" be played — everything in Chapters 1 through 12 of this book.

behind: A player who has a worse hand than another player in a hand that has not yet been fully dealt to completion.

bet: To place a wager on a poker hand. This must be done in a proper playing order (consecutively and clockwise) around a table.

Big Slick: A starting hand of Ace-King as hole cards.

blank: A card that is turned that doesn't help your hand.

blinded off: In a tournament, when a player is not at a table, he still must automatically post blinds — this is known as being *blinded off.*

blinds: "Forced" bets made by the players immediately clockwise from the dealer button to begin betting action around a table. The position immediately clockwise of the dealer button is the *small blind;* the person clockwise of the small blind the *big blind.*

bluff: Betting, or physically acting at the poker table, in such a way that people think you have a hand different from what you actually hold. Typically, people bluff to make other players fold, giving up their chances at the pot.

board: The five community cards presented in the middle of a Texas Hold'em table.

boat: Full house. Also sometimes called a *full boat.*

brick-and-mortar: An adjective used to describe real, physical card rooms or playing establishments — as opposed to online, where the experience is virtual.

Broadway: A 10-J-Q-K-A straight — the highest possible straight.

burn a card: To discard the top card off of a deck before dealing a community card. The discards are known as *burn cards*.

buy-in: The amount of money it costs to sit down and play at a ring game, or to enter a tournament.

call: To match a bet that another player has already made on the table.

calling station: A person who calls all bets.

cap: The maximum number of bets or raises that can be played on any given round. This varies by card room, but is typically four or five. In some card rooms, there is no cap on the betting after play falls into heads-up play. *See also* heads-up.

check: The option of remaining active in a hand but not betting on your turn. You may check only if no other bets have been made in the hand for that round already.

check-raise: The act of checking on your turn to bet, and then raising a bet that is made on the same turn; typically, the sign of a very strong hand.

community cards: Cards in the center of the Texas Hold'em table that can be considered to be a part of anyone's hand.

connectors: Hole cards that are in rank order (for example, J-Q).

cutoff: The player who acts immediately before the player with the dealer button.

dangling Ace: An Ace with no kicker.

dealer button: The marker used in casinos to indicate the hypothetical dealer for a hand — the person with the dealer button is the last to act on any hand. The dealer button rotates one spot clockwise at the conclusion of each hand.

double gut-shot straight: A hand containing two distinct inside straight draws like 10-5 drawing against a board of Q-9-8-7 (Jack makes the Queen-high straight, 6 makes the 9-high straight). It has the same odds as an outside straight draw.

draw: Cards to help a (presently losing) hand, typically said as being "on a draw."

drawing dead: A hand that cannot mathematically win, no matter what cards are drawn.

fifth street: The fifth community up-card, more often called the *river.*

five-card hand: A hand that needs five cards to be made (straight, flush, or full house).

floorperson: In a professional card room, the person who oversees all the dealers in the pit. This is the person you go to for any unresolved disputes at the table, or to claim your chips if you've been absent too long from a game.

flop: The first three community cards, as a group, laid out on the board.

fold: To give up on any given poker hand. A folding player mucks her cards and is no longer eligible to win the pot.

four-flush: Four cards to a flush.

fourth street: The fourth community up-card; more commonly known as the *turn.*

four-straight: Four cards to a straight.

freeroll: A tournament with no entry fee. More rarely, a situation where two players have matching hands, but one player has a possibility of drawing to improve and the other doesn't (for example: A♦ K♦ versus A♣ K♥ on a board with 10♦ J♦ Q♣).

full boat: *See* boat.

game theory: The study of strategies for how to win a game.

gapped: Cards that are one off of each other (for example, 10-Q).

Godzilla: Radioactive monster from Japan. Good poker face, bad temper.

gut-shot straight: *See* inside straight.

hand: The cards any player holds at a given time (community plus hole cards). Also refers to one full session of betting (hole cards, flop, turn, and river).

heads-up: Two players playing only against each other.

hole cards: The first two down cards dealt to everyone in a game of Texas Hold'em. Sometimes called *pocket cards*.

implied pot odds: The ratio of the size of your bet when compared to what you would win if all betting went to an obvious conclusion in subsequent rounds.

inside straight: A player needing a card in the middle of a straight draw (for example, 5-6-8-9). The probability of making this hand is half as likely as an outside straight draw. Also called a *gut-shot straight.*

kicker: An extra or outside card to a group. The hand A-A-Q-Q-K would be known as "two pair, Aces and Queens with a King kicker."

Limit: A form of poker betting where, if you bet, you must bet a specified amount. The amount you bet is doubled on the turn and river. For example, in $3/$6 Hold'em, if you bet, you must bet only $3 on your hole cards and on the flop, and $6 on the turn and the river. You may raise (or be raised), but again, it has to be by the betting units of the particular betting round you are in.

loose: A player who plays a wide array of starting hands and/or bets and raises aggressively.

lowball: A form of poker where low hand wins, or a community board in Texas Hold'em that shows only lower-ranked cards (10s or less).

main pot: The money that all betting players are eligible to win. After a player is all-in, a side pot is made for any additional wagers.

muck: To throw cards into the middle of the table (an act of folding). The cards thrown into the middle of the table are considered dis-cards and are declared dead. All discards and burn cards, as well as cards that were not dealt in a Hold'em game to a player at the end of a hand, are also called the *muck. See also* burn a card.

No-Limit: A form of poker betting where, if you bet, you may bet any amount up to your entire stack. Raises in No-Limit must be at least equal to the last bet size.

nuts: The best hand.

orbit: One complete lap of the dealer button around a card table.

out: A card that will turn a currently losing hand into a winner.

outside straight: A player needing a card on either end of a straight draw (for example, 4-5-6-7). The probability of making this hand is twice as likely as an inside straight draw.

over cards: Cards that have a higher rank when compared to other cards (for example, a King is an over card of a Jack).

pass: To fold.

piggybacking: Placing a clear plastic box over one player's chips while she is absent from the table so another player can put his chips on top and play out of the currently vacant spot. Yes, it's weird.

pocket cards: *See* hole cards.

pocket pair: Two cards of the same rank dealt as hole cards to the same player (for example, 9♣ 9♥).

post: To make a blind bet.

pot: The chips accumulated from all bets in any given hand.

pot odds: The ratio of the size of your bet compared to the size of the pot that you're calling. For example, if you have to make a $10 bet to call in a $30 pot, you have pot odds of 3-to-1. If you were to win this hand, you would be paid three times what your original bet was.

prop: A person who is paid by a professional card room to play her own money in a poker game — formally known as a *proposition player.*

proposition player: *See* prop.

quads: Four-of-a-kind.

rail: The edge of a poker venue where spectators stand.

rail birds: People who stand at the rail in a poker venue.

rainbow: Cards of all different suits. A rainbow board has no flush possibilities.

raise: To bet an additional amount over a bet that another player has already made at the table.

rake: A small percentage of each pot (typically 5 to 10 percent) that goes to a professional card room for running a poker game.

rank: The number on a card. Cards are ranked, in ascending order, 2 through Ace.

rebuy: To purchase another stack of chips in a tournament.

ring game: People playing individual hands of poker at a table in a game where they may leave at any time. Poker played around a kitchen table for matchsticks would be considered a ring game. This is different from a tournament format, where players compete until they bust out.

river: The fifth (and final) community card played to the board. *See also* fifth street.

roshambo: The formal name of the rock/scissors/paper game that you played when you were a kid.

round of betting: All players are offered a chance to bet after seeing cards in Texas Hold'em; this is known as a *round of betting*. There are four rounds of betting in Hold'em: after the hole cards are dealt, after the flop community cards are exposed, after the turn community card is exposed, and after the river community card is exposed.

runner-runner: Drawing a card on the turn *and* then drawing another on the river that makes a hand.

satellite: A smaller tournament designed to feed the winner(s) into a larger tournament.

see: Another phrase meaning *to call* a bet. *See also* call.

set: Three-of-a-kind.

shill: Similar to a prop, a shill is a person who is paid by a professional card room, but who plays with the house's money and is not allowed to keep his winnings. *See also* prop.

short-handed: A table that is missing players, or is intentionally seated with a capacity of six players or less.

showdown: When cards are exposed at the end of a hand to determine winners and losers.

side pot: A pot created by people who have more money than an all-in player. Any player eligible to win a side pot is also eligible for the main pot, whereas the all-in player is not eligible to win the side pot and may only win the main pot. During the showdown, the cards eligible for the side pot are exposed first.

singelton: A single card.

skim: A small percentage of a pot taken in home games for the house, similar to a rake.

slow play: Having a good hand but intentionally not betting it hard early on in an effort to ultimately squeeze more money out of it.

Spread-Limit: A form of poker betting where, if you bet, the amount must be within a specific range. For example, in a $1-$5 game, you may bet anywhere between $1 and $5 on any betting action. Raises in Spread-Limit must be equal to, or greater than, the previous bet.

stack: The entirety of someone's poker chips at a table.

steal the blinds: To make a raise in an effort to get the players with blinds on the table to fold. This is usually done by the player at the dealer button or in the cutoff position.

suckout: A person with a lesser hand who draws a community card to become greater and win.

suited: Two cards of the same suit.

tank: The place someone goes when she's thinking, "My all-in put Grandma into the tank."

tight: A player who only plays the best starting hands and/or bets conservatively.

tilt: Someone who plays carelessly after losing a hand he believes he should have won.

tournament: A poker game where all the entry fees are pooled and players are given a set number of chips. Prizes are awarded to the top finishers according to their exit points in the tournament. Tournaments are different from a ring-game format where players are simply competing in consecutive hands but may leave at any time.

trips: Three of a kind.

turn: The fourth community card placed on the board. *See also* fourth street.

underdog: A player at a mathematical disadvantage in a hand.

under the gun: The player immediately clockwise of the big blind. *See also* big blind.

wheel: A-2-3-4-5 straight.

World Series of Poker (WSoP): The top poker tournament in the world. Played in Las Vegas every year, the main event is a $10,000 No-Limit Hold'em tournament. The winner of the main event is considered by many people to be the top player in the world for that year.

Index

Notes

BUSINESS, CAREERS & PERSONAL FINANCE

0-7645-5307-0   0-7645-5331-3 *†

Also available:
- Accounting For Dummies †
  0-7645-5314-3
- Business Plans Kit For Dummies †
  0-7645-5365-8
- Cover Letters For Dummies
  0-7645-5224-4
- Frugal Living For Dummies
  0-7645-5403-4
- Leadership For Dummies
  0-7645-5176-0
- Managing For Dummies
  0-7645-1771-6

- Marketing For Dummies
  0-7645-5600-2
- Personal Finance For Dummies *
  0-7645-2590-5
- Project Management
  For Dummies
  0-7645-5283-X
- Resumes For Dummies †
  0-7645-5471-9
- Selling For Dummies
  0-7645-5363-1
- Small Business Kit For Dummies *†
  0-7645-5093-4

HOME & BUSINESS COMPUTER BASICS

0-7645-4074-2   0-7645-3758-X

Also available:
- ACT! 6 For Dummies
  0-7645-2645-6
- iLife '04 All-in-One Desk Reference
  For Dummies
  0-7645-7347-0
- iPAQ For Dummies
  0-7645-6769-1
- Mac OS X Panther Timesaving
  Techniques For Dummies
  0-7645-5812-9
- Macs For Dummies
  0-7645-5656-8
- Microsoft Money 2004 For Dummies
  0-7645-4195-1

- Office 2003 All-in-One Desk
  Reference For Dummies
  0-7645-3883-7
- Outlook 2003 For Dummies
  0-7645-3759-8
- PCs For Dummies
  0-7645-4074-2
- TiVo For Dummies
  0-7645-6923-6
- Upgrading and Fixing PCs
  For Dummies
  0-7645-1665-5
- Windows XP Timesaving
  Techniques For Dummies
  0-7645-3748-2

FOOD, HOME, GARDEN, HOBBIES, MUSIC & PETS

0-7645-5295-3   0-7645-5232-5

Also available:
- Bass Guitar For Dummies
  0-7645-2487-9
- Diabetes Cookbook For Dummies
  0-7645-5230-9
- Gardening For Dummies *
  0-7645-5130-2
- Guitar For Dummies
  0-7645-5106-X
- Holiday Decorating For Dummies
  0-7645-2570-0
- Home Improvement All-in-One
  For Dummies
  0-7645-5680-0

- Knitting For Dummies
  0-7645-5395-X
- Piano For Dummies
  0-7645-5105-1
- Puppies For Dummies
  0-7645-5255-4
- Scrapbooking For Dummies
  0-7645-7208-3
- Senior Dogs For Dummies
  0-7645-5818-8
- Singing For Dummies
  0-7645-2475-5
- 30-Minute Meals For Dummies
  0-7645-2589-1

INTERNET & DIGITAL MEDIA

0-7645-1664-7   0-7645-6924-4

Also available:
- 2005 Online Shopping Directory
  For Dummies
  0-7645-7495-7
- CD & DVD Recording For Dummies
  0-7645-5956-7
- eBay For Dummies
  0-7645-5654-1
- Fighting Spam For Dummies
  0-7645-5965-6
- Genealogy Online For Dummies
  0-7645-5964-8
- Google For Dummies
  0-7645-4420-9

- Home Recording For Musicians
  For Dummies
  0-7645-1634-5
- The Internet For Dummies
  0-7645-4173-0
- iPod & iTunes For Dummies
  0-7645-7772-7
- Preventing Identity Theft
  For Dummies
  0-7645-7336-5
- Pro Tools All-in-One Desk
  Reference For Dummies
  0-7645-5714-9
- Roxio Easy Media Creator
  For Dummies
  0-7645-7131-1

* Separate Canadian edition also available

† Separate U.K. edition also available

Available wherever books are sold. For more information or to order direct: U.S. customers
visit www.dummies.com or call 1-877-762-2974.
U.K. customers visit www.wileyeurope.com or call 0800 243407. Canadian customers visit
www.wiley.ca or call 1-800-567-4797.

SPORTS, FITNESS, PARENTING, RELIGION & SPIRITUALITY

0-7645-5146-9

0-7645-5418-2

Also available:

- Adoption For Dummies
  0-7645-5488-3
- Basketball For Dummies
  0-7645-5248-1
- The Bible For Dummies
  0-7645-5296-1
- Buddhism For Dummies
  0-7645-5359-3
- Catholicism For Dummies
  0-7645-5391-7
- Hockey For Dummies
  0-7645-5228-7

- Judaism For Dummies
  0-7645-5299-6
- Martial Arts For Dummies
  0-7645-5358-5
- Pilates For Dummies
  0-7645-5397-6
- Religion For Dummies
  0-7645-5264-3
- Teaching Kids to Read
  For Dummies
  0-7645-4043-2
- Weight Training For Dummies
  0-7645-5168-X
- Yoga For Dummies
  0-7645-5117-5

TRAVEL

0-7645-5438-7

0-7645-5453-0

Also available:

- Alaska For Dummies
  0-7645-1761-9
- Arizona For Dummies
  0-7645-6938-4
- Cancún and the Yucatán
  For Dummies
  0-7645-2437-2
- Cruise Vacations For Dummies
  0-7645-6941-4
- Europe For Dummies
  0-7645-5456-5
- Ireland For Dummies
  0-7645-5455-7

- Las Vegas For Dummies
  0-7645-5448-4
- London For Dummies
  0-7645-4277-X
- New York City For Dummies
  0-7645-6945-7
- Paris For Dummies
  0-7645-5494-8
- RV Vacations For Dummies
  0-7645-5443-3
- Walt Disney World & Orlando
  For Dummies
  0-7645-6943-0

GRAPHICS, DESIGN & WEB DEVELOPMENT

0-7645-4345-8

0-7645-5589-8

Also available:

- Adobe Acrobat 6 PDF
  For Dummies
  0-7645-3760-1
- Building a Web Site For Dummies
  0-7645-7144-3
- Dreamweaver MX 2004
  For Dummies
  0-7645-4342-3
- FrontPage 2003 For Dummies
  0-7645-3882-9
- HTML 4 For Dummies
  0-7645-1995-6
- Illustrator CS For Dummies
  0-7645-4084-X

- Macromedia Flash MX 2004
  For Dummies
  0-7645-4358-X
- Photoshop 7 All-in-One Desk
  Reference For Dummies
  0-7645-1667-1
- Photoshop CS Timesaving
  Techniques For Dummies
  0-7645-6782-9
- PHP 5 For Dummies
  0-7645-4166-8
- PowerPoint 2003 For Dummies
  0-7645-3908-6
- QuarkXPress 6 For Dummies
  0-7645-2593-X

NETWORKING, SECURITY, PROGRAMMING & DATABASES

0-7645-6852-3

0-7645-5784-X

Also available:

- A+ Certification For Dummies
  0-7645-4187-0
- Access 2003 All-in-One Desk
  Reference For Dummies
  0-7645-3988-4
- Beginning Programming
  For Dummies
  0-7645-4997-9
- C For Dummies
  0-7645-7068-4
- Firewalls For Dummies
  0-7645-4048-3
- Home Networking For Dummies
  0-7645-42796

- Network Security For Dummies
  0-7645-1679-5
- Networking For Dummies
  0-7645-1677-9
- TCP/IP For Dummies
  0-7645-1760-0
- VBA For Dummies
  0-7645-3989-2
- Wireless All In-One Desk Reference
  For Dummies
  0-7645-7496-5
- Wireless Home Networking
  For Dummies
  0-7645-3910-8

HEALTH & SELF-HELP

0-7645-6820-5 *†

0-7645-2566-2

Also available:

* Alzheimer's For Dummies
  0-7645-3899-3
* Asthma For Dummies
  0-7645-4233-8
* Controlling Cholesterol For Dummies
  0-7645-5440-9
* Depression For Dummies
  0-7645-3900-0
* Dieting For Dummies
  0-7645-4149-8
* Fertility For Dummies
  0-7645-2549-2

* Fibromyalgia For Dummies
  0-7645-5441-7
* Improving Your Memory For Dummies
  0-7645-5435-2
* Pregnancy For Dummies †
  0-7645-4483-7
* Quitting Smoking For Dummies
  0-7645-2629-4
* Relationships For Dummies
  0-7645-5384-4
* Thyroid For Dummies
  0-7645-5385-2

EDUCATION, HISTORY, REFERENCE & TEST PREPARATION

0-7645-5194-9

0-7645-4186-2

Also available:

* Algebra For Dummies
  0-7645-5325-9
* British History For Dummies
  0-7645-7021-8
* Calculus For Dummies
  0-7645-2498-4
* English Grammar For Dummies
  0-7645-5322-4
* Forensics For Dummies
  0-7645-5580-4
* The GMAT For Dummies
  0-7645-5251-1
* Inglés Para Dummies
  0-7645-5427-1

* Italian For Dummies
  0-7645-5196-5
* Latin For Dummies
  0-7645-5431-X
* Lewis & Clark For Dummies
  0-7645-2545-X
* Research Papers For Dummies
  0-7645-5426-3
* The SAT I For Dummies
  0-7645-7193-1
* Science Fair Projects For Dummies
  0-7645-5460-3
* U.S. History For Dummies
  0-7645-5249-X

Get smart @ dummies.com®

* **Find a full list of Dummies titles**
* **Look into loads of FREE on-site articles**
* **Sign up for FREE eTips e-mailed to you weekly**
* **See what other products carry the Dummies name**
* **Shop directly from the Dummies bookstore**
* **Enter to win new prizes every month!**

* Separate Canadian edition also available
† Separate U.K. edition also available

Available wherever books are sold. For more information or to order direct: U.S. customers visit www.dummies.com or call 1-877-762-2974.
U.K. customers visit www.wileyeurope.com or call 0800 243407. Canadian customers visit www.wiley.ca or call 1-800-567-4797.